'A valuable and thorough reading of a n
writing.'-**Professor Randy Boyagoda,** K

Salman Rushdie is one of the most widely studied and controversial contemporary British authors. This revised and expanded new edition of an established text explores all of his fiction, non-fiction and biographical writings to date. Considering the author's fiction as art, in all its richness of significance and technique, D. C. R. A. Goonetilleke examines the blend of autobiographical and historical elements and analyses Rushdie's complex position as a migrant writer.

Salman Rushdie, second edition:

- features new chapters which discuss the author's most recent novels, including *Fury* (2001), *Shalimar the Clown* (2005) and *The Enchantress of Florence* (2008)
- reviews Rushdie's texts in the light of recent research and critical developments
- focuses on Rushdie as a novelist in the context of migration, postcolonialism and globalization
- covers the 'Rushdie Affair', indicating that the situation surrounding *The Satanic Verses* is more intricate than simply 'freedom of expression versus Islamic fundamentalism'
- contains an updated Bibliography and helpful new Chronology to aid study.

In surveying Rushdie's complicated writing career and the innovative and, later, 'popular' nature of his art, Professor Goonetilleke provides fresh and original readings of all of the writer's work. This lucid and approachable study is an essential introduction to Salman Rushdie, rendering a notoriously 'difficult' author accessible to students, scholars and general readers alike.

D. C. R. A. Goonetilleke is Emeritus Professor of English at the University of Kelaniya, Sri Lanka, and has also held various academic posts in the UK and Europe. He is a well-established critic of twentieth-century and postcolonial literature, and the leading authority on Sri Lankan English Literature.

Related titles from Palgrave Macmillan:

Justin Edwards: *Postcolonial Literature* (2008)
Stephen Morton: *Salman Rushdie: Fictions of Postcolonial Modernity* (2007)
David Smale: *Salman Rushdie: 'Midnight's Children' – 'The Satanic Verses'* (2001)

Salman Rushdie

Second Edition

D. C. R. A. Goonetilleke

First edition published 1998
Second edition published 2010 by
PALGRAVE MACMILLAN

Palgrave Macmillan in the UK is an imprint of Macmillan Publishers Limited, registered in England, company number 785998, of Houndmills, Basingstoke, Hampshire RG21 6XS.

Palgrave Macmillan in the US is a division of St Martin's Press LLC, 175 Fifth Avenue, New York, NY 10010.

Palgrave Macmillan is the global academic imprint of the above companies and has companies and representatives throughout the world.

Palgrave® and Macmillan® are registered trademarks in the United States, the United Kingdom, Europe and other countries.

ISBN: 978–0–230–21721–8 hardback
ISBN: 978–0–230–21722–5 paperback

This book is printed on paper suitable for recycling and made from fully managed and sustained forest sources. Logging, pulping and manufacturing processes are expected to conform to the environmental regulations of the country of origin.

A catalogue record for this book is available from the British Library.

A catalog record for this book is available from the Library of Congress.

10 9 8 7 6 5 4 3 2 1
19 18 17 16 15 14 13 12 11 10

Printed and bound in Great Britain by
CPI Antony Rowe, Chippenham and Eastbourne

To my dear wife, Chinchi and dear sons, Suren and Dilhan

Contents

Acknowledgements

I was very pleased to find that the first edition of this book was well received and widely used. But Rushdie's relocation to the USA and his well-publicized reactions to 9/11, along with recent novels set in America, all require a re-evaluation of his oeuvre to date. Three of his works (*Midnight's Children*, *Haroun and the Sea of Stories* and *The Satanic Verses*) have been subject to major theatrical adaptations. There is no comprehensive, up-to-date study of Rushdie currently available. Clearly, there is a need for a second edition. I have revised the original chapters and added new ones to cover the recent phase of Rushdie's writing career. The Conclusion has been altered.

For invaluable assistance in preparing the second edition, I wish to thank Chinchi; Dr Lakshmi de Silva; Nirmali Amarasiri, former Outreach Coordinator of the American Center, Colombo; Mr P. Thambirajah, Chief Librarian, International Centre for Ethnic Studies (Colombo); Mr Daya Dissanayake and Mr D. Suwandaratne.

A special word of thanks is due to Ms Sonya Barker, Senior Commissioning Editor at Palgrave Macmillan, for her unflagging enthusiasm for the project – from its inception to its (hopefully) successful completion.

D. C. R. A. GOONETILLEKE

Chronology

1947	19 June: Salman Rushdie born in Bombay, in the year of Indian Independence from British rule, the only son of Muslim businessman, Anis Ahmed Rushdie, who had received his education at Cambridge, and his wife, Negin. The family includes three daughters.
1954	Begins attending Cathedral School, an English Mission school in Bombay.
1961	Sent to England for his secondary education, at Rugby School.
1964	Family moves to Karachi, Pakistan.
1965–68	Reads History at King's College, Cambridge. No longer a believer, develops a historical interest in Islam. Acts with the Cambridge Footlights review. Addicted to cinema.
1968	Returns to Pakistan, works briefly in television. Back to London.
1968–69	Continues acting at the Oval House, Kennington, London.
1969	Gives up acting to work as an advertising copywriter. Stops work to write *The Book of the Pir* (unpublished novel). Takes up copywriting again, on a part-time basis, which permits him to continue writing.
1970	Meets Clarissa Luard.
1974	Five-month trip to India and Pakistan with Clarissa.
1974	February: *Grimus* published. Begins work on *Midnight's Children*. Political involvement with Asian and black groups in London.
1976	Marries Clarissa.
1979	Son, Zafar, born.
1980	Quits advertising to write fiction full-time.
1981	*Midnight's Children* published. Wins Booker and James Tait Black prizes and an English-Speaking Union Literary Award.
1983	*Shame* published. Shortlisted for the Booker Prize; wins France's Prix du Meilleur Livre Étranger. Begins work on *The Satanic Verses*.

1984   Travels through Central Australia with the writer Bruce Chatwin. Meets Australian travel writer, Robyn Davidson.

1985   Produces documentary film *The Painter and the Pest*.

1986   Visits Nicaragua as guest of the Sandinista Association of Cultural Workers. Meets American novelist, Marianne Wiggins.

1987   *The Jaguar Smile: A Nicaraguan Journey* published. The book is dedicated to Robyn Davidson with whom he had become involved. Divorces Clarissa.

1988   Marries Marianne Wiggins. Writes and produces *The Riddle of Midnight*, a documentary for Channel 4 television. *The Satanic Verses* published. Shortlisted for the Booker Prize, wins the Whitbread Prize for the Best Novel. Book banned in India, South Africa and other countries, denounced in Pakistan.

1989   14 January: public burning of *The Satanic Verses* at a rally in Bradford, England. 14 February: Iran's religious leader, Ayatollah Khomeini, pronounces his *fatwa* (Rushdie and his publishers and translators sentenced to death for *kufr*); Iran offers a reward for his murder. A bounty of £1.5 million offered by an Iranian Foundation. Rushdie and Wiggins go into hiding under Special Branch police protection. The Rushdie Affair captures international attention. Rushdie support groups formed in England, France and in other countries. August: Wiggins separates from him.

1990   *Haroun and the Sea of Stories* published. Wins a Writer's Guild award. Meets Elizabeth West.

1991   *Imaginary Homelands: Essays 1981–91* published; concluding section devoted to essays and addresses which convey Rushdie's perspective on his situation. His Italian translator Ettore Capriolo narrowly survives stabbing in Milan. His Japanese translator Hitoshi Igarashi fatally stabbed in Tokyo.

1992   *The Wizard of Oz* published in the British Film Institute's Film Classics series.

1993   *Midnight's Children* wins Booker of Bookers. Divorced from Marianne Wiggins. His Norwegian publisher William Nygaard is shot dead in Oslo.

1994   *East, West*, a collection of short stories, published.

1995   *The Moor's Last Sigh* published. Shortlisted for the Booker Prize, wins Whitbread Prize for Best Novel.

1996   Awarded the European Union's Aristeion Prize for Literature.

1997   Publication of anthology *The Vintage Book of Indian Writing 1947–97*, edited with Elizabeth West. Marries Elizabeth West; their son Milan born.

1998   Iranian government officially distances itself from the *fatwa*. Publication of *Salman Rushdie's Haroun and the Sea of Stories* adapted for the theatre by Tim Supple and David Tushingham. Stage adaptation of *Haroun and the Sea of Stories* premièred at the Royal National Theatre, London.

1999   *The Ground Beneath Her Feet* published. India grants Rushdie a 5-year visa. *The Screenplay of Midnight's Children* published. Rushdie moves to New York. Begins a relationship with Padma Lakshmi. Separated from Elizabeth West.

2000   Travels to India with his son Zafar for the Commonwealth Writers Prize ceremony (*The Ground Beneath Her Feet* – winner of 1999 Best Novel in the Eurasian region).

2001   *Fury* published.

2002   *Step Across This Line: Collected Non-Fiction 1992–2002* published. Publication of *Salman Rushdie's Midnight's Children* adapted for the theatre by Salman Rushdie, Simon Reade and Tim Supple.

2003   January: the Royal Shakespeare Company premièrs the stage adaptation of *Midnight's Children* in London. Rushdie becomes President of PEN America. Marriage to Elizabeth West dissolved.

2004   Marries Padma Lakshmi.

2005   *Shalimar the Clown* published.

2007   Knighted by British monarchy. Divorced by Padma Lakshmi.

2008   Stage adaptation of *The Satanic Verses* in German by Uwe Eric Laufenberg and Marcus Mislin premièred at Hans-Otto-Theatre in Potsdam. *The Enchantress of Florence* published.

1
Early Life and Early Works

(Ahmed) Salman Rushdie justifies Wordsworth's view that 'the Child is father of the Man'.[1] Rushdie wrote: 'The Wizard of Oz (the film, not the book, which I didn't read as a child) was my very first literary influence.[2].... When I first saw The Wizard of Oz it made a writer of me.'[3] The other important literary influence in his childhood was The Arabian Nights which was the basis for the stories his father narrated to his children and which surfaces in the flying carpets and metamorphoses of The Satanic Verses (1988) and predictably in Haroun and the Sea of Stories (1990).

Rushdie was born on 19 June 1947, almost two months before India gained Independence from Britain (15 August) and this virtual coincidence inspired the creation of Saleem Sinai in Midnight's Children (1981) who was born at the very moment of Independence. Rushdie transforms biography into art. He acknowledges the influence of his father on his chosen vocation. He remembers him as a wonderful teller of tales. Memories of the father shade into the Oz film and into the character of Rashid Khalifa, the father-storyteller in Haroun:

> The Wizard was right there in Bombay. My father, Anis Ahmed Rushdie was a magical parent of young children, but he was also prone to explosions, thunderous rages, bolts of emotional lightning, puffs of dragon-smoke, and other menaces of the type also practised by Oz, the great and terrible, the first Wizard Deluxe.... It took me half a lifetime to discover that the Great Oz's apologia pro vita sua fitted my father equally well – that he, too, was a good man, but a very bad Wizard.[4]

The father was a barrister turned businessman (Saleem Sinai and Saladin Chamcha, the protagonists of Midnight's Children and The Satanic Verses, respectively, have businessmen fathers) and the mother, Negin (née Butt) Rushdie, a teacher from Aligarh, in North India. Both had been married earlier (Amina Sinai, Saleem's mother, begins with another name, another husband), were affluent

1

(Salman had a nanny) and lived in Bombay. Anis's law degree was from Cambridge University and he was proud of his university. He was the kind of man who would bring up his son 'in a very Anglophile and Anglocentric way'.[5] Salman was sent to a mission school, the Cathedral and John Connon School. The parents were devout Muslims, yet the family was liberal, which Salman contrasts with the attitude of some of the Muslim fundamentalists: 'there was an absolute willingness to discuss anything, there were not these anathemas, these rules, about what you must not talk about'.[6] In the household, Salman's sister, Sameen, seems virtually a model for Saleem's sister, the Brass Monkey; Salman was the proverbial good child.

After the Partition of India, many of their relatives migrated to Pakistan where the Muslims were in a majority and felt more secure. But the Rushdies decided to remain in Bombay. Salman often revisited his childhood Bombay in his fiction – in *Midnight's Children, The Satanic Verses, Haroun* and in *The Moor's Last Sigh* as typifying the rich pluralism threatened by the monolithic narrowness of religious chauvinism – and conjured it up in his mind, stimulated by the inch-high block of Indian silver with the map of an unpartitioned subcontinent (a childhood gift) which he placed like a totem before him as he wrote. His attachment to Bombay is not merely nostalgia but a component of his imagination. His technique of cuts, close-ups, juxtaposition, was influenced by the Bombay talkie (Bombay was 'the world's number-one movie city – "Bollywood" in those days produced more movies per annum than Los Angeles or Tokyo or Hong Kong'[7]) and other movies (he has mentioned the New Wave, Buñuel and Godard[8]) as well as by Sergei Eisenstein's *The Film Sense*.[9] His first literary effort, a short story titled 'Over the Rainbow', written at the age of ten, was inspired by movies – a children's fantasy, memorable for its boy–hero's encounter with 'a talking pianola whose personality is an improbable hybrid of Judy Garland, Elvis Presley and the "playback singers" of the Hindi movies'.[10]

In 1961, at the age of thirteen, Salman was sent to Rugby, the famous English public (in reality, private) school. His father accompanied him to London. What happened between them is uncertain, yet it appears that Anis drank too much (recalled in Ahmed Sinai's pink djinns in *Midnight's Children*) and Salman was relieved to leave for school. A severing had taken place. Thanks to a Kashmiri ancestor, Salman had a pale skin that could have passed for white (like Flapping Eagle in *Grimus* and Saladin Chamcha), but this did not save him from the 'wog-baiting' of the English schoolboys. His rejection and the racism in the school prodded him to write a short autobiographical novel about Rugby life titled *Terminal Report* that highlighted a conservative conventional type – such as he had been – as the hero who was changed by his experiences into an aggressive radical whenever he encountered racism. It made him think of writing as his vocation, while he himself became like his hero. He said: 'Of course, I knew that racism is not confined to the British. I come from a society where racism is commonplace, between one Indian community and another. But you have to combat racism wherever you find it.'[11]

At Rugby, a fellow-pupil recalls Rushdie submitting divinity-class essays with fake quotes from a fake authority, Professor I. Q. Gribb (recalled in *Grimus*),[12] but he did perform well academically. He turned down a scholarship to Balliol College, Oxford, in order to accept one to King's College, Cambridge.

Salman's choice of home was now problematic. Anis's business had deteriorated, his drinking had got worse and India was less hospitable to Muslims. In 1962, he and his family migrated to England and two years later moved to Karachi – both snap decisions (recalled in the story 'The Courter', in *East, West*). Salman's choice was between Cambridge and Karachi, England and Pakistan. Karachi and Pakistan were to him the antithesis of Bombay and India, which seemed secular, multifarious, tolerant, cordial. On the other hand, Salman had had enough of England.

His father (who died in 1987 – in debt) insisted that he enter Cambridge and he studied there from 1965 to 1968. He believed it was his good fortune to read History, not English. This meant he could select literary books at random and learn from them as a writer. Thus he read Sterne's *Tristram Shandy* 'with a sense of discovery as if it had been written yesterday'.[13] In his final year, Salman had chosen a special subject: Mohammed and the Rise of Islam. But only five students turned up and the lecturer cancelled the course. Yet Salman persisted and ended up as the only student following the course, coming across the incident of the Satanic Verses then. His persistence suggests a basic sense of cultural identity; the course had no value in the competitive Western society at that time.

He was influenced by the anti-Establishment spirit of the 1960s at Cambridge as elsewhere – the anti-Vietnam War attitude and the hippie style (recalled in *The Satanic Verses*). He neither wrote for the undergraduate magazines, *Varsity* and *Granta*, nor spoke in

Students' Union debates, but was involved in the theatre in the era of Clive James, Germaine Greer and David Hare. A contemporary spoke of Salman's 'radical chic'.[14] He did not study systematically, displayed an interest in the occult (recalled in Omar Khayyam in *Shame* and in 'The Harmony of the Spheres', in *East, West*) and ended up with a 2:2 (Second Class, Lower Division) degree – not surprising in the circumstances, though not commensurate with his abilities.

Salman returned to Karachi, having no real alternative, but refused to take over his father's new business, a towel factory (recalled in Ahmed Sinai and Amina Brand towels in *Midnight's Children*). He tried to work in Pakistan's new television service. He persuaded them to let him produce and act in Edward Albee's *The Zoo Story*, but, prior to the production, he had to go through 'a series of astonishing censorship conferences'. An Albee reference to the disgustingness of pork hamburgers was found offensive. Though Salman argued that it was 'superb anti-pork propaganda', he was told that 'the word pork may not be spoken on Pakistan television'. He had also to delete 'the line about God being a coloured queen who wears a kimono and plucks his eyebrows'.[15] Rushdie appears alienated and contemptuous of his illiterate countrymen, and has no sympathy for the shock or the instinctive shrinking from a birth-on religious taboo experienced by them. At the same time, censorship was a fact – pervasive and stifling.

He escaped to London which offered him far better opportunities for fulfilling his ambition to be a writer. As between Changez and Saladin in *The Satanic Verses*, alienation arose between Salman and his father, who disapproved of his son's hippie-like lifestyle and did not support him, financially or emotionally, in his ambition. To earn, he returned to acting, an immigrant in the fringe theatre circuit, occupying a marginal position, perhaps reflected and burlesqued in Chamcha's job voicing the personality of washing fluid and garlic-flavoured crisps. Salman tried to find employment in the well-known J. Walter Thompson advertising agency, but failed the test (writing a jingle about the merits of car seat belts). Soon afterwards, he was employed by a small agency called Sharp MacManus, but quit it to work on a novel. Finished in 1971, it was titled *The Book of the Pir* and featured a Muslim guru who succeeds in becoming the figurehead president of a corrupt military regime in an unnamed Eastern land. It was written in what the author calls 'sub-Joyce',[16] signifying experimentation with language. Joyce is recalled in 'The Harmony of the Spheres'; Rushdie has also said: 'I think *Ulysses* is the greatest novel of this century; it has a lot of stories in it, but its impulse is not narrative. I think one can't make that kind of naive return to the world before Joyce.'[17] Rushdie's novel was rejected even by literary agents and laid aside.

He went back to advertising and joined Ogilvy & Mather as a copywriter. Copywriting would have tended to make him word-conscious, ready to draw on surprising sources to create effects, and lead him to question the intelligence and integrity of both writer and reader, a questioning which is incorporated into the art of *Midnight's Children*.

He had already met his future wife, Clarissa Luard, in 1970. An acquaintance describes her as a 'very well-bred English-rose type',[18] and, probably, the model for Pamela Lovelace in *The Satanic Verses*, whose name ironically alludes to Samuel Richardson's characters the virtuous Pamela and the rake Lovelace. Clarissa was working with a group that was 'raising consciousness about Biafra';[19] Pamela was into Vietnam, and, later, immigrants. Clarissa's family was upper-middle-class and British. In 1973, Clarissa's mother emigrated to Spain (her father had committed suicide when she was sixteen – both Pamela's parents commit suicide together) and the daughter, Rushdie and a female lodger occupied her Lower Belgrave Street flat, next to what had been the Luard family home. The lodger was Liz Calder who had just assumed duties as an editor at Victor Gollancz. She told Rushdie of the science fiction competition Gollancz had announced as a way of finding new writers. 'He said he would enter the book he was then writing.'[20] If so, then, *Grimus* (1975), Rushdie's first published novel, like his characters Saleem Sinai, Omar Khayyam and Moraes Zogoiby, has a plural parentage.

As in *The Book of the Pir*, Rushdie tries to combine the East and the West, to use flawed but useful binaries, but in an entirely new way. His roots are in his Eastern/Islamic background though and the source of *Grimus* is a twelfth-century Sufi narrative poem, Farid-ud-din 'Attar's *The Conference of Birds*, the only novel of Rushdie that originates from another book, that has a purely literary beginning. The poem is described briefly in *Grimus* itself[21] but more fully elsewhere:

...the closest thing in Persian literature to *Pilgrim's Progress*. The characters are all birds, which is why the central character of *Grimus* is a bird, Flapping Eagle. In the poem twenty-nine birds are persuaded by a hoopoe, a messenger of a bird god, to make a pilgrimage to the god. They set off and go through allegorical valleys and eventually climb the mountain to meet the god at the top, but at the top they find that there is no god there. The god is called Simurg, and they accuse the hoopoe of bringing them on – oh dear – a wild goose chase. The poem rests on a Persian pun: if you break Simurg into parts – 'Si' and 'murg' – it can be translated to mean 'thirty birds', so that, having gone through the processes of purification and reached the top of the mountain, the birds have become the god.[22]

Rushdie adds: 'Although the plot of *Grimus* is not that of the poem, it has it at its centre, and that gave me something to cling on to. I was trying to take a theme out of eastern philosophy or mythology and transpose it into a western convention.'[23] The theme is chosen arbitrarily, in keeping with Rushdie's willed intention to be a writer. The Western convention is supplied by Dante's *Divina Commedia*. Rushdie is the kind of cloven writer produced by migration, inhabiting and addressing both worlds, the East and the West, the world of his mother country and that of his adopted country, belonging wholly to neither one nor the other. The position of the main setting of the novel is significant, an island in the Mediterranean, which straddles the West and the East.

The novel begins on this island when Flapping Eagle floats up to Virgil Jones, an intellectual with 'a tongue rather too large for his mouth' (p. 13) and Dolores O'Toole, an ugly hunchbacked grass widow. The book revels in erudition, both Eastern and Western: Jones's two Christian names are Virgil (recalling the name of the Roman poet) and Chanakya (recalling the name of the ancient Indian sage); the book's first three epigraphs are from T. S. Eliot, Farid-ud-din 'Attar and Ted Hughes. Soon the book changes into an explanatory and retrospective narrative, set in the American South West. Flapping Eagle and his sister Bird-Dog are members of an Amerindian tribe, the Axonas. Their relationship reveals that Rushdie was haunted by the figure of a dominant sister from the beginning of his career; he acknowledges his sister as being 'one of the two most important women' in his life, the other being his second wife, Marianne Wiggins.[24] Eagle is dominated by his elder sister and is, later, literally a 'sister-fucker', a term of abuse in *Midnight's Children*, *Shame* and *The Moor's Last Sigh*. It seems to me that the Axonas represent an aspect of American society and Rushdie satirizes it, as when he dwells on the Axona obsession with health and cleanliness, their credo that 'All that is Unaxona is Unclean' (p. 24) (recalling the era of McCarthyism and the prosecution of un-American activities) and the fact that 'breasted providers (such as Bird-Dog) were anathema to the Axona' (p. 17) (chiding American masculine chauvinism). Rushdie's main target is its conventionality. The gender-bender tendencies of Eagle and Bird-Dog are part of their role as nonconformists. Flapping Eagle (originally Joe-Sue) is at first a hermaphrodite and only later male. Bird-Dog hates cauldrons and cooking, is good at men's work and takes a brave's name. They were ostracized mainly because of Joe-Sue: his confused sex, the circumstances of his birth ('Born-From-Dead' was his formal given name) and his colour (ironically, the prejudice is against his whiteness). Bird-Dog, whose nature it is to adventure beyond the confines of her society, meets an itinerant pedlar Sispy, a guise of Grimus, and is given two kinds of bottle, yellow for the eternity of life and blue for the eternity of death. Joe-Sue refuses to drink any, but Bird-Dog drinks the yellow and follows Sispy as his faithful slave.

When Bird-Dog disappears suddenly, Joe-Sue is more vulnerable and has to shoulder her guilt too. He is, in effect, expelled by his tribe, but he drinks the elixir of life before leaving because, at this stage, he regarded this as lending him an advantage. He travels to the adjoining town, Phoenix, so named because it has risen out of the ashes of a huge fire that had destroyed an earlier and larger city with the same name. Rushdie proceeds to satirize another aspect of American society – the pleasure-seeking, jet-setting section, while considering exile and migration too. Eagle is a minority man, an exile, but this is no factor in his social interaction and progress; his whiteness of skin, as in the case of Rushdie himself, distinguishes him from his compatriots and draws him closer to the dominant race. An affluent white woman, Livia Cramm, picks him up to exploit him for her own pleasure (he becomes her personal gigolo), but, finally and ironically, it is she who suffers and commits not homicide but suicide.

In her will, Livia Cramm leaves her money to Eagle and her yacht to her other consort, Deggle, who offers it to Eagle to get away. His subsequent voyaging and immortality leave him unsatisfied. He wishes to grow old and be human, and seeks Sispy and Bird-Dog – in vain. His yacht sails to its home port, the port of X on the Moorish coast of Morispain (a location that points forward, perhaps, to the last scenes of *The Moor's Last Sigh*), and he meets Deggle again, who advises him about 'making a gate' to Calf Island (p. 36). He sails in the Mediterranean. It suddenly becomes turbulent and he falls through a hole in the sea, like Alice in Lewis Carroll's *Alice's Adventures in Wonderland* who fell through a hole, a rabbit-hole in her case.

The structure of the novel is a quest. After Virgil Jones resuscitates Eagle, Eagle forces the reluctant Jones to answer questions regarding Bird-Dog, Sispy/Grimus and Calf Island, and, finally, accompany him as a guide in his ascent of Calf Mountain (the dominant and only item of topographical significance on the island) towards Grimus, as the Roman poet Virgil led Dante through Hell and Purgatory towards a vision of God in Paradise. It was Virgil Jones who, while working as a digger of pets' graves, a profession arranged for him by Nicholas Deggle, found the Stone Rose, the instrument for time and dimension travel, and showed it to Deggle and Grimus, a Middle European refugee who had brought him a bird to bury. Grimus takes over the Stone Rose and uses it to create or discover or half-create, half-discover Calf Island. The fact that he cannot quite control his Effect hints that he is not the Creator.

Grimus is or, rather, becomes a kind of wizard. His origins are important:

> semi-semitic prisoner of war...the destruction of his human dignity, of his belief in the whole human race; the subsequent burrowing away, away from the world, into books and philosophies and mythologies, until these became his realities,...since he had no regard for his species he did not care what he did to them. They had done enough to him. (p. 243)

From one aspect, Grimus is the (damaged) intellectual.

Rushdie exploits the sci-fi idea of an infinity of Parallel Dimensions. As in the much-anthologized 'By His Boot Straps' (1941) by Robert A. Heinlein, America's greatest writer of science fiction, there are a million possible earths with a million possible histories, all of which do not destroy the existence of pasts or futures one chooses not to enter and exist simultaneously. Calf Island does not exist in one dimension, has existed in another, will exist in a third and does in still another. The Stone Rose is a Gorfic Object and, presumably, has been placed in the pets' graveyard by the Gorfs (an anagram for frogs). The Gorfs are the Orderers of the Universe. They inhabited the planet Thera which winds its way around the star Nus in the Yawy Klim (note the anagrams or 're-orderings' of the words Earth, Sun and Milky Way). A Gorf called Koax (the sound 'Koax' occurs in the chorus refrain of Aristophanes's *Frogs*) is an illicit observer of the ascent of Flapping Eagle and Virgil Jones. The world of Grimus is one planet in the Gorfic system or Universe, a planet where things have gone awry. The use of anagrams and, indeed, the Gorfs' belief that reality is constructed by thought forms and can be altered by the anagrammatic rearrangement of these thought forms makes sense (not as mere rather childish letter/word games), as Andrew Teverson suggests, in the context of post-structuralist theories current in the 1970s that reality is a textual construct forged out of pre-existing languages or structures and that a creative linguistic act is a mere rearrangement of earlier acts of creation and expression (Teverson, *Salman Rushdie*, p. 116).

When ascending Calf Mountain, Eagle and Jones are exposed to what Grimus calls 'Dimension Fever', to the Inner Dimensions, which is an awareness of a kind of reality that 'human kind cannot bear very much' (in the words of the epigraph from T. S. Eliot). Eagle succumbs to an Inner Dimension and is trapped, but Jones, at risk to himself, yokes energy via dance to save Eagle's sanity. Thus, Jones saves Eagle a second time and becomes Eagle's guide, rescuer and friend. They continue the arduous ascent which includes negotiating a series of concentric circles, riding on bicycles through a tunnel, and Eagle's struggle (successful) with a devotee of Axona, a conflict with himself in an 'inner' dimension. They reach the town of K, halfway up the Mountain.

They enter the bar of Flann O'Toole (the husband of Dolores) and receive an unfriendly reception. Jones is literally thrown out but finds a refuge in the town brothel, Madame Jocasta's House of the Rising Son (note the Oedipal overtones/the Oedipal pun). Eagle staggers out, but is saved by Elfrida Gribb who accommodates him as her guest in her home.

The town of K is the creation of Grimus. He had chosen its inhabitants and made them immortal and sterile, procreation being unnecessary. But the Utopia went wrong. Nicholas Deggle, one of the three founders of Calf Island, was exiled for attempting to break the Stone Rose. A disaffected Jones, the other founder, withdraws down the Mountain to the sea shore. Grimus himself is forced to leave the town and ensure his own safety by conceptualizing a mansion fortress at the peak of the Mountain, protected by a force field. He lives in this Grimushome with the Stone Rose, the source of his power, and other Dimensional paraphernalia and his recently acquired personal slave, Bird-Dog.

James Harrison argues that 'the social structure Rushdie announces as operating in K is communism in its final, ideal stage "from each according to his abilities, to each according to his needs" '.[25] It is true that 'the farmers farm, the blacksmith hammers, the tavern keeper serves all who would drink, and the quarter-master distributes provisions from his store, each for no return other than being able to benefit from everyone else's labours'.[26] But it seems to me that, in the main, K is radically different from the Marxist ideal. The State has not withered and all men are not equal, a hierarchy being discernible. Count Aleksandr Cherkassov is the chief of the town. He is very much a figurehead, yet makes his presence felt as an authority: that is why Moonshy creates a disturbance while the Count is hosting a dinner party for Flapping Eagle and the Gribbs. I. (Ignatius) Q. Gribb is respected as the town intellectual. Moonshy himself is the quarter-master and in charge of the stores, yet he feels that the State is not ideal and is an agitator, in the Marxist mould at that. Moreover, the impression produced by the society of K is not that of a positive ideal, Marxist or otherwise, but negative. The inhabitants act out their roles mechanically and this is unending. Even Moonshy is no different from the rest. He, too, is playing a part, the Opposition Man. K is, in John Hoffenden's words, 'a hell on earth'.[27] (This makes the Dante parallel particularly apt as Virgil is Dante's guide into Hell.)

Eagle's journey at the lower levels, guided by Virgil Jones, is equivalent to an interior journey, into man's earthly aspirations, his experience of satisfaction in controlling himself and others. It is suggested that life is rendered meaningless by old age and death. Yet Eagle participates in the self-destruction of old age in the shape of the hag, Livia Cramm, and has acquired everlasting life – yet finds it dooms the possessor to endless stagnation and frustration. At the town of K, it is demonstrated that eternity has not enabled man to transcend his frailties. The Two-Time Kid contrives to indulge his unrewarding sensuality (sodomizing a donkey two times is, to him, normal); the Hunter hunts; the scholar, I. Q. Gribb, cannot get beyond his mediocrity (his Universal Philosophy is simple cliché); Irina Cherkassov's son, Alexei, will not mature. The inhabitants protect themselves from Grimus and his Effect by denying his existence. The suggestion is that human beings shield themselves from awareness of self and of God by immersing themselves totally in work, drink and sex.

Eagle, however, actually entertains the idea of settling down in K rather than wandering, but the decision is taken out of his hands. He appeals to, and in turn is attracted by, both Elfrida Gribb and Irina Cherkassov, the wives of K's leading lights. When Elfrida confesses to her husband that it is Eagle she loves, the little scholar dies instantly from an attack of Dimension fever. Three other islanders succumb. The remainder close ranks after the funeral; Eagle and Elfrida, ostracized, are driven to seek refuge in the brothel. It is from here that Eagle resumes his quest.

The novel stresses gender. At the beginning, Joe-Sue (Flapping Eagle) and Bird-Dog cross frontiers of gender, whereas Grimus attracts women but is indifferent to them. He remains celibate, sterile, but has a 'son' (see p. 243). Rushdie may seem a crypto-male chauvinist. Elfrida and Irina conform to the conventional dichotomy of the innocent and the whore. Elfrida wishes to be faithful to her husband, while Irina has been a whore since seventeen. When Eagle combines the two categories and utters the word 'Elfrina', he reduces both. Worse follows: the innocent, Elfrida, ends up as a whore, a professional in the town brothel. Catherine Cundy argues that the male construction of the 'tart with a heart' is used by Rushdie in depicting the brothel[28] and her interpretation does support my view that Rushdie devalues women. But, really, it seems to me that the brothel of K is like those found in cowboy towns, brothels which the cowboys visit for relaxation and pleasure, and it is in this way that it is a stereotype. The god Axona turns out to be an old hag. She is raped by Eagle – a desecration of authority, a violent rejection of control, and a degradation of woman. Grimus, through his mouthpiece, the hypnotized Bird-Dog, thanks Liv for 'breaking down the last barrier to that meeting [between Grimus and Eagle]: his masculinity' (p. 222). Rushdie seems to gesture towards feminism. During the sex act, Liv is in command and asserts her mastery over Eagle by getting off him just before he comes. But it later turns out that she is the tool, the mere instrument, of Grimus in acting so, while Eagle himself is left anything but submissive to Grimus. Rushdie subverts feminism.

Rushdie invests his narrative with a peculiar universality by his use of myth and allusion. Many more than Attar and Dante make their presence felt. Norse myth appears. Deggle calls himself Lokki – appropriately. Loki is the God of Evil, mischief-maker, source of disharmony; gives the mistletoe to the blind God Hodur and the mistletoe causes the death of the Sun God Baldur. A giant ash shades Grimushome: Yggdrasil is the World-Tree, The World Ash. Jones refers to the town of K as Valhalla (p. 100). Grimus refers to Ragnarok, the Twilight of the Gods, and Ragnarak, the Fall, Destruction (p. 230). Livia Cramm, 'the older woman' (p. 25) who attempts to strangle Eagle and dies herself, is identified by Deggle as 'la Femme-Crampon! The clutching woman.... The Viellarde herself!' (p. 29). Thor, the strongest of the Gods, wrestled with a skinny old hag and could not overcome her. She was Elli, Old Age itself. There are Biblical allusions. Deggle is the Devil. He has been 'expelled' (p. 216). Livia Cramm would pun: 'the Deggle himself' (p. 27). Deggle is a magician; black magic is associated with the Devil. Grimus argues that 'free will really is an illusion' (p. 239) – free will is an obsessive subject of theological dispute. The novel alludes to the medieval knightly quest and the Grail mystery. There are allusions to Hindu myth, too. When a tremor shakes Calf Island, Dolores tells Virgil: 'The Great Turtle moved' (p. 50). In Hindu mythology, the turtle is an avatar of the God Vishnu. Jones describes Calf Mountain to Eagle as 'rather like a giant *lingam* weltering in the *yoni* that is the Sea' (pp. 55–6). The *lingam* is a symbol of Shiva, the *yoni* of Parvati. There is a submerged reference to Shiva when Jones explains that, in Amerindian mythology, the Eagle is the symbol of the Destroyer (p. 46). Islamic allusions are abundant. Mujeebuddin Syed points out 'the important subtext of the Prophet's *miraj*, his flight with Gabriel to Heaven and his meeting with God', the pun on Calf and the Koranic *Qaf*.[29] Myth and allusion are at the service of parody.

The journey to the higher levels (of Calf Mountain) without Virgil (Jones) is an ironic portrayal of man's spiritual aspirations, which remain unsatisfied. Dante's companion at the higher levels was the pure and beatific Beatrice, whereas Eagle's is a whore, Media. Beatrice leads Dante, but it is Flapping Eagle who leads Media. Through most of the novel, hints that Grimus is God or, at least, if not Creator, a Demiurge, a secondary creator, are present. Then, these hints are negated and the mystery is trivialized to human and sci-fi proportions. Jones tells Eagle that 'Grimus is in possession of a stupendous piece of knowledge: that we live in one of an infinity of Dimensions' (p. 189) and points out that 'he's only a man' (p. 192). There is no shock of discovery or recognition: Liv *informs* Eagle that 'Your face is as like the face of Grimus as his own reflection' (p. 205). Thus, from one perspective, Eagle, 'the spectre of Grimus', goes to meet his look-alike, the dictator (whether creator or discoverer or

creator/discoverer) of Calf Island just as Bob Wilson, the protagonist (and sole character as it ultimately turns out) of 'By His Boot
Straps', goes to find Diktor of Norkaal and meets himself. But Eagle
is not Grimus and retains his individuality despite Grimus's attempt
to subsume him. The reader's first view of Grimus is deliberately
unimpressive – he is knitting (p. 228) – and he does not proceed to
acquire any kind of exceptional stature.

It was Grimus who had arranged Eagle's quest and he wants
Eagle to succeed him. But Eagle, disenchanted with immortality,
frustrates the will of its human (and therefore necessarily limited
and imperfect) creator, Grimus. The novel reverses both the name
(Simurg) and the aim of 'Attar's *The Conference of Birds*. The birds
fuse into Simurg. Grimus desires Eagle to fuse with him. But Eagle
refuses fusion, retains his identity while rejecting Grimus and
reversing his aim, the preservation and perpetuation of Calf Island
where Eternity, the halting of time and mortality, have merely created a hell of unending patterns of thought and behaviour and
man's frailties remain. The positive implication is that quality, not
quantity, should determine life.

While the world of Grimus is dissolving and being annihilated,
Eagle is mating with Media, a confession that supreme joy lies in the
personal and human, in unmaking the rigid framework of human
aspirations. Their copulation signifies 'Consummatum est' in two
senses. Mujeebuddin Syed argues that they survive and create a
new world.[30] But the concluding words of the novel are important:
'the Mountain of Grimus danced the Weakdance to the end' (p. 253).
The suggestion is that Eagle and Media too are included in the total
destruction, a parody of Ragnarak in Norse myth.

The form of the novel fits that of the 'Menippean satire', which
has been described by Bakhtin.[31] 'Characteristic for the Menippea is
a wide use of inserted genres … . The inserted genres are presented
at various distances from the ultimate authorial position, that is,
with varying degrees of parodying and objectification.'[32] In *Grimus*,
science fiction is the most prominent of the genres, but not in its
usual guise. Eric S. Rabkin observes: 'a good work of science fiction
makes one and only one assumption about its narrative world that
violates our knowledge about our own world and then extrapolates
the whole narrative world from that difference'.[33] In *Grimus*, however, there are several areas of difference. Time is arrested. There
is life in different dimensions. There are two conflicting principles
employed for the functioning of the narrative. First, the power of

the mind. Conceptualizing is seen as a means of maintaining the status quo in Calf Island. Rather than physically dismember the Stone Rose, Eagle conceptualizes Calf Island minus the Rose, and the Rose disappears. He refuses and thwarts Grimus's plan to keep Calf Island going, and helps it to disintegrate – purely through the mind. Second, what seems to be gadgetry or chemicals are brought in from other dimensions where Grimus and Deggle have travelled: immortality and death come in bottles. The heterogeneous genres in the novel include Absurd Drama (used in rendering the 'romantic life' of Jones and Dolores) and the cowboy film. The tavern in the town of K is called Elbaroom – a triple pun (L-Bar – cowboy; Elba – exile; Elbowroom). Peckenpaw's name alludes to Sam L. Peckinpah, the famous Hollywood film director, who specialized in making cowboy movies foregrounding violence. Peckenpaw in the novel is violent: he helped to throw Jones out of the bar after he enters the town; he is one of those who lynched Grimus. The Two-Time Kid is a cowboy-like sobriquet. Punishments like punching and ostracism in the novel convey the feel of the cowboy film and cowboy books too. (Phoenix is located in Arizona in the United States, and Arizona has the largest American Indian population and includes the Old West.)

Bakhtin notes: 'The most important characteristic of the Menippea as a genre is the fact that its bold and unrestrained use of the fantastic and adventure is internally justified by and devoted to a purely ideational and philosophical end.'[34] The aim of science fiction is purely entertainment, but *Grimus* is different. 'It was written with all kinds of high and serious intentions' (in Rushdie's words)[35] and does make ideational and philosophical statements. Bakhtin adds: 'A very important characteristic of the Menippea is the organic combination within it of the free fantastic, the symbolic, at times even a mystical-religious, with an extreme (and from our point of view) crude slum naturalism.'[36] This is true of *Grimus*; there is 'crude slum naturalism' in the bar and brothel scenes. The genre expresses in its own sense the intimate connection of truth with the simplest, most sensual, earthy reality as well as the highest levels of thought.

Bakhtin goes on to remark: 'The presence of inserted genres reinforces the multi-styled and multi-toned nature of the Menippea; what is coalescing here is a new attitude to the word as the material of literature.'[37] Surely, very true of Rushdie with his interest in the craft of presentation. Bakhtin concludes by 'emphasising the organic unity of all these seemingly very heterogeneous features, the deep internal integrity of this genre'.[38] *Grimus* fails in this respect. Perhaps its plural parentage obstructs a deep unifying impulse like the 'saeva indignatio'[39] behind *Midnight's Children* and *Shame*, but the parts of *Grimus* fit in neatly, though without a narrative flow. Rushdie's style is rather wooden, his humour rather strained. He satirizes ideas and social systems – but in the abstract. The next stage is to locate this in the real world. Rushdie himself has observed of *Grimus*: 'a fantasy without any roots in the discernible world. It's too cerebral a book and it's clever in a kind of pejorative sense.'[40] In *Grimus*, Rushdie is practising his notes; in *Midnight's Children*, he finds his voice and a real subject congenial to his talent. In *Grimus*, the East and the West are grafted. The next stage is fusion, true cultural translation, with *Midnight's Children*. Rushdie's view that he 'had to reject *Grimus* to write *Midnight's Children*',[41] is true, in a sense, but his failure in *Grimus* remains the pillar of his success.[42]

2

Midnight's Children (1981)

Rushdie was a writer without a subject. After attaching himself to a woman from his adopted country, Rushdie did what comes naturally: took her with him to visit the mother country (to celebrate the acceptance of *Grimus* for publication by Gollancz for 'some paltry sum'[1]). There his subject, India, hit him on the nose, with an immediacy of impact, the sights, the smells, the scenes, especially Kashmir where he had holidayed as a child (this explains the luminous beauty with which he invests it in *Midnight's Children* and *Haroun*), while Indian politics, Indira Gandhi's state of emergency, aroused his indignation.

Rushdie returned to England for the publication of *Grimus* – 'to the worst reviews I have ever seen for a first novel',[2] in the opinion of Liz Calder, his friend and most important supporter in his early career, and his publisher too. This failure, though a disappointment, could not deter a man of Rushdie's character and, moreover, he realized what was wrong with the book. In 1974, he insisted at Ogilvy & Mather, despite the agency's reluctance, that he work part-time – to have sufficient leisure for writing. His superior, Keith Ravenscroft, observed Rushdie's 'very, very strong sense of self. Quite unshakable. Work and dignity. The right to be as he is and to say what he says.'[3] For Clarissa Luard, this aspect of Rushdie's personality caused strains, but they married in April 1976.

Rushdie rejected upper-middle-class Belgravia and the couple moved to Kentish Town in North London, a very different environment, where South Asian immigrants were made to feel second-class citizens and treated as such. In 1977, Rushdie became involved in a local project to create employment for Bangladeshi immigrants. It seemed to him that racism had 'seeped into every part of British culture' and that 'Britain is now two entirely different worlds, and the one you inhabit is determined by the colour of your skin.'[4] Rushdie himself got off lightly: 'I have this accidental fair skin, speak with an English accent and don't go round in Nehru topees.'[5] But his experience had a deep impact and is, probably, the basis for *The Satanic Verses*.

In the meantime, his fictional self was in the grip of India. His first effort was titled *Madame Rama* and its chief character bore some resemblance to Indira Gandhi. He offered it to Gollancz but Liz Calder rejected it. 'It had some great stuff in it', she admitted; 'he plundered it for *Midnight's Children'.*[6] He continued to tap the same rich vein and became aware of his true position as a writer. In one way, he allied himself to the non-realist, alternative tradition in Western fiction – Cervantes, Rabelais, Sterne, Swift, Melville, Gogol, Joyce, Günter Grass, Borges, Garcia Márquez. He said: 'In almost every country and in almost every literature there has been, ever so often, an outburst of this large-scale fantasized, satiric, anti-epic tradition, whether it was Rabelais or Gogol or Boccacio…. That simply was the literature I liked to read. So it seemed to me that it was also the literature that I would like to write.'[7] T. S. Eliot said:

> A very young man, who is himself stirred to write, is not primarily critical or even widely appreciative. He is looking for masters who will elicit his consciousness of what he wants to say himself, of the kind of poetry that is in him to write. The taste of an adolescent writer is intense, but narrow; it is determined by personal needs. The kind of poetry that I needed, to teach me the use of my own voice, did not exist in English at all; it was only to be found in French.[8]

Rushdie found his 'masters', and his voice especially via Grass. In fact, the relationship of *Midnight's Children* to *The Tin Drum* is seminal as well as intertextual. Rushdie himself has said: 'I'm sure that Grass is somewhere behind the book. I hadn't read it for many years at the time I wrote *Midnight's Children*, but *The Tin Drum* is one of my favourite novels.'[9] He had chosen a Western language, English, as the medium of his creative work, not his mother tongue, not surprisingly since the affluent in Bombay used English freely and he had been educated at the Cathedral and John Connon School until he went to Rugby.

Rushdie has also allied himself to Eastern tradition. He has stated that the narrative method of *Midnight's Children* was inspired by traditional Indian storytelling:

> One of the strange things about oral narrative – which I did look at very closely before writing *Midnight's Children* – is that you find there a form which is thousands of years old, and yet which has

all the methods of the modernist novel, because when you have somebody who tells you a story at that length, a story which is told from the morning to the night, it probably contains roughly as many words as a novel, and during the course of that story it is absolutely acceptable that the narrator will ever so often enter his own story and chat about it – that he'll comment on the tale, digress because the tale reminds him of something, and then come back to the point. All these things, which are absolutely second nature in an orally told story, become bizarre modern inventions when you write them down. It seems to me that when you look at the old narrative and use it, as I tried to do, as the basis of a novel, you become a modernist writer by becoming a very traditional one. By going back to the very ancient traditions you have done something which is very bizarre and modern.[10]

The narrative strategies of the novel do include a first-person narrator, chat, digressions, a considerable length which permits a range of characters and stories. But Rushdie denies the influence of classical Indian allegory. He has said:

I usually resist the idea of allegory. In India there's too much of it, allegory is a kind of disease. People try to decode everything, every story or text allegorically, and although clearly there are elements that you could call allegorical in *Midnight's Children* and *Shame*, the books are not allegories in the way that *The Pilgrim's Progress* is, where everything stands for something and the real story is a story that is not told. Allegory asks readers to make a translation, to uncover a secret text that has not actually been written. In that sense I don't think my books operate as allegories.[11]

In Sanskrit poetics, there is a category of prose called *Akhyayikas*, which combines fact and fiction, and a category of fiction called *Sakalakatha*, which is a cycle of stories,[12] which may have influenced Rushdie, at least unconsciously, and which surface consciously in *The Satanic Verses* (p. 342) and in the very title of *Haroun and the Sea of Stories*, directly recalling the *Kathasaritsagara*, and in its form. Indian myth is a part of the background of his novels. (In *Midnight's Children*, myth functions as a kind of shorthand to convey concepts though it is rarely fully and elaborately worked out, unlike in Joyce's *Ulysses* and Eliot's *The Waste Land* which use myth as a framework.)

Faced with this dual inheritance, Rushdie seems to be stating his own credo in 'The Courter':

> But I, too, have ropes around my neck, I have them to this day, pulling me this way and that, East and West, the nooses tightening, commanding, *choose, choose.*
>   I buck, I snort, I whinny, I rear, I kick. Ropes, I do not choose between you. Lassoes, lariats, I choose neither of you, and both. Do you hear? I refuse to choose.[13]

He confirms this as not disadvantageous: 'Our identity is at once plural and partial. Sometimes we feel that we straddle two cultures; at other times, that we fall between two stools. But however ambiguous and shifting this ground may be, it is not an infertile territory for a writer to occupy.'[14] He has also called himself 'a translated man';[15] the specific etymological (from the Latin) meaning of translation as 'bearing across' lies at the root of the dual kind of identity based on cultural negotiation, interaction and assimilation; a hybrid, a man who remains a unity, 'makes both one, each this and that' (to echo John Donne's 'The Exstasie'). As such, Rushdie's kind of 'magic realism', whatever the affinities to Grass or Gabriel Garcia Marquez, is uniquely his own. The immediate artistic imperative was to find a method to hit off reality different from restrictive orthodox realism of, say, Zola; Rushdie himself put it thus: 'I think of fantasy as a method of producing intensified images of reality ... one thing that is valuable in fiction is to find techniques for making actuality more intense, so that you experience it more intensely in the writing than you do outside the writing.'[16] The liberation of the imagination, as it functions in this way, affords Rushdie the maximum opportunity to be the artist as 'maker' (to use a traditional term in an extended sense) and a way of transcending the politics of dominance (literary as well as political), whether European or subcontinental.

Rushdie spent five years in writing *Midnight's Children*, time enough for him to mature. He began it as a third-person narrative which would have been useful in setting up a framework, but the change to the first-person was crucial in making his satire come alive and ensuring an immediacy of impact (imagine *Gulliver's Travels* as a third-person narrative!). The novel was completed in June 1979, two weeks before the birth of his son. He dedicated it to Zafar as an inheritor of India's legacy and as a sign of his own connection to it and to Islam (his son is given a distinctively Islamic name, though he had settled down in Britain and married a British woman).

In his 1989 essay, 'Outside the Whale', Rushdie observed that 'the British Raj, after three and a half decades in retirement, has been making a sort of comeback' and instances Attenborough's *Gandhi*, *Octopussy*, the TV serials *The Far Pavilions* and *Jewel in the Crown*, the 'documentary' *War of the Springing Tiger* and David Lean's film of *A Passage to India*.[17] But when Rushdie wrote *Midnight's Children*, India was not yet a subject in vogue or important in the West. 'The received wisdom in those days', said one publisher, 'was that books on India didn't sell, big fat books on India didn't sell and big fat books on India by writers whose last book had been rubbished were worst of all.'[18] Yet Liz Calder, who had moved from Gollancz to Jonathan Cape, London's most prestigious house for literary fiction at that time, was enthusiastic and almost all the referees' opinions were in favour, especially Tom Maschler's view that 'this was a work of genius'.[19] Still, Cape's first print run was only 1,750 copies. The reviewers were rhapsodic. *The New York Review of Books* hailed *Midnight's Children* as 'one of the most important (novels) to come out of the English-speaking world in this generation'.[20] In October 1981, it won the lucrative Booker Prize, Britain's most prestigious award for fiction; twenty-five years later, the Booker of Bookers; and in 2008 the Best of Booker prize as voted by the public, beating five other former Booker winners, shortlisted by a panel of experts from the Prize's forty-year-old history. Rushdie, having succeeded in the West as a man (at the stages of schoolboy, undergraduate and later), had now done so as a writer.

The opening of *Midnight's Children* is arresting and a fine introduction to the novel:

> I was born in the city of Bombay... once upon a time. No, that won't do, there's no getting away from the date: I was born in Doctor Narlikar's Nursing Home on August 15th, 1947. And the time? The time matters, too. Well then: at night. No, it's important to be more.... On the stroke of midnight, as a matter of fact. Clock-hands joined palms in respectful greetings as I came. Oh, spell it out, spell it out: at the precise instant of India's arrival at independence, I tumbled forth into the world. There were gasps. And, outside the window, fireworks and crowds. A few seconds later, my father broke his big toe; but his accident was a mere trifle when set beside what had befallen me in that benighted moment,

because thanks to the occult tyrannies of those blandly saluting clocks I had been mysteriously handcuffed to history, my destinies indissolubly chained to those of my country.[21]

It begins like a fairy tale ('once upon a time' is a leitmotif in the novel), suggesting the level of fantasy, but this is rejected in favour of actual historical dates and facts, suggesting a responsibility to history. At a simple level, the novel is the story of Saleem Sinai, a *Bildungsroman*, and, at a deep level, the story of his country. Saleem is important as an individual, a representative of Independence and a literary mechanism. The humour does more than produce the dominant tone of the novel. Rushdie's wit and humour are unpredictable and destabilize the reader and, thereby, open up new areas of perception, like T. S. Eliot and unlike his heir, Shashi Tharoor, whose humour tends to run along predictable lines (for instance, at the opening of *The Great Indian Novel* it is asserted that India is not 'an underdeveloped country' but 'a highly developed one in an advanced state of decay'[22]). Rushdie has said: '*Midnight's Children* was written as a comic novel. It seemed to me that the comic epic was the natural form for India, and it was amazing that nobody was writing it then, not just in English, but in *any* language that I know of in India. It was as if the richest soil was virgin.'[23] But Rushdie, given his lack of knowledge of the vernacular literatures of India, is unaware of Satinath Bhaduri's classic comic epic in Bengali, *Dorai Charit Manas* (1951) and Srilal Shukla's uproarious saga of a village (in Hindi), *Raag Darbar* (1968), both published before Rushdie became a writer. In the field of British fiction, the term 'comic epic' was coined by Henry Fielding in the Preface to *Joseph Andrews* (1742), while *Tom Jones* (1749), given its larger scale, fits the term better. Yet the fact remains that *Midnight's Children* is a departure in British fiction and in Indian literature *in English* – in its time.

Rushdie wrote: 'It is normally supposed that something always gets lost in translation; I cling, obstinately, to the notion that something can also be gained.'[24] Thus, he is free of the blinkers of a national/cultural identity, is able to offer the reader a critical, alternative view of India and its destiny, and 'give the lie to official facts'.[25] The hi/story begins in early spring, early in the morning, in Kashmir, in 1915 – with the first man (in the family) Aadam (pun on Adam) Aziz, a doctor, Saleem's grandfather. Rushdie is also alluding to the main Indian character in E. M. Forster's *A Passage to India*, thereby evoking the preceding stock of literature about India and the colonial period it dealt with, filling out an era for which Rushdie himself cannot afford much space in his own text. The painting of the Boy Raleigh and the fisherman in *Midnight's Children* alludes to the painting, 'The Jewel in Her Crown', in Paul Scott's *The Raj Quartet* and this allusion too serves the same purpose.

The most prominent feature of Aadam's physique is his extraordinarily large nose, the point at which the inner meets the outer world (suggesting intelligence – a pun on the Greek *nous*) through perception of the external world, both as breath and smell. It is the sign of a patriarch and the head of a 'dynasty'. Aadam is a Westernized intellectual. He was educated as a doctor in Germany, but he could not have got there if not for the British Empire. He is a product of Empire as well as a witness to its break-up. The scientific, rational knowledge, which Aadam brings back, provokes the virulent disapproval of Tai, the boatman, a representative of tradition. Tai abuses the doctor's pigskin (anathema to a Muslim) bag, the symbol of his knowledge: 'makes one unclean just by looking at it... from Abroad full of foreigners' tricks.... Now if a man breaks an arm that bag will not let the bone-setter bind it in leaves' (p. 20). Tai chooses to stink (Rushdie takes a Swiftian interest in excrement) as 'a gesture of unchangingness in defiance of the doctori-attache' (p. 28). Aadam later notices a soldierly young man in a street in Amritsar and thinks: 'the Indians have fought for the British; so many of them have seen the world by now, and been *tainted* by Abroad' (my emphasis, p. 33). Rushdie is conscious of the narrowness, rigidity and the hold of tradition as well as both the value and the danger of hybridization.

Aadam is called upon to treat Naseem, the daughter of the rich landowner Ghani, and he later marries her. Naseem is a representative of the traditional East. Her upbringing is extremely orthodox. She is hidden away in the house, guarded by women. Her husband is chosen by her father. She is given in marriage in traditional style, with dowry and ceremony. When Aadam examined Naseem in her role as patient, he was permitted to see the supposedly afflicted parts of her body through a perforated sheet. The implication is that woman cannot be, at first, seen whole, but a more serious point emerges as Naseem appears to represent Bharat-Mata (Mother India) – that India can be seen, and understood, only in fragments. Naseem as wife is transformed into a formidable figure, known by the title of Reverend Mother. She is a typical Indian (female) figure in this respect – dishing out or not dishing out food, fasting as a protest (like Gandhi). Aadam tries to change her character. He asks her to move during the sex act and come out of purdah. He fails in regard to the first but, though he succeeds in regard to the second, Naseem resents it and the concession is on the surface. She is typically Indian in stipulating religious instruction for her children and in that their first important conflict (in 1932) is over religion – when the atheistic Aadam flings out the guru. In fact, she is often at loggerheads with her Heidelberg-returned mate. Aadam's failure to alter Reverend Mother's character suggests the difficulty, if not impossibility, of changing traditional India.

Pressurized by Tai, Aadam leaves – with Naseem, for Amritsar, from where they were to catch the Frontier Mail to Agra (Aadam had found employment there as a university medical officer). He arrives in Amritsar on 6 April 1919. Saleem's life and that of his family are linked to landmarks in Indian and world history:

> ...my grandfather was holding a pamphlet...looking out of his [hotel] window, he sees it [the message on the pamphlet] echoed on a wall opposite; and there, on the minaret of a mosque; and in the large black type of newsprint under a hawker's arm. Leaflet newspaper mosque and wall are crying: Hartal! Which is to say, literally speaking, a day of mourning, of stillness, of silence. But this is India in the heyday of the Mahatma, when even language obeys the instructions of Gandhiji, and the word has acquired under his influence, new resonances. *Hartal – April 7*, agree mosque newspaper wall and pamphlet, because Gandhi has decreed that the whole of India shall, on that day, come to a halt. To mourn, in peace, the continuing presence of the British. (p. 33)

Indian nationalism grew after the First World War, promoted by the Indian National Congress. Gandhi's call for self-rule and for the removal of untouchability, and his non-violent, civil disobedience campaign spurred the independence movement. David W. Price's claim that 'Mahatma Gandhi hardly appears at all' and that 'primary emphasis on the great figures' is avoided, is a misrepresentation.[26] Here Rushdie is highlighting Gandhi's power, his magic, his ability to transform and influence. This is of a piece with the reactions and atmosphere of the announcement of Gandhi's death in the scene at the cinema hall (men prostrate on the floor weeping and the general shock and desolation indicated); with Lifafa Das's peepshow with 'untouchables being touched, educated people sleeping in large number on railway lines' (as in John Masters's *Bhowani Junction*); and with the leitmotif 'Gandhi dies at the wrong time' (actually, a pun in the novel) which underlines regret and loss. Passive *hartal* mourning turns to *hartal* resistance in the context of nationalism. Rushdie goes on to present the Jallianwala Bagh massacre. Aadam began as a Kashmiri who loses his faith. After his Amritsar experience, he becomes an Indian. Ernest Renan argues:

> A heroic past, great men, glory ... this is the social capital upon which one bases a national idea ... . One loves in proportion to the sacrifices to which one has consented, and in proportion to the ills one has suffered ... . More valuable by far than customs posts and frontiers conforming to strategic ideas is the fact of sharing, in the past, a glorious heritage and regrets, and of having, in the future, [a shared] programme to put into effect, or the fact of having suffered, enjoyed, and hoped together.[27]

Renan is articulating a nineteenth-century position and concepts, yet these are what people and leaders of the colonial and postcolonial world lived and acted by, certainly on the subcontinent, whether it be India against Britain or Bangladesh against Pakistan.

The scene changes to Agra – in the 1930s and, then, the 1940s. One of the closest friends of Aadam was the Rani of Cooch Naheen, 'who was going white in blotches, a disease which leaked into history and erupted on an enormous scale shortly after Independence ... . "I am the victim", the Rani whispers ... "the hapless victim of my cross-cultural concerns. My skin is the outward expression of the internationalism of my spirit" ' (p. 45). She is an admirable kind of liberal but ineffectual, as signified by Naheen (meaning 'nothing', 'nowhere'). Aadam supports Mian Abdullah, the Hummingbird, who invited the leaders of the dozens of Muslim splinter groups to form the Free Islam Convocation, a loosely federated alternative to the dogmatism and vested interests of Muhammad Ali Jinnah's Muslim League. Mian Abdullah is assassinated; Jinnah succeeds in partitioning India and creating a new nation for the Muslims, Pakistan. Mian Abdullah's secretary, Nadir (literally, the bottom-most) Khan, escapes the assassins. Khan in his roles as Muslim politician, as poet (a modernist – rhymeless, verbless), as husband and, later, as revolutionary idealist, a Communist politician (a change of name to Qasim Khan/Lal Qasim signifying his changed identity) is ineffective in all of them; his impotence is symbolic of his powerlessness.

The Rani, Mian Abdullah and Khan are treated in comic terms but the positive values they embody are not negated by the comedy or by their failure (Dickens portrays Pickwick as a comic figure but his positive worth is not erased thereby). Nationalism as an obscurantist and divisive force incurs Rushdie's condemnation, especially when it leads to sectarian massacres as during Partition.

In Agra, Aadam and Reverend Mother raise a family of five. The third daughter, Mumtaz, marries Nadir Khan, who hid in their basement after escaping assassination. Unable to consummate his marriage, Khan divorces her in summary Islamic fashion. But Mumtaz soon after wins the leather-cloth merchant, Ahmed Sinai, who was the chosen of her elder sister, Alia, and, after marriage, is renamed Amina. She accompanies Ahmed to Old Delhi where he lives and conducts a prosperous business. Here the Ravana gang make a cynical use of chauvinism for purposes of extortion, a criminal aspect of the commercialism of India, foreshadowing *The Moor's Last Sigh*. The Muslims who give in to these Hindu blackmailers are not touched, whereas those who resist find their businesses set on fire. The ransom money of Ahmed Sinai, Mr Kemal and S. P. Butt unfortunately does not reach the hands of the Ravana gang and their godowns are burnt down. Ahmed decides to get out of the leather-cloth business and also to move to Bombay to enter the property business, lured by his friend there, Dr Narlikar the gynaecologist. Rushdie emphasizes the historicity of Bombay as does Grass in respect of Gdansk in *The Tin Drum*.

Soon after arrival, Ahmed enters into a bargain with William Methwold, one of the Englishmen projected as a representative of the Raj. Saleem indicates that Methwold is named after the East India Company officer who in 1633 was the first to envision Bombay as a British stronghold and was involved in the emergence of Bombay as a great city. Methwold explains to Ahmed: 'My notion is to stage my own transfer of assets…. Select *suitable persons* … hand everything over absolutely intact: in tiptop working order' (my emphasis, p. 97). He sells his Estate, consisting of four identical houses named after palaces in Europe, on two conditions: that the houses be bought with the entire contents which were to be retained by the new owners; and that the actual transfer takes place at midnight on 15 August 1947, the moment of Independence for India. Thus, Methwold's transaction is symbolic of the transfer of political power. The 'suitable persons', in his view, as the new owners (one Villa was divided into flats) were Ahmed Sinai, a representative of the world of business; Homi Catrack, film magnate and racehorse-owner, a representative of the world of entertainment; Ibrahim Ibrahim, one of the 'idle rich'; Dubash, the physicist, a representative of the world of science and technology; Dr Narlikar a representative of the professional classes; and Commander Sabarmati, a high-flyer in the navy, a representative of the armed forces. David W. Price argues that Methwold wishes to preserve 'the Imperial tradition of the British Raj',[28] but it seems to me that he is only attempting to control India through imposing Western patterns of culture – and, consequently, behaviour – on the power elite of post-Independence India. Actually, the subtext has it that power has been transferred to those already inclined towards the West, the Anglicized Indians. Methwold's buyers agree to accept his terms and even follow his routine regarding habits such as the cocktail hour because they were of a cast of mind already predisposed to such manners. Imperialism does not end when the imperialists leave. When the sun finally set on Methwold's Estate, Methwold's head of hair with its centre-parting which had been a focus of attention, contributing to his impressiveness and being irresistible to women, is shown to be a hairpiece, revealing him in a less attractive light and suggesting deception, the difference between the professions and practice of Empire.

Saleem Sinai is introduced through his voice. He is born after a considerable part of the narrative is over – more than a mere Shandian trick: Saleem's begetting is important. His birth is more so. Rushdie's major concern is post-Independence India, the subject of the bulk of the book. The birth is not fully auspicious. There are rumours in Bombay that the statue of Shivaji, the Marathi hero-king, had galloped the previous night, suggesting the rise of the Shiv Sena, a warning of incipient fissiparous tendencies, and that the stars were unfavourable. Ahmed Sinai lets a chair fall and it breaks his big toe. Rushdie stresses that India was 'a nation which had never previously existed ... quite imaginary ... a mythical land, a country which would never exist except by the efforts of a phenomenal collective will – except in a dream we all agreed to dream ... a mass fantasy shared in varying degrees by Bengali and Punjabi, Madrasi and Jat' (p. 112). It looks as though Rushdie is anticipating Benedict Anderson in his view of the nation as an 'imagined community'. But, at a deeper level, he is showing that this is not true of India, that it is composed of communities (not unified except as in a rare instance in the past under King Asoka and at present, as V. S. Naipaul has it in *India: A Million Mutinies Now*, falling out into its component parts). During the freedom struggle, Indians are shown as united, but only by opposition to the British, and even that did not last. The Muslims opt for a separate state; Pakistan is almost Midnight's Child, the Partition taking place a day before Indian Independence; 'the mass blood-letting' is noted, though not described. Later, the Muslims themselves divide and Bangladesh is born on 16 December 1971.

Nevertheless, at Independence India's expectations are high, caught by Nehru's lofty rhetoric: 'At the stroke of the midnight hour, while the world sleeps, India awakens to life and freedom.... A moment comes, which comes but rarely in history, when we step out from the old to the new.... We have to build the noble mansion of free India, where *all* her children may dwell' (my emphasis, pp. 116–18). Correspondingly, Saleem's birth is invested with great promise. Newspapers celebrate his arrival. Nehru himself ratifies his position in a personal letter: 'We shall be watching over your life with the closest attention; it will be, in a sense, the mirror of our own' (p. 122). Saleem announces that he is a prophet, alluding to Oskar in *The Tin Drum* identifying himself with Jesus. Guru Purushottam comes to witness the birth of the Mubarak, the Blessed. Shri Ramram Seth the seer's forecast regarding Saleem's life sounds cryptic when uttered to Amina but turns out to be meaningful and true stage by stage – imparting to his life a sense of destiny. On his bedroom wall hung a picture of the Boy Raleigh and an old fisherman with a pointing finger – pointing to history. August was the month of Saleem's birthday; it is Krishna's as well. The walls of Saleem's room, his crib, his pram, his eyes were all sky-blue – Krishna's and (on p. 136 'the sky-hued Jesus of the missionaries', for example) Jesus' colour, the liturgical colour of hope. The descriptions in these pages of the novel abound in the colours saffron and green, colours of the flag of independent India.

At Dr Narlikar's Nursing Home, two children were born at midnight – the child of Ahmed and Amina Sinai and the (illegitimate) child of Vanita (the minstrel Wee Willie Winkie's wife) and, presumably, William Methwold. The nurse Mary Pereira, who was the girlfriend of Joseph D'Costa, an orderly at a Peddar Road clinic and a revolutionary who believed that the struggle in India was not between Hindus and Muslims but between the rich and the poor, performed her own act of social adjustment for the sake of her beloved: she switched the babies. So Saleem is not the child of Ahmed and Amina; yet, later, when the truth is revealed, they continue to accept him as their son. Midnight's Child is thus a hybrid of dubious parentage; he is a product of India (Vanita) and, perhaps, the Raj (Methwold). Saleem becomes a representative Anglicized, middle-class intellectual; his nose, his most prominent physical trait, signifies intelligence. The true heir of India is dispossessed and brought up in the slums by Wee Willie Winkie (Vanita does not survive her child-bearing). Despite his hidden Muslim parentage and 'Anglo' foster-father, he carries a Hindu name, Shiva, which indicates deep historic roots, since Muslim culture was a latecomer to India, and has a further appropriateness, given that he represents the indigenous (predominantly Hindu) proletariat. His most prominent physical trait is his knees, suggesting strength, basis, foundation, someone nearer the soil. Saleem is not India, but a segment of India. So is Shiva. Nose is no whole, any more than Knees. Saleem and Shiva turn out to be antagonists; Rushdie's positive implication is that there should be unity, not opposition. What the transfer of power means in terms of class (an important issue in postmodernism), is clear at the very birth of the nation.

Rushdie suggests further justification for the exchange of babies: 'this very melodramatic device...was a genuine kind of Bombay-talkie, B-movie notion, and I thought that a book which grew out of a movie city ought to contain such notions...these are children not so much of their parents, but children of the time, children of history'[29] (the latter point is made by Saleem, too [p. 118]).

Rushdie suggests more justification for Saleem's very large nose: 'the map of India...for me resembled a very large nose hanging into the sea'.[30] Emil Zagallo, the geography master, is crazed and derisive, but the fact that he sees the map of India in the face of Saleem possesses a seriousness of which he is unaware: 'See here [the nose] – the Deccan peninsula hanging down!.... These stains are Pakistan! Thees birthmark on the right ear is the East Wing; and thees horrible stained left cheek, the West!...Pakistan ees a stain on the face of India!' (pp. 231–2). Saleem appears the identical twin of his country. The significance of his nose is even richer; Rushdie explains:

> the god Ganesh, having the head of an elephant, also has a very large nose, and it seemed to me that he was a proper mythological ancestor to place behind Saleem. Partly for that reason, and partly for two other reasons. One is that Ganesh is the kind of patron deity of literature, and since Saleem is the story-teller, I thought that he should have as an ancestor the god of literature.

The legend of Ganesh is the legend of disputed parentage; that's to say the reason he has the head of an elephant is because Shiva and Parvati quarrel over who the father of the child is. Shiva becomes convinced that his wife has been fooling around, that this child is not his, and so in rage he cuts off its head and then, repenting, looks around heaven for a head; and what comes to hand is the head of an elephant. This is stuck on, and so you have a god with an elephant's head ... since Saleem's entire ancestry is also very murky and disputed ... it was correct to give him, as a mythological ancestor, somebody with disputed ancestry ... [31]

Ganesh, the God of Wisdom, of Knowledge, took down the *Mahabharata* at the dictation of the sage Vyasa. Like the scribe of the *Mahabharata*, Saleem too is a historian of sorts. Ganesh is the myth central to *Midnight's Children.*

The history Saleem records is that of himself and his family and that of his country to which the personal history is linked. Saleem feels the mantle of greatness has fallen upon him; the country's aspirations are soaring. The hopes in both spheres are impaired as the histories unfold; *Midnight's Children* is postmodern in that, as Linda Hutcheon notes, 'in general terms, postmodernism takes the form of self-conscious, self-contradictory, self-undermining statement'.[32] In the personal sphere, Saleem's father, deprived of wifely attention, supplanted by his son, his vision blurred by whisky and djinn, tries to raise his fortunes by investing in tetrapods, Dr Narlikar's entrepreneurial dream. The dream is not inconceivable, given that 'Bombay is a city built on reclaimed land',[33] but its futility is suggested by the fact that concrete tetrapods have never been used for this purpose. (From another perspective, 'land reclamation' is a metaphor for the task Rushdie is undertaking in his novel.[34]) In the national sphere, Gandhi is murdered by a Hindu assassin. Thus, in both spheres, expectations are undermined by disasters.

Snakes play a prominent and ambiguous part in the narrative. Snakes and ladders, a metaphor for the vicissitudes of life, is a leitmotif in the novel. Snakes are also invested with the power to save or slay, recalling Robert Graves's line 'Athene had previously given two drops of this ... to Erichthonius, one to kill, the other to cure, and fastened the phials to his serpent body ...'[35] as well as the Indian belief regarding *kundalini*, a vital form of cosmic energy embodied in everybody and pictured as a coiled serpent at the base of the spine, both portrayals of a latent force equally capable of redemption

and destruction. The text (p. 136) records a rumour about a mad
Bengali snake-charmer who frees snakes from snake-farms (such
as Dr Schaapsteker's Institute where their medical functions were
studied and anti-venenes devised), leading them by the Pied Piper
fascination of his flute, the instrument traditionally associated
with Krishna. Rumour added that the Tubriwallah was seven feet
tall with a bright blue skin and 'that he was Krishna...he was the
sky-hued Jesus of the missionaries'. Blue is the colour associated
with hope, and the identification with Jesus as well as the liberating influence of his flute marks him out as a saviour. But the colour
has a further significance. Krishna signifies 'dark' and the God is
invariably painted blue/blue-grey in contrast to other figures; this
is seen in the traditional Barahmasa paintings of India in which the
classical artist sought to evoke the essence of each of the months of
the Hindu calendar. This factor has stimulated speculation as to the
rise of his importance as a deity from a position on the margins of
the Vedic pantheon. Mythology presents him as the son of Devaki,
smuggled out to save him from the wicked uncle who, it is proph-
esied, will die at his hands, and consequently brought up as the son
of the Chief of the herdsmen, stealing butter as a child and dallying
with the cowgirls or *gopis* as a youth, instead of leading the life of a
scion of the *Kshatriyas*, the royal warrior-clan. Such a god may well
be sympathetic to the lower classes and their aspirations. When
the revolutionary Joseph D'Costa is found dead, he is in the clock-
tower which is a landmark in Bombay and the tower is described
as 'peeling, inoperational' (p. 146), suggesting that 'the time is out
of joint' and needs someone 'born to set it right'; Joseph himself is
surrounded by the bombs of an incipient revolution, and has died by
the fangs of a banded krait, a venomous snake, since a would-be liberator may unleash forces that are violent, destructive. Picture Singh
too, Communist and magician, charms snakes yet survives, though
drained of vitality. On the other hand, when Baby Saleem falls very
seriously ill, the sickness is diagnosed as typhoid by his grandfather
and his life is saved by the diluted venene of the King Cobra, provided by Dr Schaapsteker. Rushdie is also evidently concerned here
with the nature of good and evil which continues to preoccupy him
in *The Satanic Verses*. From one angle, the snake is evil as in the case
of Joseph D'Costa, from another angle the snake is positive as in the
case of Baby Saleem: good may emerge from evil.

Schaapsteker, the old European doctor, claims the status of father
in respect of Saleem fairly enough, as a life-giver because his snake

venom had saved Saleem. He is one of the eight different types who are presented as fathering Saleem – the Anglo Wee Willie Winkie who is an entertainer; Ahmed Sinai – the native businessman; Nadir Khan poet and leftist; his uncles, Hanif Aziz, the failed realist in films, and General Zulfikar who introduces him to Pakistani realpolitik, and, finally, Picture Singh, both entertainer and political activitist.

The links between the personal history and national/world history are coincidental or circumstantial. In the summer of 1956, Saleem's sister, the Brass Monkey, developed the curious habit of setting fire to shoes and thereby tried to impede family progress, while Nasser sank ships at Suez and thereby slowed down the movements of the world by obliging it to travel round the Cape of Good Hope – a matter of coincidence on the plane of a parallelism. The British imposition of English during the Raj as the single most important and dominant language led to the dormancy of Indian language rivalries.

With Independence, these surface. In February 1957 the Marathi language march has already started when Saleem crashes into it on his runaway bicycle. The demonstrators then take up his chant as their song of war and clash with the Gujarati marchers; Saleem himself flees. Saleem does not cause the language violence (which ended with the partition of the state of Bombay), though he thinks he does; it is Independence that does it. Saleem merely makes an accidental contribution through force of circumstances. Rushdie's uneasiness regarding the fissiparous tendencies in India, noted at Independence, has reason to deepen after it. 'While parliamentarians poured out speeches about "Chinese aggression" and "the blood of our martyred jawans", Saleem's eyes began to stream with tears; while the nation puffed itself up, convincing itself that the annihilation of the little yellow men was at hand, Saleem's sinuses, too, puffed up and distorted a face...' (p. 299) – again, a coincidence, this time on the metaphorical plane. Thus, Saleem's connection to history is remote. In two instances, however, he appears to be at the hub. He is at his uncle General Zulfikar's dinner table when Pakistan's soldiery plot Ayub Khan's coup: 'With the fate of the nation in my hands, I shifted condiments and cutlery, capturing empty biriani-dishes with water-glasses, stationing salt cellars, on guard, around water-jugs' (p. 290). As the Buddha, he led the Pakistani troops to the lair of Sheikh Mujib-ur-Rahman who had proclaimed the state of Bangladesh. Yet, even in these instances, Saleem's association with history is tangential. His voice proclaims his place as 'at the centre of the universe' (p. 126) but the text undermines it, clearly revealing it as peripheral. In the end, Saleem realizes this himself. After all, in the painting with the Boy Raleigh, the pointing finger is that of the fisherman – a peripheral figure.

As I stated earlier, Saleem feels that greatness has been thrust upon him, but, after the excitation over his birth, this notion is subverted by the treatment accorded to him by those around him. His romantic hopes are not only given short shrift by the American Evie Burns but are clearly misplaced, given that, two years later, Evie, back in America, knifes an old woman and is sent to reform school. Emil Zagallo jeers at him and pulls out a clump of his hair. His head in a bandage and ascribing it to 'a sporting accident' (p. 233), he becomes soft on Masha Miovic at the Cathedral School Social. Goaded by Masha, he takes on two bullies, then turns tail and loses a segment of his middle finger as his hand is caught in a door slammed by one of them. When he hears voices in his head for the first time and announces this to his family and ayah, he expects 'pats on the back, sweetmeats, public announcements, maybe more photographs' (p. 104), but his mother calls him 'a madman' and his father delivers a huge blow on the side of his head, which permanently impairs the hearing in his left ear. Saleem's life turns out to be a series of mishaps and misfortunes; his physique is disfigured and maimed. Far from emerging as a hero, he becomes an anti-hero – the two notions being in constant collision in the text. As Rushdie points out, 'the nature of heroism is one of the concerns of the book'.[36] He adds that 'heroism is something that is very alive in Indian culture and narrative tradition'.[37] The text has it that heroes are a rarity; only Gandhi measures up to one. His urge to unite, through peace, the religions; through moral means, the castes; is a major positive in the novel. Even Nehru at the moment of Independence and especially later seems a pontifical figure; his obsession with astrology does not redound to his credit. Commander Sabarmati, 'the most popular murderer in the history of Indian jurisprudence' (p. 262), poses an ambiguous instance, based on the real life Nanavati case,[38] on a lesser level.

At the age of nearly nine, fearing that his much-trumpeted existence might turn out an empty one, Saleem took to hiding in his mother's large washing-chest and it was there that he discovered voices in his head. He then receives a jolt in a bicycle accident and realizes in full his telepathic powers. He is able to tune in to

Midnight's Children, those born between midnight and one a.m. on 15 August 1947 – a total of 1,001. The figure is 'roughly accurate' according to the Indian birth-rate,[39] alludes to *The Arabian Nights* and is a lucky number, according to Indian belief. This was the 'generation which was too young to remember the Empire or the liberation struggle'.[40] Inevitably for a country like India, a large number failed to survive – 420 'since time immemorial, the number associated with fraud, deception and trickery' (p. 196). The children were gifted (a few were freaks) and 581 lived. They could get in touch with one another through Saleem's mind. This conception could have been inspired by science fiction such as John Wyndham's *The Chrysalids* or the supernatural side of Indian literature or both, and (as Rushdie suggests) has a psychological basis at the beginning in that lonely children like Saleem invent imaginary companions.[41] The 'companions' spill over into the real world. The Midnight's Children's Conference takes the initials of the Metro Cub Club in the novel and ironically alludes to the imperial emblem, the Marylebone Cricket Club. The Indian MCC is a kind of alternative parliament. Westminster-style democracy, whether in India or Pakistan, did not seem to be succeeding. The alternative could have been a kind of resistance as put together by Midnight's Children. But it takes a conspiratorial form, remains at a verbal level and on the fringe, without any coherent programme of action. Dissension sets in and, more seriously: 'the prejudices and world-views of adults began to take over their minds, I found children from Maharashtra loathing Gujaratis, and fair-skinned northerners reviling Dravidian "black-ies"; there were religious rivalries; and class entered our councils. The rich children turned up their noses at being in such lowly company; Brahmins began to feel uneasy at permitting even their thoughts to touch the thoughts of untouchables; while among the low-born, the pressures of poverty and Communism were becom-ing evident ... and, on top of all this, there were clashes of personal-ity ...' (pp. 254–5). The Midnight's Children's Conference gradually disintegrates; the younger generation succumbs to the divisions characteristic of India; instead of forging a unity, it becomes a victim of the fissiparous tendencies of the country. Only three of the chil-dren are sufficiently individualized to become characters as such – Saleem, Shiva and Parvati. The rest remain, in Rushdie's words, 'a kind of vague collective entity ... a kind of metaphor of hope and of possibility, which, one day, was destroyed. A metaphor of hope betrayed and possibilities denied.'[42]

Their destruction is partly the work of Indira Gandhi, ironical given that she is the daughter of Nehru, one of the founding fathers of Independence. In the novel, she is called the Widow. She was, in real life, a widow, and a widow is a figure of ill-omen in Indian culture. Whereas green and saffron, the colours of the Indian flag, were prominent in descriptions at Independence, the Widow and her virtual dictatorship are presented in green and black (the negation of saffron): 'And children torn in two in Widow hands which rolling halves of children roll them into little balls the balls are green the night is black' (p. 208). Rushdie is actually tapping strong sources of emotion and intertextuality: '*The Wizard of Oz* goes for bold, expressionist splashes ... . So striking were these colour effects that, soon after seeing the film as a child, I began to dream of green-skinned witches; years afterwards, I gave these dreams to the narrator of my novel *Midnight's Children* ... the nightmare of Indira Gandhi is fused with the equally nightmarish figure of Margaret Hamilton: a coming-together of the Wicked Witches of the East and of the West.'[43] There is also an allusion here to Niobe, the killer of men, of the green paint and amber eyes, to the black, wicked witch, in Grass's *The Tin Drum*. Indira Gandhi's hair has a centre-parting, like William Methwold's. The Britisher is alienated, but Indira Gandhi is not: the symbol chosen for her party is the sacred cow and calf; she is given to consulting astrologers. But they are alike in symbolizing kinds of oppression. Under the rule of the Widow, India is being made impotent, literally, through vasectomy and, metaphorically, too, as exemplified by the Midnight's Children and Saleem himself. Midnight's Children have no power, no hope and no future.

The destruction of the Children is also made possible by one of their own number, Shiva, appropriately so in that his name signifies Destruction in one of its aspects. The text says that Shiva had the gifts of war – of Rama, who could draw the undrawable bow, and Bhima, the mightiest and most militaristic of the five Pandavas (p. 200). He is the voice of expediency and self-interest and ultimately sells out to the world of power. But this is the result of his deprivation and dispossession. Shiva is the God of Procreation as well (the *lingam*, the phallus, is his symbol), and it is Saleem who shoulders the major responsibility for the debacle:

The questions I'd [Saleem] been dreading and trying not to provoke began: *Why is Shiva not here?* And: *Why have you closed off part of your mind?* ... when ... the children of midnight launched a concerted assault on me, I had no defence ... accusing me of secrecy, prevarication, high-handedness, egotism; they tore me apart; because, despite all their sound-and-fury, I could not unblock what I had sealed away; I could not bring myself to tell them Mary's secret [that Shiva was the heir, the leader, and Saleem the bastard child of Methwold and Vanita] ... now, as the midnight children lost faith in me, they also lost their belief in the thing I had made for them. I continued ... to attempt to convene – our nightly sessions, but they fled from me, not one by one, but in tens and twenties; each night, less of them were willing to tune in ... (p. 298)

Perhaps the hope of a modern, integrated nation lay in the liberal intellectuals, the haves, with their hybrid culture, but the haves denied, ignored, suppressed the need to share their inheritance of India with the non-intellectual but practically and *physically* power-ful masses, the dispossessed, the true heirs. The fisherman's finger, from a longer perspective, was 'an accusing finger which obliged us to look at the city's dispossessed' (p. 123) and open to an interpreta-tion as a warning.

The blueness of Saleem's eyes – underlined later in the novel, too – and other items in blue connected to him, because of the asso-ciation of blue with Krishna and Jesus, is a clue of possible (potential but never realized) saviourhood, just as Independence might have meant hope for India (but was not). Saleem is endowed with extraor-dinary powers – telepathic and, later, olfactory – but he is not able to use these to bring about anything worthwhile. The only promising action of his is when he uses his telepathic powers to convene the Midnight's Children's Conference, but this ends in complete fail-ure – and mainly owing to his own shortcomings. For the most part, he employs his gifts for purposes which bring him no credit – such as cheating at school or behaving as a kind of Peeping Tom as he spies on his mother when she carries on a Platonic association with her former husband, Nadir Khan. His olfactory powers are made use of by others and for destructive purposes – in a role no more important than as a tracker-dog; his only significant action even in this respect is to sniff out Mujib-ur-Rahman. Perhaps the trait most disadvantageous to him is his passivity (things seem to happen to him rather than he shape events) – for the most part, until the phase in Bangladesh and after.

The heirs of William Methwold sell their Villas – Ahmed Sinai holds out to the last. The heirs of the heirs of Methwold are the

Narlikar women – the dour respectable commercialism of India. Saleem's inflamed sinuses are drained; as a result, he loses his telepathic powers but acquires olfactory gifts instead. His family moves to Pakistan. He himself is not unhappy to leave 'the city in which Shiva lurked...like a landmine' (p. 345), but Karachi proves hardly a suitable alternative: 'Beset...by the knowledge the name of the faith upon which the city stood meant "submission", my new fellow-citizens exuded the flat boiled odours of acquiescence, which were depressing to a nose which had smelt – at the very last...the highly spiced nonconformity of Bombay' (p. 308). He studies at his aunt's college, 'but not even learning could make him feel a part of this country...in which my fellow-students took out processions to demand a stricter, more Islamic society – proving that they had contrived to become the antithesis of students everywhere else on earth by demanding more-rules-not-less' (p. 310). Saleem's (and Rushdie's) feelings could hardly be plainer.

In India, Saleem's sister occupied a peripheral position and did things to gain attention, given that Saleem was at the centre. On the other hand, in Pakistan, she reaches stardom as a singer and is at the centre of things. The Brass Monkey acquires a new name, Jamila Singer, and this is a sign of a new identity. Saleem's is the voice of secularism and multiculturalism, ideals at Indian Independence; Jamila Singer is, literally and metaphorically, the voice of the highly religious, non-secular nationalism of Pakistan. Again, a perforated sheet appears; Jamila sings through the hole, suggesting that she is playing a role. As the Brass Monkey, in response to Sonny Ibrahim's overtures of love, she with the assistance of three beefy female swimmers rips every scrap of clothing off his body. The fires remain: as Jamila Singer, in reply to Saleem's late-flowering love for her (not incestuous; he now knows that she is not a genuine sister of his), she turns him over to the army and he is sent to Bangladesh. Perhaps the match is not a suitable one and Rushdie is suggesting that the demands of art (Jamila is a singer) will prevent a man from getting to grips with rough reality.

The course of history seems downhill. Gandhi is assassinated soon after Independence. Nehru dies before his time. He is succeeded by the Widow. Moraji Desai follows – a urine-drinking dotard. Rushdie's treatment of Indian Independence in comic terms and his critical view of India's leaders is, in one way, linked to Western tradition. Churchill trivialized Gandhi by calling him 'a half-naked fakir'.[44] Westerners have been critical of Gandhi's testing of his chastity at the expense of the women who slept beside him and being supported in old age by young girls. On the other hand, Indians respect, even revere, their nationalist leaders, especially Gandhi and Nehru, and the moment of Independence. Yet, there is a long-standing Indian tradition which is critical, even cynical, about politics. *The Mahabharata* suggests that no leader is totally innocent or guiltless: Indra tells Yudhisthira, 'Hell must be seen by all kings without fail.'[45] *Kissa Kursi Ka (Story of the Chair)*, a Hindi play in the 1970s by Amrith Nahata, was a severe parody of the tyrannical years of Indira Gandhi.

Saleem records how India is humiliated by China in their border conflict, how Five Year Plans do not achieve their targets, how Pakistan ceases to be a democracy, how Indo-Pakistani relations deteriorate and how the countries go to war in 1965. The war eliminates his family (he suggests this was its purpose!). Saleem himself is brained by his mother's silver spittoon, which surfaces in the narrative as one of its leitmotifs. He is styled the buddha, an almost reborn identity. The buddha simply records, impersonally, minus Saleem's individual perspective. The narrative strategy is rather like John Dos Passos's *Camera Eye*, where the narrative is interspersed with sections of prose, comprising headlines, fragments of striking news and scraps of pop songs from the appropriate period, but, unlike the *Camera Eye*, comment does leak in via irony: neutrality is neither achieved nor actually sought. Nevertheless, the voices of Saleem and the buddha, who is numb and neither remembers nor feels – not even an electric shock (p. 353) – are different.

Saleem/buddha divides present from past – as Pakistan was divided. The buddha secedes from history and his example is followed by Sheikh Mujib who led the East Wing into secession – as Bangladesh. Emptied of history, the buddha is completely submissive. He becomes the 'man-dog' of a 'Canine Unit for Tracking and Intelligence Activities', composed of Ayooba Baloch, Farooq Rashid and Shaheed Dar, sent from Pakistan to Bangladesh.

The reader is informed that the Urdu word 'buddha' meant 'old man' whereas Buddha meant 'he-who-achieved-enlightenment-under-the-bodhi-tree' (p. 349). Yet Saleem is shown sitting under a chinar tree, apparently since no 'bodhi-tree' is available (p. 350), and, later, in the jungle, the parallel to the Buddha is closer: Saleem has taken to sitting cross-legged (the Buddha's posture) under a sundri-tree (p. 364). Saleem-the-saviour motif continues. The buddha, finally unable to pursue his submissive role, his soul seared by pessimism, futility and shame, deserts into the historyless ano-nymity of the Sundarbans, dragging the three (child) members of the 'CUTIA' unit after him. The jungle chapter, 'different in texture from what was around it', is the most impressively written section of the novel and represents the 'descent into hell' in Rushdie's (comic) epic.[46] The magical jungle, having tortured Ayooba, Farooq and Shaheed, with their misdeeds, was leading them towards adult-hood. The forest found a way through to the buddha when a blind, translucent snake bit, and poured venom, into his heel. Robert Graves remarks that the heel was 'the one vulnerable point of sacred kings'[47] – an allusion appropriate to the B/buddha. This is the sec-ond time that snake venom enters Saleem's body and also saves him. He is rejoined to the past, his self is unified, except that he could not remember his name.

When the buddha and his unit emerge from the jungle, it is October 1971. The Indian attempt to intervene in the Bangladeshi rebellion proves decisive in December the same year. When the characters return to Dacca, interesting connections arise between *The Tin Drum* and *Midnight's Children*. In *The Tin Drum*: 'the ants were in no way affected by the arrival of the Russian army. They still had the same interest – potatoes and sugar…. The ants found themselves facing a new situation but, undismayed by the detour, soon built a new highway round the doubled-up Matzerath; for the sugar…had lost none of its sweetness….'[48] In *Midnight's Children*, Shaheed, bisected by a grenade, wants to enter a minaret, and the buddha carries him there. 'Shaheed babbled of light-bulbs while red ants and black ants fought over a dead cockroach…. Down below…antlike people were emerging, preparing for peace; the ants, however, ignored the ant-like, and fought on…when the screams began; [the buddha] looked up to see an abandoned cockroach. (Blood had been seeping along trowel-furrows; ants, following the dark viscous trail, had arrived at the source of the leakage, and Shaheed expressed his fury at becom-ing the victim of not one, but two wars.)…. Shaheed, fulfilling his father's dearest wish, had finally earned his name…' (pp. 376–7). Shaheed means martyr; he has died in war, in a *jihad* of a sort; Matzerath chokes on his Nazi-party pin, suffocates and is shot by the Russians. There are ideological parallels. The Pakistani war to retain East Pakistan forcibly is Fascist. In both cases, a background of war, preceding peace; in both cases, the dead are identified with aggressors, are active supporters of a cause. Earlier, the buddha had recorded the Pakistani violence: '… the intelligentsia in the city being

massacred by the hundred ... slit throats being buried in unmarked
graves ... lady doctors were being bayoneted before they were raped,
and raped again before they were shot' (pp. 375–6). The account is
horrifying. In Rushdie's view, 'The Emergency and the Bangladesh
war were the most terrible events since Independence.'[49]

The Indian advance into Dacca was a triumphal march with
sideshows. A hundred and one of the finest Indian entertainers
and conjurers from the famous magicians' ghetto in Delhi had
been transported, including Parvati-the-Witch and Picture Singh,
a seven-foot giant known as the Most Charming Man in the World
because of his unsurpassable skills as a snake-charmer and striding,
twined from head to foot with deadly snakes with their poison-sacs
intact, evoking the snake leitmotif in the novel. Parvati sees the buddha and gives him back his name, Saleem. Parvati and Picture Singh
smuggle Saleem back into India. Saleem's Pakistani phase is over.
He is reunited with his earlier life.

He lives in the magicians' ghetto in Delhi. The magicians were
Communists almost to a man and their colony reflected the many
divisions and dissensions of the Party at large. Magicians can try to
influence a crowd. Magicians can change the world. They can also
be illusionists. Magicians can be taken on a metaphorical level as a
representation of politicians. The leader of these particular magicians was Picture Singh – an inspirational figure. His advocacy of
an Indian type of socialism is a positive. He beats a challenger in his
field, in a snake-charming contest, but 'the efforts of his struggle had
broken something inside him, his victory was a defeat' (p. 456) and
his ultimate fate is uncertain. Yet, as in the case of the Rani of Cooch
Naheen, Mian Abdullah and Nadir Khan, his positive worth is not
negated. As Linda Hutcheon observes, 'postmodernism ultimately
manages to install and reinforce as much as undermine and subvert
the conventions and presuppositions it appears to challenge'.[50]

Saleem uses impotence as an excuse – it soon becomes a fact – to
avoid marrying Parvati, but does so when she begets a child by
Shiva. Parvati herself later disappears, presumably a victim of the
State destruction (under the Widow) of slums, even of the entertainers who had earlier adorned the triumphal march of the Indian
army in Dacca. Saleem's class has proved sterile. The indigenous, the
working class it had suppressed and marginalized, those with the
roots in the soil, not necessarily rural but those in touch with the real
world, are needed by India – those like Shiva and Parvati. In Indian
myth, Parvati is the consort of Shiva. Hope in the novel is associated

with the child of parents such as Shiva and Parvati. (The bastards Shiva fathers on rich women are a mere exhibition of class-revenge and the potency of him and his class.) In the case of Saleem, what is extra large is the nose; in the case of this child, it is the ears. The nose is the agent of experience; Saleem savours the period of tragic experience in his country. The ears are superior to the nose: what the child takes in, goes straight to the mind. The child knows what it wants and how to get it; his silence (while the Emergency lasted) is ambiguous and suggests reserves of strength. 'He was elephant-headed Ganesh' (p. 420), suggesting a promise of intelligence and prosperity (Ganesh is the patron deity of shopkeepers) and rooted in the soil, tradition. As Rushdie intends, the book shows 'the end of a particular hope', but it 'implies that there is another, tougher generation on the way'.[51] (By 1988, this seemed to Rushdie 'absurdly, romantically optimistic'.[52])

Uma Parameswaran argues that 'the central issue' in all Rushdie's novels is 'the dichotomy of good and evil in oneself and the world'.[53] In *Midnight's Children*, evil can appear clear and unalloyed as in the case of the Widow. The good, however, is mixed, whether it is represented by Saleem or Shiva. Good does not triumph over evil in the present, but, as the child suggests, it survives and may triumph in the future. Rushdie argues that optimism, 'the Indian talent for non-stop self-regeneration', is suggested by the fact that 'the narrative constantly throws up new stories, it teems; the form – multitudinous, hinting at the infinite possibilities of the country'.[54] But it seems to me that this kind of optimism is more a product of the vitality of the rhythm of the novel and of its comic tone.

From one perspective, *Midnight's Children* is a fiction about fiction, an allegory about writing, a deconstruction of the text. Saleem is writing his novel and he relates it to Padma. She is not a reader but a listener, an audience. She is a pickle-maker (at Mary Pereira's Braganza pickle factory where Saleem is presently the supervisor), and such a woman, in an Indian context, would be illiterate, at least in regard to reading in English. The story is always told to her, the transmission always oral. Hence the presence of retrospective and prospective summaries of the narrative at regular intervals. Padma is a native non-intellectual, but not unintelligent; the author is a formidable intellectual. Her judgements are comments not to be accepted as valid assessments, but sometimes they serve as a critique of Saleem's views and actions. Her credo as a critic is 'whatnextism', conventional, yet not to be discounted. She keeps the actual reader of the novel alert, critical, and prevents him/her from getting absorbed into the world of the novel; the novel, not mimetic, not presented as an illusion of the real world, remains, in a postmodern way, a self-reflexive artefact. But Padma is not only audience but also co-creator. The mythological associations of her name suggest that she is a sort of Muse. Padma has been named after the lotus goddess. Saraswathi, the goddess of creative arts, is always portrayed as carrying a *veena* and seated on a lotus. Saleem needs Padma's support; his memory tends to fail without it. The writer and the audience collaborate to create the text. This is in keeping with postmodern belief as well as Anandavardhana's ninth-century aesthetics in *Dhvanyaloka* (the *sahrdya*, the critical yet appreciative reader, is his equivalent for the co-creator). It is important to note that Saleem also proceeds with his writing in Padma's absence (though admittedly seldom), yet with no difference in the quality of his writing, suggesting the inner compulsion of the writer and that the text can exist independently of the audience, the autonomy of art.

Padma enjoys an important surrogate status. She is also important as a character. Like Shiva and Parvati, she represents the working class and is in touch with the real world. She embodies a practicality, warmth, a comforting quality – not to be discounted. She is, indeed, a positive presence, and her traits, including her interest in Saleem's other pencil, impart a tangible reality. Saleem has been cracking up and he has been rendered impotent by the Widow, but Padma affectionately accepts him as her husband, with no sense of self-sacrifice, in keeping with her Hindu background and conjugal tradition. The intellectual requires a companion like Padma. The lotus is the only beautiful object in Saleem's muddy world. Timothy Brennan interprets: 'What seems like sexual attraction is really a cold respect. "Perfect harmony" exists only as a lull between crises, in a relationship of mixed loathing and submission.'[55] I read it as a warmly comic and satisfying relationship.

Saleem adopts the child of Shiva and Parvati: the intellectual can contribute to but not father the new generation. Significantly, the child's foster parents are from the middle and working classes: the union of these classes is desirable, and necessary, for India's welfare and progress. That Saleem's surname is Sinai is significant. Moses saw the Promised Land from Mount *Sinai*, but Moses was told that *he* would never enter the Promised Land himself – only show the way. Saleem Sinai shows the way he himself cannot go – but his successor *may*. Finally, while on his way to Kashmir for a holiday with his newly wedded wife (the novel began in Kashmir and has now come full circle), Saleem disintegrates, not reaching his destination, literally and metaphorically, like the generation he represents. But the festive feeling of the atmosphere at this point in the narrative and his disintegration like a firework suggest a kind of apotheosis, something positive gained from the journey.

In *Grimus*, Rushdie's portrayal of women was seemingly feminist, yet subverts feminism. *Midnight's Children* marks a mixed kind of advance. His portrayal offers a greater range and positiveness, yet incorporates a curious negativity as well. Naseem is, at first, a nubile girl and devoted wife, as evident in her reaction to mercuro-chrome. She later becomes a tough matriarch, often trying to impose her will. The Widow is destructive, her hand sleek yet lethal. Evie Burns is seductive/destructive. The Brass Monkey repels love, yet is no Islamic fundamentalist: she finally seeks virginal sanctuary in a convent. Parvati is protective, tender – and powerful; a kind of mother goddess, the source of new hope; yet not beautiful. Padma is protective, tough, vigorous, loving, powerful too; she, too, is not beautiful as such. The Narlikar women are tough financiers, powerful. The ayah Mary Pereira is the nurturer of Saleem's crea-tive/chutnifying power and his fate in that it is she who switches the babies. The preponderance of women, powerful yet exerting a certain attraction, suggests the altered view of women in *Midnight's Children*. 'In *Shame*, the women seem powerful only as monsters, of one sort or another', remarks Gayatri Spivak[56] – with reason.

Rushdie's innovativeness in *Midnight's Children* includes his use of language. It is different from that of British writers about India such as Kipling, Forster and Paul Scott, and from that of Indian writers in English, except G. V. Desani. It is more complex than a use of the Indian variety of English, and he learnt from Desani's *All About H. Hatterr*: 'it showed me that it was possible to break up the language and put it back together in a different way .... I found I had to punc-tuate it in a very peculiar way, to destroy the natural rhythms of the English language; I had to use dashes too much, keep exclaiming, putting in three dots, sometimes three dots followed by semicolons followed by three dashes .... That sort of thing just seemed to help to dislocate the English and let other things into it.'[57] Rushdie's use of English is available only to those writers adopting his kind of milieux, but his example can, certainly, benefit users of other varieties of English, including British English, and users of other languages as well. He has demonstrated a method of revitalizing language.

Postmodernism problematizes not only fiction but also history. Saleem's – and Rushdie's – version of history is different from the traditional, which is logical, imposes patterns, a chain of cause and effect, is seemingly objective, definitive, unitary, repressive and closed. History in *Midnight's Children* is, in a postmodern way, fragmented, provisional, openly subjective, plural, unrepressive, a construct, a reading. It is different from European master (in three senses of the word: apparently all-encompassing, of the dominant race, male) narratives. For one thing, Rushdie alludes to both European and indigenous sources. He gives voice to a whole range of sections in society – from the leaders to the slum-dwellers, men as well as women. Rushdie himself has written an essay on the 'errata' in *Midnight's Children*.[58] Some of the errors in the text – such as Ganesh sitting at the feet of the poet Valmiki and taking down the *Ramayana* or General Sam Manekshaw accepting the surrender of the Pakistani army at the end of the Bangladesh War – have to be inferred as such by the reader, but due warning is given in that certain errors – such as the date of Gandhi's death or inverting the order of Saleem's own tenth birthday and the 1957 elections – are declared as errors by Saleem and nevertheless not changed. Saleem can permit open contradictions to remain in the historical discourse: in the Indo-Pakistani War of 1965, 'aircraft, real or fictional, dropped actual or mythical bombs' (p. 341). Rushdie's convention is that Saleem's 'mistakes are the mistakes of a fallible memory, compounded by the quirks of character and of circumstance',[59] but not only does this keep the reader alert and involved in a role as co-creator, it also carries important messages regarding the nature of historiography and the unreliability of the writer. Rushdie adopts a homely, Indian image for his construct: 'the chutnification of history' (p. 459). Each chapter falls into the mould of a pickle jar. Chutnification is also a method of preserving. Saleem acknowledges that both processes involve distortions. One jar is left empty, reserved for the future. Therefore, the novel ends on a note literally and metaphorically against closure.

In regard to the structure of *Midnight's Children*, Rushdie aims at rich inclusiveness rather than neat or mechanical unity, which is against his principles. Concurring with Elfrida Gribb in *Grimus* that 'stories should be like life, slightly frayed at the edges' (p. 141), Rushdie wants 'to leave loose ends' and imply 'a multitude of stories'.[60] Commander Sabarmati's trial, Cyrus Dubash's reincarnation as Lord Kushro, the lady wrestler who threatened to marry whoever defeated her, are instances. Saleem himself embodies the principle of inclusiveness ('To understand just one life, you have to swallow the world' [p. 109], he declares hyperbolically). So does Lifafa Das – on the level of popular entertainment (his cry was 'See the whole world, come see everything!' [p. 75] and he desperately added picture postcards into his peepshow to make good his claim). So too does the painter friend of Nadir Khan (he set out to be a miniaturist and 'got elephantiasis instead!' [p. 48]). (*Midnight's Children* expresses totalizing impulses while questioning their realization.) The leitmotifs 'provide a network of connections and so provide a shape'.[61] In the main, it is Saleem's character and voice, his pervasive consciousness, that hold the novel together.

A consciousness of India's history is imposed subtly on the reader. The opening pages announce that 'Tai…is about to set history in motion' (p. 13), and he does so in more than one sense. His references to Alexander and Jehangir evoke the Western invader and the Muslim Empire, respectively. A folk figure, he introduces a leitmotif, the folk belief that Christ spent his last days in Kashmir. His folk image of Christ is not the traditional, ascetic one but bald and gluttonous. The belief implies that Christianity is not only a religion imported and imposed by the imperialists (as in Mary Pereira's Goa with its Francis Xavier cult) but possesses a native strain; and that no rigid division between East and West exists. The Hindu and Islamic inheritances are naturally more prominent in the novel. The fact that all these form a mix is important. This is underlined by Saleem's multiple parentage and character. The name Braganza Pickles (Private) Ltd (where Saleem and Padma work) is relevant. Catherine of Braganza's dowry for Charles II included Bombay and this brought Britain and India closer together. Braganza suggests Portuguese/Goanese, too. Pickles, of course, are unmistakably native. Rushdie states:

> My view is that the Indian tradition has always been, and still is, a mixed tradition. The idea that there is such a thing as a pure Indian tradition is a kind of fallacy, the nature of Indian tradition has always been multiplicity and plurality and mingling…. I think that the idea of a pure culture is something which in India is, let's say even politically important to resist. So the book comes out of that, that sense of a mixed tradition.[62]

S. Nomanul Haq is right in praising Rushdie's 'formidable grasp of history and, through that, of the psyche of a complex culture in all its variations that formed the substratum of [his] tale'.[63] Rushdie specifies the ideals that *Midnight's Children* celebrates: ' "My" India has always been based on ideas of multiplicity, pluralism, hybridity: ideas to which the ideologies of the communalists are diametrically opposed. [In *Midnight's Children*] the defining image of India is the crowd and a crowd is by its very nature superabundant, heterogeneous, many things at once.'[64]

In the last paragraph, the novel is handed over to the reader. The final note is pessimistic, not regarding the future of India, but in respect of the writer. The sentences are richly suggestive. Each writer prevails only for a time. Fate will soon give a different version of India to the Indians. Generation after generation of writers must reinterpret India for the Indians. The writer is both master and victim; he reinterprets and suffers. He, as a martyr, is not a private person, but must identify with the masses. He saves others but himself he cannot save. In course of time, he will be obliterated.

3

Shame (1983)

Midnight's Children soon made Rushdie world famous. It was translated into more than a dozen languages. His lifestyle changed into that of a celebrity and he became a public intellectual, engaging in polemics in the newspapers, journals and on TV. As a writer, his view of himself as a radical was confirmed; *The Tin Drum* had taught him: 'Go for broke. Always try and do too much. Dispense with safety nets. Take a deep breath before you begin talking. Aim for the stars. Keep grinning. Be bloody-minded. Argue with the world.'[1]

Shame appeared in 1983. Rushdie thinks it is 'wrong to see *Midnight's Children* as the India book and *Shame* as the Pakistani book',[2] as readers generally tend to do. In this case, I would say, wholly trust neither the writer nor the generality of readers. *Midnight's Children* and *Shame* are companion pieces. Both India and Pakistan are shown as not having fulfilled the expectations of their founding fathers, Gandhi and Jinnah, respectively. The settings and concerns of *Midnight's Children* do extend beyond India as such, into Pakistan and Bangladesh. In a sense, the structure of the novel is a postmodern version of the picaresque: Saleem's family and/or Saleem himself journey from Kashmir to Amritsar, Agra, Delhi, Bombay, Lahore, Dacca and back again to Delhi, Bombay and Kashmir. But Rushdie's emotional investment in the novel relates only to India, with its original stimulus located in his attachment to Bombay. Similarly, the settings and concerns of *Shame* extend beyond Pakistan, into India – the 1947 Partition phase in Delhi is integral to the novel and important – and Pakistan includes both the West Wing and the East Wing (later Bangladesh), before and after Pakistan's own partition. But the impetus behind the novel derives from Rushdie's revulsion from Pakistan, clear in his critical attitude to Karachi in *Midnight's Children* and his satiric references to Pakistan as the Land of the Pure in both *Midnight's Children* and *Shame*. What Bombay and India stand for in *Midnight's Children*, the ideals that novel celebrates, are the antithesis of what Karachi and Pakistan represent – singularity rather than plurality, religious extremism rather than tolerance, 'a closure of possibilities' rather than 'multiple possibilities'.[3] Rushdie has said that *Shame* is 'not written as affectionately' as *Midnight's Children* 'although – as I say somewhere in the book – Pakistan is a place I've grown to have affection for, so that it's not written entirely without affection'.[4] This may be granted qualified acceptance. But readers would concur wholly with Rushdie's admission: 'It's a book which comes from a very different place from *Midnight's Children*.'[5]

The origins of Pakistan are not propitious. The narrator of *Shame* refers to 'the famous moth-eaten partition that chopped up the old country and handed Al-Lah a few insect-nibbled slices of it, some dusty western acres and jungly eastern swamps that the ungodly were happy to do without'.[6] Economically, the country is disadvantaged. 'To build Pakistan it was necessary to cover up Indian history, to deny that Indian centuries lay just beneath the surface of Pakistani Std Time. The past was rewritten; there was nothing else to be done' (p. 87). The country is an artificial creation. Yet the text, in fact, points up Pakistan's stores of history not merely through statement but also through drama as when Omar Khayyam Shakil in the grip of insomnia 'in the silence of the night and the first sounds of dawn explored beyond history into what seemed the positively archaeological antiquity of "Nishapur", discovering in almirahs the wood of whose doors disintegrated beneath his tentative fingers the impossible forms of painted neolithic pottery in the Kotdiji style; or in kitchen quarters whose existence was no longer even suspected he would gaze ignorantly upon bronze implements of utterly fabulous age; or in regions of that colossal palace which had been abandoned long ago because of the collapse of their plumbing he would delve into the quake-exposed intricacies of brick drainage systems that had been out of date for centuries' (p. 31). Precise items suggest untold antiquity – pre-Islamic and non-Islamic. The narrator supplies an account of how the name, Pakistan, was invented:

It is well known that the term 'Pakistan', an acronym, was originally thought up in England by a group of Muslim intellectuals. P for the Punjabis, A for the Afghans, K for the Kashmiris, S for Sind and the 'tan', they say, for Baluchistan. (p. 87)

In fact, the name was coined by Chaudhri Rahmat Ali, a Muslim graduate student, in 1933 (the date is significant – this was in the era of simple Indian nationalism), at Cambridge, England (he died there)[7] – along the lines indicated by Rushdie's narrator. Though the fiction and fact do not tally completely, the two accounts are agreed that the name was invented in England – remote from the aspirations and experience of the people of Pakistan. In *Midnight's Children*, much is made of how India was, at one level, an imagined country. On the other hand, the narrator of *Shame* suggests that Pakistan was '*insufficiently imagined*, a picture full of irreconcilable elements ... Urdu versus Punjabi, now versus then' (p. 87). He adds later: 'that country divided into two Wings, a thousand miles apart, that fantastic bird of a place, two Wings without a body, sundered by the land-mass of its greatest foe, joined by nothing but God' (p. 178). The potentiality for unrest, tension and division was inbuilt into the nation. The West Wing tended to treat the East Wing virtually as a colony and was disdainful of its people ('savages, breeding endlessly, jungle-bunnies good for nothing but growing jute and rice ...' p. 179). The Bengalis of the East Wing were not historically or racially homogeneous with the West Wing. India's position facilitated intervention in Pakistani affairs. The basis of Pakistan was the rigid one of religion and that alone. Rushdie observes: 'Whether or not it is desirable or not that Pakistan should exist is really a question that the book doesn't discuss.'[8] After all, this is a *fait accompli*. But it seems to me that the book does raise the question whether it should have been carved out, a question already raised in *Midnight's Children* through Mian Abdullah, the Hummingbird.

The parameters of *Midnight's Children* do not extend beyond the subcontinent and the novel is tied to India. But the narrator of *Shame* announces:

> The country in the story is not Pakistan, or not quite. There are two countries, real and fictional, occupying the same space, or almost the same space. My story, my fictional country exists, like myself, at a slight angle to reality. I have found this off-centring to be necessary; but its value is, of course, open to debate. My view is that I am not writing only about Pakistan. (p. 29)

The narrator's words are demonstrated in the novel to be true. The immediate subject of *Shame* is Pakistan, but the novel's significance and relevance is not limited to that country. Rushdie is once tempted to name his fictional country Peccavistan (p. 88). It stands for both

Pakistan and the Third World (referring not only to countries in Asia and Africa, but also in South America).

From one perspective, *Shame* is different from *Midnight's Children*, yet its technique remains a variant on that of the earlier novel. Whereas *Midnight's Children* was narrated by its protagonist, Saleem, the narrator of *Shame* appears to be the novelist and this persona overlaps with Rushdie himself. Although the narrator/Rushdie writes from England, he chooses to write about Pakistan, admitting that 'although I have known Pakistan for a long time, I have never lived there for longer than six months at a stretch. Once I went for just two weeks.... I am forced to reflect that world in fragments of broken mirrors.... I must reconcile myself to the inevitability of the missing bits' (p. 67) – a warning to the reader of the novel as fiction and as history. The broken mirrors in *Shame* are the equivalent of the perforated sheet in *Midnight's Children*. But the narrator/Rushdie poses the question whether he possesses a right to his subject and then validates the right of an expatriate to write about his mother country: 'is history to be considered the property of the participants solely? In what courts are such claims staked, what boundary commissions map out the territories?' (p. 28).

The narrator/novelist seems generally omniscient, but occasionally confesses to ignorance as when he suggests reasons, scientific and otherwise, why Omar Khayyam Shakil falls in love with Sufiya Zinobia yet is unable to be conclusive. He intervenes in the fictional narrative to comment on the real world as when he has his say on the Islamic revival (p. 281) or makes Kundera-like jokes about regimes ('You can get anywhere in Pakistan, if you know people, even into jail' [p. 28]).

The narrator/novelist ascribes the origins of Sufiya to three incidents in the real world, in London. In the first, an immigrant Pakistani father murdered his only child, a daughter, because by making love to a white boy she had brought such ignominy upon her family that only her blood could wash away the defilement. In the second, an Asian girl is beaten in a late-night underground train by a group of teenage white boys. In retrospect, she feels not anger but shame. In the third, a boy is found blazing in a parking lot, apparently having ignited spontaneously. In regard to the first, the narrator/novelist is horrified, having recently become a father himself, but understands it, not finding it alien to him, having been brought up in the same culture. The second is a blowing-up of an actual tiny incident involving Rushdie's sister Sameen (to whom he dedicates *Shame*) in a tube during the Brixton riots.[9] He conjures up an alternative image of the victim, a slightly built, lone girl, turning upon her assailants in a fury, with awesome strength; then, the relation to Sufiya's case is clear. The narrator/novelist does not comment on the third incident and the reader may well find it hard, if not impossible, to swallow as fact, but it is reflected in Sufiya's blushing (literally) heatedly when she experiences shame and in the final 'fireball of her burning' (p. 286).

Though not as convoluted as *Midnight's Children*, *Shame* is a distinctly postmodern novel. Rushdie transgresses the boundaries of fact and fiction. The intervention of the narrator/novelist makes for an alertness comparable to Brecht's alienation effect and does not permit mimesis. Both the fiction and history are constructs. The narrator/novelist/Rushdie confesses: 'As for me: I, too, like all migrants, am a fantasist. I build imaginary countries and try to impose them on the ones that exist. I, too, face the problem of history: what to retain, what to dump, how to hold on to what memory insists on relinquishing' (p. 87). Both the fictional and historical accounts are similar and openly not definitive.

In postmodern fiction, the boundaries of the past and the present, too, are often transgressed. In *Shame*, Rushdie's use of the Hegiran calendar permits him to suggest two periods and cultures existing simultaneously: the Muslim (Hegiran) fourteenth century with its suggestion of the medieval hangover and outdatedness alongside the modern twentieth century. The boundaries of the past and the present are not blurred but remain, are challenged and are investigated.

The opening setting of the town of Q. possesses as its orbs, the old town, the native quarter, and the cantonment of the whites. The symbol of the latter is the Hotel Flashman, recalling the decaying imperial Hotel Majestic in which Major Brendan Archer stays in J. G. Farrell's *Troubles* (1970), but distinguished by only a single splendidly effective image: 'The Hotel Flashman ... whose *great golden dome was cracked* even then but shone nevertheless with the tedious pride of its *brief doomed glory*' (p. 12, my emphasis). The Hotel Flashman suggests that the sun was setting on the Empire but that its influence continues after its demise. Old Mr Shakil, a widower, the grandfather of the 'hero' of the novel, dies cursing both sections of society and, finally, himself. His house is equidistant from both orbs and is named 'Nishapur'. In Sanskrit, *'nisha'* means 'darkness', 'night' and *'pur'* 'city'. The house is a symbol of Pakistan, its closed society, the name of the house suggesting the country's 'benighted' state, and its contents the country's long history. The exaggeration of the art imparts the meaning with force, even shock. Within the house, Shakil imprisons his daughters, Chhunni, Munnee and Bunny, and brings them up according to an inflexible, mostly Islamic, morality. The three sisters, too, are themselves a symbol of aspects of Pakistan – of its static society, made stagnant by Islamic patriarchy.

The sisters had been so dominated and repressed by their father that the life had virtually been crushed out of them. After his death, they nevertheless cannot help but remain immured, except for two brief periods of liberation which his death permits and during which they conceive two sons. Their virtual imprisonment forges between the three sisters a bond of intimacy so close that they even resolved to share their babies. This is the explanation in the novel for the triune maternity. The multiple mothers in *Shame* recall the multiple fathers of Saleem Sinai in *Midnight's Children*. Farid-ud-din 'Attar's *The Conference of Birds* seems a permanent ingredient in Rushdie's imagination; there are recurrent references to it as from *Grimus*. In the study of 'Nishapur' was a walnut screen on which was exquisitely carved the mythical circular mountain of Qaf, complete with the thirty birds playing God (p. 33). The thirty birds form One, like the three mothers form one – like the Christian Trinity and the Hindu triad.

The sisters conceive their first child when, ironically, they throw a party as a reaction to the news of their ruin, that their dead father had squandered his wealth. This suggests Pakistan's bankruptcy, literally and metaphorically. The capital of the sisters, and the country, is the past. Both have no future. The sisters invite only the white inhabitants of the cantonment to their party. Like Saleem Sinai, Omar Khayyam Shakil has an unidentified Angrez father and is Westernized. Through his father, he inherits an Anglicized colonial strain and, through his mothers, a native strain. Thus, he is a product of the two sections of society his grandfather cursed. Yet, paradoxically, his grandfather himself leaves him the same kind of dual inheritance. Old Mr Shakil's business acumen and his scholarship were a sham, the former trait like Ahmed Sinai in *Midnight's Children* and both traits like Salman Rushdie's own father, Anis.[10] Just as Anis's impressive library may have been purchased *in toto* from a British Colonel, Shakil's study boasted of books which 'bore the *ex libris* plates of a certain Colonel Arthur Greenfield and many of their pages were uncut' (p. 33). These books and the grandfather's own personal books give Omar access to both Eastern and Western learning as they included volumes such as the poetry of Ghalib and the tales of Hatim Tai as well as an account of the hypno-exorcisms of Father Gassner of Klosters and a study of the 'animal magnetism' theory of Franz Mesmer. Yet it is his Western legacy that empowers Omar – his skill as a doctor and his mesmerizing ability.

Omar Khayyam's name recalls the ancient Persian poet (1048–1131) and the name of his house recalls the home town in Iran of the poet, 'Naishapur' (in Persian *'nai'* means 'city' and 'Shapur' is an ancient Persian king; that is, the city of Shapur). The narrator/novelist of *Shame* comments accurately: 'Omar Khayyam's position as a poet is curious. He was never very popular in his native Persia; and he exists in the West in a translation that is really a complete reworking of his verses, in many cases very different from the spirit (to say nothing of the content) of the original' (p. 29). The original poem would run:

> I was in the potter's shop last night
> And saw two thousand jugs, some speaking, some dumb;
> Each was anxiously asking,
> *'Where* is the potter, and the buyer and seller of pots?'[11]
>
>   (my emphasis)

Edward Fitzgerald (1809–83) would translate:

> And, strange to tell, among the Earthen Lot
> Some could articulate, while others not;
> And suddenly one more impatient cried –
> 'Who *is* the Potter, pray, and who the Pot?'[12]

The 'Where' in the original refers to the Creator and Preserver of clay vessels whereas the atheistic nineteenth-century Fitzgerald uses 'Who'. The original would run:

> Today is the time of my youth,
> I drink wine because it is my solace;
> Do not blame me, although bitter it is pleasant,
> It is bitter because it is my life.[13]

'Wine' is ambiguous here, unlike Fitzgerald's booze. Fitzgerald is more cynical, sceptical/atheistic and more hedonistic. In fact, the

Shame *(1983)* 53

translation celebrates hedonism and this is the chief trait of Omar Khayyam Shakil, apart from his professional skill as a doctor. It is the same trait, the animal side to him (to use conventional terminology), that is suggested by the references to him as a wolf-child, alluding to Rudyard Kipling's Mowgli, and supported by the fact that Omar is brought up by a pack (of mothers). The reader is prepared for the wild side to him from his very (inauspicious) birth – significantly symbolic – on the death-bed of his austerely Islamic, traditionalist grandfather.

Omar Khayyam Shakil 'entered life without benefit of mutilation, barbery or divine approval' (p. 21). That is, he is not a traditional Islamite and, like Saleem Sinai, is totally secular. Like Gibreel Farishta in *The Satanic Verses*, he experiences nightmares and gives up sleep to avoid these, and is an autodidact. He immerses himself in his grandfather's books. But, unlike the Persian poet with whose name he is associated, he never writes although he is expected to. Rushdie regards it as a duty of the writer to safeguard freedom, writing as a weapon of protection. The narrator/novelist speaks of a friend, a poet who 'had been hung upside-down by the ankles and beaten, as if he were a new-born babe whose lungs had to be coerced into action so that he could *squeal*' (p. 28, my emphasis; note the macabre pun and fun). After having been tortured, this poet does not write again. Unlike this poet, Shakil is never suppressed and his silence is an abdication of responsibility. He is, therefore, guilty of complicity in the turn of events in Pakistan.

Shakil is all the more culpable because he has a kind of character which could have enabled him to be a writer: 'his voyeurism, which revealed to him both the infinitely rich and cryptic texture of human life and also the bitter-sweet delights of living through other human beings' (p. 45). Rushdie's language suggests how the voyeur and the writer occupy a position in common. Omar Khayyam Shakil's association with the Persian poet is ironic from one perspective, but, from another, it is not. The Persian survives in Fitzgerald's translation rather than in his own right and, as such, is a subsidiary/peripheral figure. It is this kind of role that Shakil plays in the novel: 'it was the fate of Omar Khayyam Shakil to affect, from his position on the periphery, the great events whose central figures were other people' (p. 108). His character is a development from Saleem Sinai's. Whereas Saleem was a peripheral character who thought he was central until towards the close of *Midnight's Children*, Shakil is aware from the beginning that he is 'a peripheral man' (p. 283). In fact, he describes himself to Iskander Harappa as 'not even the hero of his own life' (p. 24). The constant references to him as the hero in the text appear, and are meant by Rushdie to be 'a piece of fun'.[14] *Shame* possesses no hero or heroine, no dominant central figure as Saleem Sinai was in *Midnight's Children* despite his marginal status.

While being confined in Nishapur and shortly before his twelfth birthday, Omar sees through a telescope, and finds appealing the figure of Farah Zoroaster, at the time no more than fourteen. His voice changes with adolescence and he also becomes aware of sexuality. These motivate him to ask his mothers for a present on his twelfth birthday – his freedom. It is granted and the mothers forbid him to feel shame, which is the title of the novel, thereby signalling its importance. Rushdie has clarified it: 'Because shame and its opposite, which is honour, seem to me to be kind of central to the society I was describing, to such an extent that it was impossible to explain the society except by looking at it through those concepts.'[15] The narrator/novelist takes pains to spell out (literally, too) the word:

> *Sharam*, that's the word. For which this paltry 'shame' is a wholly inadequate translation…. A short word, but one containing encyclopaedias of nuance. It was not only shame that his mothers forbade Omar Khayyam to feel, but also embarrassment, discomfiture, decency, modesty, shyness, the sense of having an ordained place in the world, and other dialects of emotion for which English has no counterparts…. What's the opposite of shame? What's left when *sharam* is subtracted? That's obvious: shamelessness. (pp. 38–9)

The narrator/novelist defines the cultural and semantic gap between '*sharam*' and 'shame'. The word in its Eastern, Islamic context represents a potent, rich concept.

Omar is permitted to go to school and soon becomes the private pupil of Eduardo Rodrigues who had discovered Omar's brightness. Eduardo's only other private pupil was Farah Zoroaster who was also bright. Farah's father was a customs officer who had volunteered to serve at a desolate post on the Iranian frontier to be close to erstwhile Persia, his ancestral land where Ahuramazda was worshipped, and loses his mind there, making invocations in the nude to the Sun God to destroy earth. Farah, known as 'Disaster', was also called 'the ice-block' on account of her sub-zero coldness towards

her many admirers, a frigidity which also extended to her relations with Eduardo. Her iciness is similar to the Brass Monkey's in
Midnight's Children. Yet, at her father's outpost, Omar breaks through
it by interesting her in a hypnosis session. She gets pregnant and
Omar believes he is responsible. But Eduardo marries her and takes
her away. Omar takes to drink. Forbidden to feel shame by his
mothers, his descent into dissoluteness is the result. Nevertheless, at
eighteen he wins a scholarship to the best medical school in Karachi.
His teacher selects for him the profession appropriate to his character. The narrator/novelist comments:

> What Eduardo saw in Omar ... the possibilities of his true, periph-
> eral nature. What's a doctor, after all? – a legitimized voyeur, a
> stranger whom we permit to poke fingers and even hands into
> places where we would not permit most people to insert so much
> as a finger-tip ... anonymous, a minor character, yet also, paradoxi-
> cally, central, especially at the crisis. (p. 49)

'Legitimized voyeur' applies to writers, too, and refers to the literary
allusiveness embedded in Shakil's forenames. The words fit Omar's
role in the narrative.

In *Midnight's Children*, Aadam Aziz's skill as a doctor, though he
qualified in Germany, is not shown as exceptional. He is called upon
to treat his future wife, Naseem, but this is really a ruse on the part
of his father-in-law to ensnare him matrimonially. He does tend to
wounded Indians on the streets of Amritsar during the troubles
there in 1919, but this is routine stuff. On the other hand, Omar in
Shame becomes an expert in immunology and is Pakistan's leading
specialist in the field. His prowess is shown when he repairs Sufiya
Zinobia's immune system when it breaks down totally after the
turkey-decapitating episode. Rushdie has been alert to a new health
problem and is, perhaps, the first to bring it into literature: *Shame* was
published in 1983 and it was only in 1981 that the Acquired Immune
Deficiency Syndrome (AIDS) was identified.[16] Omar becomes a representative middle-class intellectual of Pakistan.

Shame is not allegorical in the usual technical sense of having a
parallel meaning generated by a surrogate narrative; the fable and
the allegorical meaning are not two things. The novel is wholly a
political and moral parable. The parable is personalized and blends
with reality. Rushdie does not intend his major characters, Raza
Hyder and Iskander Harappa, to be portraits of Zia ul-Haq and

Zulfikar Ali Bhutto, respectively.[17] They are freely modelled on the originals so as to make them fully fictionalized as characters in novels, yet they are identifiable with the real historical figures and this, too, is intended.[18]

Yet the first important character the reader encounters is neither Raza nor Iskander but Raza's future wife, Bilquis, and the scene is Delhi during the Partition. The Red Fort in Delhi is identified as Al-Hambra, The Red One – like the Muslim remains in Spain, pointing forward to *The Moor's Last Sigh* which emphasizes the unity of Muslim conquest. Tolerance is shown as a casualty during this period and Bilquis's father who possessed this quality, loses his Empire (his cinema and livelihood – notice Rushdie's pun) because of it. His Talkies exhibited both Randolph Scott and Gai-Wallah (in *Midnight's Children*, Nadir Khan is rescued by a lad imitating Gai-Wallah) to cater to both 'veg' and 'non-veg', Hindus and Muslims, and 'his double bill was settled' (p. 62 – again, notice Rushdie's pun) when he offended both sides, lost his audience and even his own life when his cinema was bombed. Bilquis is nicknamed by the street urchins as the Rani of Khansi (that is, queen of coughs – of expelled air, of sickness and hot wind), a parody of the heroic Rani of Jhansi, yet appropriate to Bilquis's militant and self-aggrandizing stance, very different from the harmlessness of the Rani of Cooch Naheen in *Midnight's Children*. Bilquis is left totally destitute. She loses everything except her dupatta, the traditional Islamic emblem of womanly modesty, and enters the Red Fort where Muslims were given refuge from the massacres during the Partition. There she encounters Raza and the conquest is on both sides. Raza treats Bilquis well. During these days of their courtship, he brings her fine clothes. It is true these belong to dead women caught in the pogrom at this time and all his gifts are thus tainted, yet he is only a Captain and perhaps cannot afford to do more. The same kind of equivocalness attaches to Bilquis's acceptance of the presents. Bilquis accepts the fine clothes gifted by Raza even though she is aware that these have been removed from the dead bodies of victims of the massacres.

Just as India was partitioned, so was the army, and Raza is one of those Muslims who opt for Pakistan. Raza is a man of the people, unlike Iskander. He is peasantish, proper, Islamic, stolid in his ambition. In Karachi, his wife lives with his extended family and that is, in effect, his home. His energy aids his ambition. He quickly makes his mark. He is acclaimed as a hero for seizing Aansu and promoted to the rank of Major, though the narrator/novelist subversively comments that Aansu was 'a mountain valley so high that even goats had difficulty in breathing up there' and that 'you must not believe that propaganda which says that the enemy did not bother to defend the place' (p. 79). Nobody knows what to do with it except Iskander who purchases it cheaply from the Tribal Agencies Department and in a few years makes it a lucrative tourist resort. Nothing of the profits goes into Raza's pockets. Raza and Iskander form a contrasting pair of characters. Raza is stupid, Iskander brainy; Raza an immigrant, Iskander native; Raza religious, Iskander profane; Raza virtually moral, Iskander permissive. Iskander marries Raza's cousin, Rani Humayun. His crony is Omar Khayyam Shakil.

Bilquis Hyder's first child, a boy, is stillborn. Her next child, her first born, is a girl and, as such, a disappointment to both her parents in this patriarchal society. Bilquis is subservient to patriarchy in regarding the birth of a daughter, Sufiya Zinobia, the 'wrong miracle', as a shame. Sufiya soon contracted a brain fever that turned her into an idiot. Sufiya is innocent and good and, like Stevie in Conrad's *The Secret Agent,* she is able to preserve these qualities in a corrupt world because she is an idiot. She is sensitive to shame which others do not feel and is, from one perspective, a saint – 'a person who suffers in our stead' (p. 141). Rushdie realizes: 'Somebody who behaved like an ordinary person could not carry the kind of metaphorical weight that I wanted the character to have!'[19] Raza's later fondness for Sufiya seems to reflect Zia ul-Haq's open affection for his mentally retarded daughter and strengthens the historical parallel, though Rushdie himself claims that he was ignorant of Zia's daughter when he was writing the book. Rushdie adds 'I actually discovered it before I finished the book but by that time it was much too late to do anything about it. I couldn't very well unmake the character, because I needed her to be like that.'[20]

Raza's career advancement is rapid. Already a full Colonel, he is considered the right officer to protect the gas fields discovered in Needle Valley against local tribals. He warns the Chief Minister Gichki: 'Army is watching these days.... All over the country the eyes of honest soldiers see what they see, and we are not pleased.... The people stir, sir. And if they look away from politicians, where will they turn for purity?' (p. 102). Raza formulates the common justification for military takeovers. Martial law is soon declared, the Chief Minister arrested, and Raza appointed administrator of the region. Maulana Dawood, the fanatical divine, is Raza's adviser. Raza inaugurates his programme of making examples of arrested tribals by hanging them. The official version of Raza's period of power in the West is that it was an unqualified success. He is appointed national minister of education, information and tourism. His career, however, registers a slump when his actual dubious deeds lead to his removal from the post of minister. He is assigned the futureless job of commanding the Military Training Academy.

Ironically, the stupid and fundamentalist Raza treats his wife, Bilquis, in a much better fashion than the brainy and Westernized Iskander does his wife, Rani. Isky adopts the attitude of an oriental despot towards Rani and exiles her to his country estate when she does not bear him a son. He takes Pinkie Aurangzeb as his mistress. He shows a modicum of courtesy towards Rani and a slight twinge of conscience when he visits her once a week with his friends, without Pinkie, and Rani is 'queen for the day'. He shows her off as his wife when it is politically to his advantage. Raza looks after Bilquis not only during their days of courtship but even when her early traumatic experiences cause a neurosis. He shuts her off only when she becomes impossible and there is no alternative. He is sincere in his emotional response to Bilquis's death in the Shakil household. It is also noteworthy that Rushdie, while stressing the casual brutality of the approach to women encouraged by patriarchal attitudes via Rani's reference to the commonness of episodes of wife-beating in the dormitory, makes her point out that Raza is exceptional in sparing Bilquis. Raza's affection for Sufiya even though she is mentally retarded and even when she is dangerous, is genuine. On the other hand, his cruel side is evident in his personal relations, too. He is responsible for the shame-inspired murder of Sinbad Mengel who had enjoyed a liaison with Bilquis and is, perhaps, the father of the second daughter, Naveed, 'Good News'. Rushdie's opposition to fundamentalism does not simplify his view of individual human beings.

Rushdie's portrayal of Pakistani males is, indeed, complex. Talvar Ulhaq is a complete male chauvinist. He selects Naveed to be his wife because his clairvoyancy shows him her fertility, her capacity to bear children. He uses her solely to gratify his lust for sex and procreation. He impregnates her regularly on the day she is bound to conceive. He disregards the problems caused by children increasing in arithmetical progression. He is responsible for her suicide – brought about by the terror induced in her by this fact. The text is silent as to his reaction to her death.

Their wives abandoned in their separate exiles, Raza and Isky are invitees at a reception of Marshall Aurangzeb. Their duel begins here, the initial prize the body of the Marshall's wife, Pinkie. Isky whisks her away under Raza's nose and she becomes his loyal mistress. When Omar recalls this episode to Bilquis at a get-together at the Harappa estate, she complains to Raza and he tethers himself to a stake and issues a challenge (which no one takes up) to vindicate his honour – a memorable episode.

Raza's success in being appointed a minister, followed by Little Mir's similar achievement, stings Iskander Harappa into engineering his own advancement. His first name alluding to Alexander the Great and his surname referring to the ancient Indus valley civilization, suggest the co-presence of Westernized and Eastern components in his personality as well as, by ironic contrast, his own debasement of the heroic and culture. His dissolute life as a playboy ('Bhutto *was* a playboy and Zia *was* puritanical'[21]) also lends 'Iskander' an underlying appropriateness because Alexander in personal life – not a part of the legend – was no less dissolute. He has the intelligence to see the need to change his ways completely if he is to succeed: he repudiates both Omar and Pinkie. Succeed he does, with calculated brilliance.

Rushdie states that what interests him in regard to Bhutto and Zia is 'not so much the personalities of the two men as the relationship of the two men'.[22] In *Shame*, Raza is not so much a personality as a type whereas Isky is a personality. Isky, like Bhutto, is a self-contradictory man, the scion of an enormously wealthy landowning family (the surname Harappa is doubly appropriate because the site of the Harappan civilization borders Bhutto's family estate in the Sind province), patrician, Westernized, yet he adopts a populist manner to succeed as a politician – rhetorical speeches, bad language, histrionics. 'Bhutto deserves a place in history, if only for the way he rescued his country from demoralization and defeat after the 1971 war with India, when the eastern part of Pakistan split off to become the nation of Bangladesh.'[23] This does come across as Isky's main achievement in *Shame*, when he becomes prime minister. Isky answers his critics:

At a rally attended by two million people, Iskander Harappa unbuttoned his shirt. 'What have I to hide?' he shouted. 'They say I have benefited; but I have lost fully half my beloved country. Then tell me, is this gain? Is this advantage? Is this luck? My people, your hearts are scarred by grief; behold, my heart bears the same wounds as yours.' Iskander Harappa tore off his shirt and ripped it in half; he bared his hairless breast to the cheering, weeping crowd. (The young Richard Burton once did the same thing, in the film *Alexander the Great*. The soldiers loved Alexander because he showed them his battle scars.) (p. 180)

'On the campaign trail, Bhutto would rip off his jacket or vest or even his shirt and proclaim his willingness to die for his followers. "Come on, fire bullets at me", he would shout. "I am prepared to die for the sake of the people." '[24] Rushdie is writing for two different reading publics. He is warning his Pakistani readers against being taken in by histrionics, whereas the parallel to Alexander would make Isky appear one of the epigoni to Western readers. Isky's standing is also undercut when he is shown as putting his brains to frivolous use as when he gets rid of Western ambassadors in Pakistan by means of practical jokes. More importantly, he is guilty of serious political crimes.

Shame does not depict Raza and Isky as having a 'relationship' as such, whatever Rushdie's intentions and interests. There is interaction but it is occasional. At a time when Raza's career had slumped, Isky picks him up from the wilderness and appoints him Commander-in-Chief of the Army, promoting him over the heads of many other Generals, on the grounds of his stupidity; Isky believes that Raza is in his pocket. The protégé becomes the supplanter, even the executioner, of his patron. These ironies are true to history. The text records Raza's permanent resentment over Isky carrying off Pinkie Aurangzeb and over Isky's slap when Raza visits him to discuss the defence budget, and Isky's intemperate conduct (towards Raza) when in detention. These interactions provide motivation, but not justification, for Isky's murder. The subtext suggests that the main motive is political and this is historically true: that Isky remains the only political alternative to Raza and that Raza uses Isky's elimination as a method of ensuring the continuation of his own power.

When Raza ousts Isky in a coup, he proclaims that the Army's role is that of an honest referee or umpire. But it is more than a joke when his self-styled acronymic position CMLA stands for not only Chief Martial Law Administrator but also Cancel My Last Announcement, in popular usage. Raza's rule is different from Isky's in that his is military and Isky's civilian, and in his use of religion. The *gatta*-bruise on Raza's forehead – a sign of devotion to religion – is highlighted as the distinguishing feature of his appearance. He exploits

Islam to legitimize his rule and project an image of himself as a God-fearing ruler. He brazenly justifies the introduction of Islamic law and punishment (barbaric to Western eyes) and uses these as an instrument of terror; this is a State application of fundamentalism. It is to the point that his name incorporates a submerged allusion to the cruel 'raja' Hyder (Ali) of Mysore (1761–82).

Isky and Raza are contrasting characters and they appear to form an opposition. Yet the opposition is superficial: both are evil. The drift of the whole novel is one way – towards evil. Rushdie thinks that he is writing 'about the nature of evil',[25] but the result is not quite that. *Shame* is not an exploration of evil but a presentation of an aspect of evil, mainly political evil. The crimes of Isky the civilian and Raza the military man amount to the same thing, tyranny (perhaps Isky is more culpable as he is an elected leader), and tyranny of a commonplace kind. There is nothing splendid, glorious or extraordinary about the evil in *Shame*. The political evil illustrates what Hannah Arendt called 'the banality of evil'.

The ironies in the roles of Raza and Isky make the situation tragic, tragic for others and, indeed, for Pakistan, but the figures themselves are low-grade and comic. Rushdie's intention was to 'write a book whose story was more or less unrelieved tragedy but I would write it as a farce'.[26] The result is a black comedy. Rushdie 'didn't want to make cartoons',[27] but his basic technique remains the cartoon, yet, as in Ben Jonson's *Volpone*, it does not trivialize and is effective, especially when it incorporates dimensions and resources beyond the cartoon. Isky and Raza are presented as buffoons but what they inflict on Pakistan is not farcical but tragic. The political situation in Pakistan is blatant and simple, and does not call for subtlety of art: Dryden employed a fine nib for Achitophel and Zimri but a poster pen for Og. Yet Rushdie does go beyond the cartoon as in the scene of Isky in detention, deprived of his Havanas, spewing betel-juice and, consequently, the walls appearing as if spattered with blood, while (with symbolic prognosis) the red fluid dribbled off Raza's fingertips 'as if his hands had been washed in a bowl of Iskander's lifeblood' (p. 225); or as when Rushdie suggests the humane side of Raza. Moraes Zogoiby's comments in *The Moor's Last Sigh* apply here:

> So was this a Mahabharat-style conflict, then, a Trojan war, in which the gods took sides and played their part? ... there's no need to hear echoes of Yudhisthira's loss of his kingdom on a fatal

throw of the dice…. Tragedy was not in our natures. A tragedy
was taking place all right, a national tragedy on a grand scale, but
those of us who played our parts were – let me put it bluntly –
clowns. Clowns! Burlesque buffoons, drafted into history's theatre on account of the lack of greater men. Once, indeed, there were
giants on our stage; but at the fag-end of an age, Madam History
must make do with what she can get.[28]

The dynamics of politics in Pakistan is such that power is concentrated in the hands of a minute ruling class. In *Shame*, Rushdie
shows the ruling class as members of a single family. Isky marries
Raza's cousin, Rani, though the families of Bhutto and Zia were
not connected. Rushdie even places a family tree at the beginning
of his novel – an unconventional one with details such as 'many
illegitimate offspring', '11 legitimate sons', '32 boys', '27 children', as
grotesque as the politics. The common people are not much in the
picture in the real situation and also in the world of the novel; they
are not decisive. As Aijaz Ahmad observes, 'this plot device of turning all the antagonists into relatives is a wonderful technical resolu-
tion for reflecting the monopolistic structure of dictatorial power
and the very narrow social spectrum within which this power in
Pakistan circulates. It also helps him [Rushdie] to bypass the easy
liberal dichotomy between military villains and civilian innocents;
they are all of the same stripe.'[29]

Shame possesses another (important) side to it. The narrator/nov-
elist remarks:

I had thought, before I began, that what I had on my hands was
an almost excessively masculine tale, a saga of sexual rivalry,
ambition, patronage, betrayal, death, revenge. But the women
seem to have taken over; they marched in from the peripheries of
the story to demand the inclusion of their own tragedies, histories
and comedies, obliging me to couch my narrative in all manner of
sinuous complexities, to see my 'male' plot refracted, so to speak,
through the prisms of its reverse and 'female' side. It occurs to me
that the women knew precisely what they were up to – that their
stories explain, even subsume, the men's. Repression is a seamless
garment; a society which is authoritarian in its social and sexual
codes, which crushes its women beneath the intolerable burdens
of honour and propriety, breeds repressions of other kinds as
well. Contrariwise: dictators are always – or at least in public, on

other people's behalf – puritanical. So it turns out that my 'male' and 'female' plots are the same story, after all.

...

In the end, though, it all blows up in your face. (p. 173)

The terminology and general feel suggest that Rushdie is setting off on a feminist/gender track, a deliberate tapping of a trendy timely vein and adding support for feminism to his liberal standpoint. He speaks as if he is opposed to oppression in sex relations just as in the political sphere. He appears critical of the conventional attitude to women as inferior beings: he spotlights the sign (at the Sind Club in Karachi) which reads 'Women and Dogs Not Allowed Beyond This Point' (p. 69). Women bulk large in the novel, yet it is the men who make all the important decisions. The women are not decisive; they are victims and, except for Rani Harappa, powerless. Bilquis is a victim partly of her early traumatic experience, her mental state aggravated when she is unable to bear Raza a son and heir. Rani is a gossipy young thing at the beginning, but she becomes a victim of her husband's philandering and power-hunger and is exiled to the Harappa family residence in the provinces. She is not subservient to patriarchy as Bilquis is, and maintains her dignity. Their female bonding when cast aside by their husbands, though their telephone conversations sound a kind of one-upping, is supportive, nurturing and positive, but does not last, being severed by the deeds of the men. Rani acts as a judge of Isky and (recalling Philomela) embroiders eighteen shawls depicting his misdeeds ('the torture shawl', 'the swearing shawl' and so on) under the collective title 'The Shamelessness of Iskander the Great'. She signs them with her maiden name, 'Rani Humayun', not to restore her pre-marital identity, but to repudiate her connection to Isky and to dissociate herself from his misdeeds. Her shawls have no public function and have no effect on Isky's public reputation, yet she does send them to her daughter – not jealous of Arjumand's close relationship with Isky, but as a maternal and political warning to one nursing illusions regarding Isky and important for Pakistan's future. Her resistance is thus virtually passive and ineffectual in the immediate context; she does appear in public with Isky after he comes into power. Rani is the only character in the novel clearly not a cartoon. Rushdie does evoke a touch of sympathy for Bilquis and Rani and, for Rani, a touch of respect too. The three Shakil sisters, Chhunni, Munnee and Bunny, possess a collective identity. Moreover, when they are divided over Omar's birthday wishes (for freedom and knowledge of his father's name), they interchange identities, though this is not brought to life in artistic terms.

'To say Arjumand Harappa is Benazir Bhutto is nonsense, she isn't, that was never the intention', says Rushdie.[30] Whatever Rushdie states, the resemblance is marked. They have in common the view of the father as someone who can do no wrong and both exploit the father's name to come into power. Rushdie writes in 1983 in *Shame*: 'the daughter ... telling herself the time will come for Iskander to be restored to history. His legend is in her care' (p. 178). The gender division in Pakistani society is sharp. A woman cannot do without patriarchy if she wishes to come into power. Arjumand ('Virgin Ironpants') wishes to appear masculine for this reason, for empowerment. When she conceives a love for Haroun Harappa (not reciprocated), it is because he resembles her father (in his dissoluteness and potential).

The women in the novel, except for Rani, are more or less repellent. Sufiya Zinobia is literally part monster. When she fills up with shame, this conflicts with her innocence/goodness, and the result is a beast. Abandoned by Isky and her now dead husband, Pinkie Aurangzeb turns to business – turkeys. Sufiya first explodes when she kills these turkeys not merely because they disturb her mother but because her father decides to do nothing about this due to his earlier feeling for Pinkie, and this shame seeps into Sufiya. The second time she explodes is because of the shame over Naveed's marriage to Talvar Ulhaq, who had supplanted Haroun Harappa as the bridegroom at the eleventh hour. She twists his neck but is dragged away, yet not before burying her teeth in his neck. These explosions do not deter Omar Khayyam Shakil from marrying her. Shame and Shamelessness unite; 'they are both the repositories of the society, and that's why they are married'.[31] D. J. Enright thinks that 'it helps somewhat' if we see these two as 'the book's symbolic poles'.[32] But this is not operative in the text. Sufiya, as Shame, is merely reactive and engages in no constructive action, while Omar, as an intellectual, is inactive.

Given Omar's nature, he needs someone to satisfy him sexually; if not Sufiya, the Parsee *ayah*, Shahbanou. On learning this, Sufiya goes in for sex with not one but four youths (a multiple deflowering) and tears off their heads afterwards. She is not disturbed by the infidelity of her husband but by shame because she cannot/is not performing her conjugal function. This explosion of hers instils fear into Omar and Raza, and soon they decide to keep Sufiya unconscious in an attic room, Omar believing that treatment was no longer possible.

In *Midnight's Children*, the Rani of Cooch Naheen and her circle, Nadir the modernist left-oriented poet, the secularist Hummingbird, the scientific Aadam Aziz, all intellectuals, do have a political conscience despite their ineffectualness. On the other hand, Omar, an intellectual, an equal of Raza and Isky, who is a crony of Isky and marries into Raza's family and therefore has access to both rulers, is content with his position, never exerts himself to protest or attempt to change their courses, does nothing politically, good or bad. He has simply abdicated his responsibility and is, therefore, implicated in both tyrannies and is as guilty as the rulers are. He admits: 'I am a peripheral man.... Other people have been the principal actors in my life-story. Hyder and Harappa, my leading men.... And several leading ladies. I watched from the wings, not knowing how to act. I confess to social climbing, to only-doing-my-job...' (p. 283). Indeed, Omar is just like all of us non-politicians, a non-contributory yet guilty victim. Rushdie is warning the Pakistani people against adopting such an attitude. The other son of the Shakil sisters, Babar, is politically committed to an extremist position, a terrorist, and is guilty and culpable in this way. His name (the nickname given him by the guerrillas was 'the emperor') is a parodic allusion to the heroic historical Babur, a descendant of Tamerlane and Genghis Khan, who invaded northern India, founded his own dynasty in India in 1526 and whose descendants, the Moguls, achieved the dream of the Delhi Sultans, to rule an Indian empire.[33]

Timothy Brennan concludes: 'Rushdie has been able to give more people than ever before in the West the issues of Pakistan – an imagined Pakistan, perhaps, and only one version, but one replete with a sense of its history and territorial contexts.'[34] But *Shame* would have generated much more active, either combative or acceptant, reactions in English-reading Pakistanis, more aware of Bhutto, Zia and their actual effect on the land, who might have picked up little gossipy allusions and felt it so much nearer their own skin, than in Western readers.

The novel ends with an explosion of evil. Sufiya explodes. She breaks out of the room in the attic at the moment Isky is murdered, that is, when the most shameful deed in the novel is committed, given that Isky had been Raza's patron and Isky's was a civilian, democratic government. 'What now roamed free...was not Sufiya Zinobia Shakil at all, but something more like a principle, the embodiment of violence, the pure malevolent strength of the Beast' (p. 242) – brought about by shame. She is white whereas Kali is black, and she is not an embodiment of the goddess, but she resembles Kali in her fierce aspect, 'a fury rather than a goddess'[35] and, like Kali, she is ubiquitous. Kali is represented with 'a hideous and terrible countenance, dripping with blood, encircled with snakes, hung round with skulls and human heads',[36] while Sufiya moves 'on all fours, naked, coated in mud and blood and shit, with twigs sticking to her back and beetles in her hair' (p. 286). According to ancient Indian theories regarding the duration of the universe, the present age is *Kali-yug*, the fourth and last cycle, the age of moral degradation, which will end in universal dissolution. *Shame* does apply to more than Pakistan.

Sufiya topples the regime of her father, Raza. He and Omar escape from Hyder's house, with Raza acutely aware of the 'humiliation' of having to disguise themselves as women, and, together with Bilquis, reach the Shakil residence. Bilquis dies there. The Shakil sisters revenge themselves on Raza as he is responsible for the death of their son (Babar is killed during a sortie lead by Raza); they kill him in the dumb-waiter by releasing, for the first and last time, the stiletto blades fitted therein. From one perspective, this is retribution – and for more than Babar's killing. The reason why Sufiya and Omar 'arrive as opposite figures in the final moment is that in their different ways they are both the repositories of the society', Rushdie explains.[37] Sufiya murders not Raza (a surprise) but Omar. The suggestion is that he is more an embodiment of shame and more culpable, especially given that his intellect endows him with a capacity above the average.

In *Shame* (as in Jonson's *Volpone*), Rushdie is portraying a world of evil – not wholly evil, of course, for such a world could not be conceived, but one in which evil preponderates – which works out its own destruction. The text makes it plain that Rushdie is aware that the novel's ending is artificial. Yet this is no flaw in a postmodern novel. The typical Rushdie 'loose ends' are there: Farah, presumably made pregnant by Omar, goes away with Eduardo, but returns with neither husband nor child; their fate remains an unknown. The fabulistic and realistic modes in the novel are not compartmentalized but intertwined. *Shame* is not so much 'darker than *Midnight's Children*' (as James Harrison thinks)[38] as simpler and more schematic.

It is a success of a lesser order. Understandably, it took half the time of *Midnight's Children* to complete (two and a half years).

The narrator/novelist confesses that he has learned Pakistan 'in slices' (p. 69). An informed writer would adopt a perspective and be selective about the realities he takes into account. In Rushdie's case, omission could easily be the consequence of ignorance. *Shame* has it that, in Pakistan, Islam has not provided a space for nationhood. This is suggested by Farah's father's yearning for his native land, the rebellion which Raza suppresses, and the terrorists whom Babar joins. But Aijaz Ahmad's complaint that Rushdie does not bring in the possibility of social regeneration through ordinary people,[39] is beside the point. Rushdie simply does not know the ordinary people and could not have included them in his novel. His admission of ignorance is frank and defensive, too. His artefact has its inbuilt limits, yet is nevertheless a reading and has its value. Superior informedness does not necessarily bring about superior art. An insider's view is not necessarily superior to a migrant's.[40]

4

The Jaguar Smile (1987) and *The Satanic Verses* (1988)

Shame was banned in Pakistan immediately after publication. When Zia died in an unexplained air crash in August 1988, Rushdie was reported to have said: 'Dead dictators are my speciality. I discovered to my horror that all the political figures most featured in my writing – Mrs G [Gandhi], Sanjay Gandhi, Bhutto, Zia – have now come to sticky ends. It's the grand slam, really. This is a service I can perform, perhaps. A sort of literary contract.'[1] Rushdie had nothing to do with their deaths but speaks as if he were the Scourge of God. *Shame* was acclaimed and shortlisted for the Booker Prize. Nobody had won it twice and Rushdie had reason to believe he might, judging by the reviews of his novel and those of the other competitors. He was a sore loser.

The Rushdies moved into a splendid five-storey house in elitist Highbury Hill, in Islington. Clarissa visualized a new life for herself, as the wife of a celebrity. But on a visit to Australia in 1984, Rushdie met Robyn Davidson. Their two-year relationship was described by Liz Calder as 'volcanic'.[2] Clarissa bought a new house for herself and Zafar. Robyn Davidson moved into Rushdie's new house in St Peter's Street, also in Islington.

Like Harold Pinter, Rushdie grew more political with success and time. His leftism of the 1960s resurfaced. In 1988, John Mortimer suggested to Pinter that meetings of the anti-Establishmentarians should be convened to express their mounting dissatisfaction with Margaret Thatcher. Because of the date of the first meeting, the colloquy came to be known as the 20th June Group. Besides the Pinters and the Mortimers, among those who participated were David Hare, Margaret Drabble, Michael Holroyd, Germaine Greer, Ian McEwan, Angela Carter and Rushdie. There were also other immigrant voices critical of the Thatcher regime – Tariq Ali, George Lamming,

A. Sivanandan, C. L. R. James and Faruq Dhondy. 'Charter 88', a manifesto demanding a Bill of Rights and a written constitution for Britain, was signed by leading left-wing intellectuals, including Pinter, John Mortimer and Rushdie. In the case of Rushdie, the point is not only that his position, anti-Establishment, was the same in regard to both the subcontinent and Britain but that his anti-imperial attitude too applied to both, given his view that imperial racist attitudes were entrenched in white British society, endorsing E. P. Thompson's view that Britain was the last colony of the Empire, and that the shades of Empire hovered around Mrs Thatcher herself, pronounced in her policy regarding the Falklands (Malvinas) Islands.[3] James Harrison notices 'those who find – in his [Rushdie's] wealthy middle-class Indian family background, his upper-class English education, his very English accent, and even his pale skin – too many barriers to his really understanding or representing the underprivileged, whether from the third or the first world'.[4] But the fact is that the immigrant, whether privileged like Rushdie or not, never slots into the system.

Being political as a writer in fiction and non-fiction as well as in ordinary life, Rushdie goes to Nicaragua (in July 1986), probably, to demonstrate that he was a man true to his ideals. In 1984, he had written:

> The modern world lacks not only hiding places, but certainties. There is no consensus about reality between, for example, the nations of the North and of the South. What President Reagan says is happening in Central America differs so radically from, say, the Sandinista version, that there is almost no common ground. It becomes necessary to take sides, to say whether or not one thinks of Nicaragua as the United States' 'front yard'. (Vietnam, you will recall, was the 'back yard'.) It seems to me imperative that literature enter such arguments, because what is being disputed is nothing less than *what is the case*, what is truth and what untruth. If writers leave the business of making pictures of the world to politicians, it will be one of history's great and most abject abdications.[5]

Omar Khayyam Shakil in *Shame* is guilty of precisely such an 'abdication'.

The Jaguar Smile (1987) is the product of Rushdie's three-week visit to Nicaragua. It is more than a travelogue, given its political commentary, but not a tract either, and occupies an intermediate position between these two forms. Rushdie does 'take sides', the same side Harold Pinter took.[6] Rushdie became a sponsor of the Nicaragua Solidarity Campaign in London. He went to Nicaragua as the guest of the Sandinista Association of Cultural Workers (ASTC). He openly states: 'I did not go as a wholly neutral observer.'[7] The Sandinistas, for their part, would have had a vested interest in placing before world opinion, the centres of power and their own people the fact that an eminent writer from the West had graced the seventh anniversary celebrations of their triumph. It was on 17 July 1979 that Nicaragua was liberated from the dictatorial Somozas. The United States backed the Somozas and, then, the Central Intelligence Agency invented, assembled, organized and armed the Contras, the counter-revolutionaries (which the International Court of Justice in the Hague had ruled was in violation of international law). Rushdie asks Daniel Ortega, the Sandinista leader, to explain the US fixation regarding Nicaragua. His reply:

'It isn't only us. What Reagan wants to do, by defeating us, is to send a message to the region'...give up, folks. Accept that you belong to the American empire. Resistance is useless; you only end up worse off than you were to begin with. 'Just do as we say.'
'That is why we believe we are fighting for the whole of Central America. We are fighting to say, this is not somebody else's back yard. This is our country.' (pp. 162–3)

His Indianness is of the essence of Rushdie and Nicaragua is seen through 'eyes trained in India and Pakistan' (p. 17). He observes parallels between the countries: 'the city's [Managua's] few buses...were crammed to bursting point with people, who hung off them in a very subcontinental way. And the roadside shanties put up by the *campesinos* (peasants)...echoed the *bustees* of Calcutta and Bombay' (p. 17); the original guerrilla leader, Augusto Cesar Sandino, had been almost as thoroughly mythologized as Gandhi (p. 21); the three tendencies of the FSLN (the Sandinista movement) resembled the rifts and arguments of the Left in India and many poor countries of the South (p. 167). Rushdie has stated elsewhere: 'the likes of General Zia ruled by permission of the Western alliance...Europe and America...Thatcher and Reagan and the Common Market....'[8] In *The Jaguar Smile*, Rushdie confesses:

I was myself the child of a successful revolt against a great power, my consciousness the product of the triumph of the Indian revolution. It was perhaps also true that those of us who did not have our origins in the countries of the mighty West, or North, had something in common – not, certainly, anything as simplistic as a unified 'third world' outlook, but at least some knowledge of what weakness was like, some awareness of the view from under-neath, and of how it felt to be there, on the bottom, looking up at the descending heel. (p. 12)

Perhaps the root of his sympathies for Nicaragua lies here.
Nicaragua forces Rushdie to adopt an unusual position:

For the first time in my life,...I had come across a government I could support, not *faute de mieux*, but because I wanted its efforts (at survival, at building the nation, and at transforming it) to succeed. It was...disorienting.... I had spent my entire life as a writer in opposition, and had indeed conceived the writer's role as including the function of antagonist to the state. (p. 70)

He stresses the romance, idealism and martyrdom of the Sandinistas (pp. 15–23), the popular support for them (pp. 84–5) and the freedom of speech as when a wounded woman calls the revolution 'junk' and says she is against it 'in the presence of several officers of the state' (p. 90). But Rushdie's account is flawed on occasion – when he gets startlingly and uncharacteristically evangelistic and sentimental (p. 74) or when he repeats the Sandinista tale that the last ruling Somoza fed men to panthers in his private zoo, without entertain-ing any doubt as to its veracity (p. 21) or, more importantly, when he deconstructs Dona Violeta Chamorro. Rushdie writes:

Dona Violeta also complained, several times, that the Nicaraguan government was the only body with the resources to 'travel eve-rywhere, make any propaganda they want, to tell the whole world their version of what is happening here'. Yet during our interview she mentioned at least two very recent speaking tours of her own. (pp. 148–9)

Surely, Rushdie is biased, his point not valid: Chamorro's resources could hardly match the government's.
Yet Rushdie does try to remain independent-minded. He is criti-cal of both American aggression and the Nicaraguan revolutionary government's suppression of freedom of expression, especially the

closure of the opposition newspaper, *La Prensa*. He is overtly critical
of the Minister of Culture, Ernesto Cardenal's stone-wall defence of
Cuban violations of human rights (pp. 46–7). Rather than leftist or
revolutionary, Rushdie seems liberal – strongly in favour of democracy and pluralism, aware of the importance of the vote and many
voices. The epigraph to the book is a limerick (which provides the
title):

> There was a young girl of Nic'ragua
> Who smiled as she rode on a jaguar.
> They returned from the ride
> With the young girl inside
> And the smile on the face of the jaguar.

At the conclusion, Rushdie glosses it:

> it occurred to me that the limerick, when applied to contemporary
> Nicaragua, was capable of both *a conservative and a radical reading*,
> that there were, so to speak, two limericks, two Misses Nicaragua
> riding two jaguars, and it was necessary to vote for the version
> *one preferred*. If the young girl was taken to be the revolution,
> seven years old, fresh, still full of the idealism of youth, then the
> jaguar was geo-politics, or the United States; after all, an attempt
> to create a free country where there had been, for half a century,
> a colonized 'back yard', and to do so when you are weak and the
> enemy close to omnipotent, was indeed to ride a jaguar. That was
> the 'leftist' interpretation; but if the young girl was Nicaragua
> itself, and the jaguar was the revolution?
>
> I *closed* my eyes and looked through my collection of Nicaraguan
> snapshots. Finally I *chose* between the two girls on the two jag-
> uars. I *tore up* the picture that *looked, well, wrong*, and *threw* it away.
> In the one I preserved, the girl on the jaguar looked like the Mona
> Lisa, smiling her Gioconda smile. (p. 161, my emphasis except for
> 'wrong')

Rushdie suggests the subjectivity of interpreting Nicaragua (the
possibility of alternative readings and the question of personal
choice), plays safe as unreliable narrator (note the emphasis on
'closed', 'looked'), is tentative ('well') and engages in willed action
('tore', 'threw'). The last line suggests enigma, ambiguity. Moreover,
Rushdie believed that the 'moment' he went to Nicaragua was 'a

crucial and revealing one because it was neither a beginning nor an end, but a middle' (p. 13). Given this stance, later vicissitudes of history such as the defeat of Daniel Ortega by Dona Violeta Chamorro at the next election and by Arnoldo Aleman in the 1996 election, and the return to power of Ortega in 2006, do not invalidate Rushdie's reading of Nicaragua.

V. S. Naipaul's non-fiction is important – an integral part of his development and his oeuvre and a basis for his creative work. *The Jaguar Smile* appears extrinsic to Rushdie until his estimation of America emerges in *The Ground Beneath Her Feet*. We also recall the lighter, satiric note regarding America in *Grimus*.

The Jaguar Smile did sell 33,000 copies in the first two months of its publication,[9] and a second edition was issued ten-years later, in 1997, understandable as Rushdie was a writer in vogue and after *The Satanic Verses* the centre of global controversy; but the book never caught on. It is dedicated to Robyn Davidson, who soon returned to Australia for good. Rushdie had begun *The Satanic Verses* before he visited Nicaragua, but the country's strong impact on him demanded immediate expression if he was to come to terms with his experience. *The Jaguar Smile* was the solution and the result.

These are eventful years for Rushdie. At a Thanksgiving dinner in 1986, Rushdie meets another strong-willed writer, an American, Marianne Wiggins. Soon, early in 1987, she moves into Rushdie's house and they marry in 1988. Suzie MacKenzie recalls how lovingly he used to talk of Marianne Wiggins and called her 'one of the two most important women in my life, the other being my sister'.[10] He dedicates *The Satanic Verses* (1988) to her. In 1987, after spending several weeks in India, he completes a film for Britain's Channel Four – 'The Riddle of Midnight', India seen through the eyes of Rushdie's forty-year-old generation, recording the shattered dreams of Independence. He dedicates it to his father who died in 1987 and with whom there took place a rapprochement at the end, like that between Salahuddin and Changez at the close of *The Satanic Verses*. In 1987, he signs up with Andrew Wylie, the New York literary agent. He breaks with his British agent and friend, Deborah Rogers, and with Liz Calder to whom he had promised *The Satanic Verses* for her new publishing house, Bloomsbury (she had moved from Cape). Calder called it 'the most blatant and unfeeling piece of daylight robbery I've ever seen'.[11] Rushdie's new literary agent sold the novel abroad first – to a German and an Italian publisher – as a measure of its value in the market and, then, offered it to English-language publishers. Viking Penguin bought both the British and US rights for $850,000, a stunning sum for a novel, more so for a literary novel.

'This is the first time', said Rushdie, 'that I have managed to write a book from the whole of myself. It is written from my entire sense of being in the world.'[12] It incorporates the Indian subcontinent, Britain and Islam. Whereas *Midnight's Children* and *Shame* focus on the modern nation-space designated 'India' and 'Pakistan', respectively, *The Satanic Verses* is transnational and bridges the present and the seventh century (Asia). It deals with themes close to Rushdie's heart – migration, Islam/fundamentalism (both prominent and growing points of contemporary history) and love. Its point of view is Rushdie's own: as he said, 'If *The Satanic Verses* is anything, it is a migrant's-eye view of the world. It is written from the very experience of uprooting, disjuncture and metamorphosis... that is the migrant condition, and from which, I believe, can be derived a metaphor for all humanity.'[13] There are striking parallels between the life of Saladin Chamcha, the character in *The Satanic Verses*, and Rushdie's own, though Rushdie is right to assert 'not that Chamcha is me', and there is an important autobiographical referent on the plane of thematics too: Rushdie states, 'I wanted to write about a thing I find difficult to admit even to myself, which is the fact that I left home. And my relationship with India, although it remains quite close, is with a country I know I'm not going to live in. I wanted to write about someone who does, maybe provisionally, find his way back.'[14]

The novel begins metaphorically as well as literally – with a bang. Hijackers explode an Air India jumbo jet over the English Channel. It is based on a real occurrence: the blowing-up of an Air India Boeing 747 off South-West Ireland in 1985 by Sikh militants. Though it is not examined, Rushdie does present terrorism, another prominent and growing aspect of recent history. The three male hijackers shilly-shally and are curiously ineffectual and unimpressive. But especially via the woman hijacker, Tavleen, who obviously meant business though she does not seem particularly clever, terrorism is shown as frightening and perverse (nestling in her cleavage were grenades like extra breasts, seen by her captives when she stripped). The jet is named Bostan – a Farsi word, the title of the great didactic poem by the thirteenth-century Persian poet, Saeli, affirming orthodox virtues such as justice, self-restraint, gratitude and generosity, and also the name of one of the gardens of Paradise, as the text itself points out. It is intimated that violence has shattered traditional life and beliefs.

Two Indians, Gibreel Farishta and Saladin Chamcha, tumble from the plane without parachutes and land safely, the only survivors. That the novel is fabulated is clear from the outset. Gibreel and Saladin are immediately confronted by the question 'Who am I?'[15] This is partly a social matter, particularly important to immigrants: are the Indians and other immigrants British or Indian, West Indian, African and so on? This is also a philosophical matter, especially problematical for immigrants: what is the truth about themselves? Rushdie has described the fall of Gibreel and Saladin into England as a 'drastic act of immigration'.[16] Rushdie has also said: 'I have a theory that the resentments we *mohajirs* engender have something to do with our conquest of the force of gravity.'[17] The last phrase applies literally, too, to Gibreel and Saladin.

Saladin is actually entering England a second time. He was born in Bombay as Salahuddin Chamchawala and, like Rushdie, was privileged, came to Britain for public school and university education, was estranged from his father and settled down in his adopted country. On the very day he was born, his father, Changez, had planted with his own hands the tree of Saladin's life, a walnut tree – an important many-faceted symbol. Saladin remarks: 'In Kashmir, your birth-tree is a financial investment of a sort. When a child comes of age, the grown walnut is comparable to a matured insurance policy; it's a valuable tree, it can be sold, to pay for weddings or a start in life' (p. 65). The tree is a symbol of the Indian way of life and an integral part of it. Saladin's first choice of profession, to be an actor, alienated Changez further, but Changez did write irregular letters, including ones in a sentimental vein: 'I have your soul kept safe, my son, here in this walnut-tree. The devil has only your body. When you are free of him, return and claim your immortal spirit. It flourishes in the garden' (p. 48). Saladin pays a visit home in search of forgiveness. Whether to give or receive it, he was unable to say. In fact, neither happens. He asks his father to cut down the walnut tree, sell it and send him the cash – which Changez does. The symbolism underlines the widening breach between father and son and the severing of Saladin from Indianness. When Saladin is on his way to his father's death-bed at the close of the novel, he observes the stump of the felled walnut tree and it disturbs him.

Rushdie is aware of the Anglophile tendencies of the English-educated and the elite in British colonies before and after Independence. These tendencies in Salahuddin Chamchawala, typical of his class, began in Bombay and develop fully when he settles down in London. He changes his name to Saladin Chamcha, signifying a change of identity. The heroic associations of his name – the great champion of medieval Islam who defeated the Crusaders and restored Sunni Islam to Egypt was Saladin – are deflationary. 'Chamcha' has the same effect: it means, in Urdu, 'spoon' (hence Gibreel's nickname for him – 'Spoono') and, in Bombay slang, 'sycophant' (which is what he is, culturally, in regard to Englishness). Thus, the name is instinct with Rushdie's critical attitude.

In London, Salahuddin tries to transform himself into a 'goodand-proper Englishman', Saladin, cultivating an English accent, English manners, English dress; love for English food, emblems of England such as Big Ben, Nelson's Column, the Tower of London and the Queen; acquiring membership of Actors' Equity, the Automobile Association and even the Garrick Club, and nursing a colonial concept of England as a land of stability, moderation and fairness. He wishes to identify completely with the English and his interest in having a woman like Pamela Lovelace for a wife is part of this desire. Pamela 'had woken up one day and realized that Chamcha was not in love with her at all, but with that voice stinking of Yorkshire pudding and hearts of oak, that hearty, rubicund voice of ye olde dream-England which he so desperately wanted to inhabit' (p. 180). On the other hand, Pamela was rebelling against stuffy Englishness, embracing Third-World and immigrant causes and desired a husband from her area of interest. 'It had been a marriage of crossed purposes, each of them rushing towards the very thing from which the other was in flight' (p. 180). This authorial comment is true. Moreover, Pamela was from a broken home, harboured panic within and was neurotic. The marriage was not a success but they kept up appearances. Saladin yearned for culture. His list of favourite movies included *Potemkin, Kane, Otto e Mezzo, The Seven Samurai, Alphaville* and *El Angel Exterminador* – cosmopolitan and conventionally arty.

Saladin possesses the background and education to invent an English personality-front, but the British system can only permit him a profession where this is erased. He does find work as an actor, but an actor of an invisible kind, a mere voice, an impersonator of voices, though much in demand over radio and television (he knew how a ketchup bottle should talk or a packet of garlic-flavoured potato crisps) and quite a virtuoso in his line: 'Once, in a radio play for thirty-seven voices, he interpreted every single part under a variety of pseudonyms and nobody ever worked it out' (p. 60).

His big break was to star in *The Aliens Show* – 'a situation comedy about a group of extraterrestrials ranging from cute to psycho, from animal to vegetable, and also mineral, because it featured an artistic space-rock that could quarry itself for its raw material, and then regenerate itself in time for the next week's episode' (p. 62). Even here, Saladin does not appear as a person, not even as the voice of a human being.

Saladin's English personality does not develop into anything deeper than a front. Moreover, place influences personality. This is revealed when Saladin leaves London, en route to India, to visit his father:

> an air stewardess bent over the sleeping Chamcha and demanded, with the pitiless hospitality of her tribe: *Something to drink, sir? A drink?*, and Saladin, emerging from the dream, found his speech unaccountably metamorphosed into the Bombay lilt he had so diligently (and so long ago!) unmade. 'Achha, means what?' he mumbled. 'Alcoholic beverage or what?' And, when the steward-ess reassured him, whatever you wish, sir, all beverages are gratis, he heard, once again, his traitor voice: 'So, okay, bibi, give one whiskysoda only.' (p. 34)

His inner Indian self, reflected in the variety of English he speaks at this moment, bursts through. Moreover, within forty-eight hours of arriving in Bombay, though his wife, Pamela, is not out of his mind, he makes love to an Indian woman (for the first time), his friend, Zeeny Vakil. She challenges his invented self:

> You know what you are, I'll tell you. A deserter is what, more English than, your Angrez accent wrapped around you like a flag, and don't think it's so perfect, it slips, baba, like a false moustache – (p. 53)

and it proves/has proved vulnerable. He steps into Indian life.

Saladin, however, had become so habituated to his English front that it proves too strong for his Indian self. On the return flight, 'his voice had begun of its own accord to revert to its reliable, English self' (p. 73), a sign of a larger personality reversion. When the plane explodes, and Gibreel and he fall, the first spoken words of the novel are Gibreel's: 'To be born again, first you have to die' (p. 3). After their fall, which, in normal circumstances, would have ended in death, they are reborn. Gibreel was afflicted by bad breath before the fall, but, after his rebirth, he loses it. Saladin's breath is fresh before the fall, but, after his rebirth, he is visited by halitosis.

Gibreel Farishta translates literally, from Urdu, into Gabriel Angel – the revered archangel who, according to Islamic tradition, brought down the Koran from God to Prophet Mohammed. Soon after landing, Gibreel develops a halo, recalling his archangelic namesake, while Saladin acquires horns, goat hooves and a tail and an enlarged and erect phallus, exhibiting uncleanness, sexuality and lust which the British associate with coloured immigrants, and exuding suggestions of the devil, the ultimate bogie regarding blacks in the white man's mind. Both are welcomed by Rosa Diamond, a widow in her late eighties. But others too spot them and inform the police, who come to Rosa's house by the beach in quest of illegal immigrants. The police do not touch Gibreel because of his halo but Saladin, without his background, appears to them an illegal immigrant, a stinking one at that. Saladin turns to Gibreel for assistance but is deserted by his friend.

He is taken away by the police in a van in which he is laughed at, beaten, forced to eat his own (goat) faeces by his captors. He thinks, 'This isn't England' (p. 158) – not the England of his colonial concept but an England where the immigrant is demonized and is helplessly at the mercy of the law. When the police find out that Saladin's claim that he is a British citizen is true, they knock him unconscious and dump him at a special medical facility in a detention centre for illegal immigrants. There he encounters more coloured people, also wrongly categorized as illegal immigrants, who have also undergone metamorphosis – an Indian male model as a manticore, a woman as mostly water-buffalo, businessmen from Nigeria with sturdy tails, holidaymakers from Senegal as snakes. The Indian model explains: 'They have the power of description, and we succumb to the pictures they construct' (p. 168).

Saladin escapes from the detention centre during a mass breakout and reaches his home where he astonishes his friend Jumpy Joshi and his wife Pamela, who had become lovers after his supposed death in the plane explosion. Jumpy offers Pamela protection and consolation when he hears of the explosion. The Western mores he has acquired enable him to have sex with her even after they learn that Saladin is alive and, at a later stage, even while Saladin resides in the same house, his house, in fact. But a certain Easternness remains in Jumpy and he pays *pooja* to Saladin, pays him the respect due to him: Jumpy carries food to Saladin, newspapers and mail, visits him, brings him little presents and even invites him to accompany Pamela and himself to the public meeting convened to protest against Dr Simba's arrest. Pamela, for her part, entertains no qualms about her adultery, given that her marriage to Saladin was a mismatch.

Saladin suffers acutely in his transformed state. He doubts the value of his earlier invented English self. He loses his wife. He feels the absence of a son, about whom he dreams: 'an avenue of mature elms, whose overarching branches turned the avenue into a green tunnel...Chamcha ran along behind his imagined son, holding the bike.... Then he released it, and the boy (not knowing himself to be unsupported) kept going.... "Aren't you pleased with me? Aren't you pleased?" It was a dream to weep at; for when he awoke, there was no bicycle and no child' (p. 400). Jumpy is happy that he has made Pamela pregnant and he experiences a dream similar to Chamcha's: 'an avenue of overarching trees, helping a small boy to ride a bicycle. "Aren't you pleased with me?" the boy cried in his elation' (p. 411). The dream looks back to snide *Midnight's Children*, Saleem's love for Evie Burns and the bike episode. Here Rushdie aims at, and achieves, poignance, rare in his earlier novels. To add to Saladin's misfortunes, he loses his job. He is so much at the mercy of the system that he is discontinued once the 'ethnic universe' in the mass media shrinks.

In *The Satanic Verses*, the importance of migration in the thematics is signalled by the epigraph of the novel which suggests that Satan is, in a sense, a migrant. Rushdie contemplates the subject in an all-sided way – in its social, cultural, political, psychological, sexual and religious aspects. When Saladin first enters the house in his unkempt, animal-like state, Pamela refuses to tolerate him and Jumpy takes him to the Shaandaar Café, a restaurant and rooming house run by Muhammad and Hind Sufyan, immigrants from Bangladesh. Migrants tend to live in ghettos. Brickhall is the street of the Bangladeshi immigrants or Pakies/Pakis. The familial and labour relations of migrants change. In Bangladesh, Muhammad Sufyan, as a teacher, was the breadwinner and Hind simply the housewife. In London, Hind is the breadwinner: her cooking is the basis for their flourishing restaurant, a situation typical of Asian migrants, and she manages the finances too; Muhammad merely waits on the customers.

I connect Sufyan with Sufism just as Timothy Brennan – with less reason – does Sufiya Zinobia.[18] Its central tenet is that 'love rather than fear (should be) the determinant of man's relationship with God'.[19] In Farid-ud-din 'Attar's *The Conference of Birds*, a poem about Sufism, the hoopoe advises the birds:

> If you are told: 'Renounce our Faith', obey!
> The Self and Faith must both be tossed away;
> Blasphemers call such action blasphemy –
> Tell then that love exceeds mere piety.[20]

Sufyan's belief in the value of prayer is in line with Sufi thought. In *The Conference of Birds*, the hoopoe tells the birds:

> ... don't imagine that you need not pray;
> We curse the fool who tricks you in this way.
> Pray always, never for one moment cease,
> Pray in despair and when your goods increase.[21]

The connection to Sufism suggests Sufyan's nature – an undoctrinaire, kindly Muslim, kindly even at cost to himself and his family, as when he offers Saladin refuge free of charge despite Saladin's shocking metamorphosis and Hind's opposition. There is something to be said for Hind's dissatisfaction regarding this cost though. Ironically, Saladin is protected by his own people from whom he had been fleeing during his earlier phase in England and still wishes to. Sufyan is so unworldly that he is unaware of the high rents Hind is charging the lodgers.

Sufyan's character evokes sympathy and pathos. He is a man of learning and culture, a true cosmopolitan. He is capable of quoting effortlessly from Rig-Veda as well as Quran-Sharif, from the military accounts of Julius Caesar as well as the Revelations of St John the Divine. He had imbibed the multiple cultures (including Western) of India. His profession in Bangladesh as a school teacher is more suited to his character than his present position in London. But he is forced to leave Bangladesh because of his (Communist) political leanings and, therefore, one cannot conclude that his situation in his home country is any better than the one in his adopted country. Moreover, he comes to England by choice. His status in London, as an immigrant, is that of a second-class citizen but that is a consequence of his own free will and he does not seem to have expected or aspired to anything better. Unlike his wife, he does not suffer as such because of the loss of his position back at home. He adapts himself to his new role, is cheerful and prospers, though this last is not wholly his doing.

Sufyan's daughters, Mishal (seventeen years old) and Anahita (fifteen), are healthy growths. Unlike their mother, they have adjusted culturally to Britain and adopted Western mores, which are anathema to Hind. They have, in effect, severed relations with their home country. Mishal confides in Saladin: 'Bangladesh isn't nothing to me. Just some place Dad and Mum keep banging on about.' Anahita adds conclusively: 'Bungleditch' (p. 259). Mishal goes to bed with Hanif Mohammed as members of British permissive society. Their relationship begins as mere sex, but later develops into something deep and lasting. They share a Muslim background. Though Hanif is from Trinidad, both are Asians. Hanif is a smart professional with a command of 'the vocabularies of power' (p. 281), a lawyer. When they get married, their love is obvious to the guests, the registrar and the onlookers! D. J. Enright is right to suggest that Mishal and Anahita 'hold out some hope for a racially integrated future, more or less'.[22] They do represent positives.

The political aspect of migration is important. Dr Uhuru Simba, an Afro-Caribbean, is a political activist (significantly, he discards his earlier ordinary name, Sylvester Roberts). He advocates political freedom (*'uhuru'* is an African word for 'freedom') but not gender freedom and is tainted by a record of sexual aggression. Timothy Brennan thinks that he is named 'Simba' after Tarzan's elephant;[23] 'Simba' is, surely, the lion, as the text itself notes (p. 413). Dr Simba is not a very pleasant or pleasing portrait of a black leader: 'we shall also be the ones to remake this society' (p. 414). If the migrant is a victim of stereotypes invented by the dominant race, he counters this by duplicating this power.

Billy Battuta, a Pakistani, an operator, is a part of the fun side of the novel. His relationship with Mimi Mamoulian is a defiant alliance of survivors. Mimi had been Saladin's professional partner. Through her, Rushdie touches on wider issues. She is conversant with postmodernist critiques of the West: a society capable only of pastiche, a 'flattened' world. When the supposedly dead Saladin telephones her, she, surprised, blurts out 'Who can ask for reason in these times?' (p. 259) and imparts reverberations beyond the immediate situation.

The Satanic Verses confirms Khachig Tololyan's view: 'To affirm that diasporas are the exemplary communities of the transnational moment is not to write the premature obituary of the nation state, which remains a privileged form of polity.'[24] Rushdie's cast of migrants possesses the variety and range necessary for his far-reaching survey of conditions relating to them within Britain. Mimi, a British Jew, is part of the Jewish strain in the novel. Otto Cohen, a Polish Jew, wishes to be English – like Saladin. His change of name from Cohen to Cone is an attempt to wipe out his Jewish identity. He wishes his family to follow suit. His Anglicizing of the names of his daughters – Yelyena into Ellaynah and Elena, Alleluia into Allie – signifies more than a change of names. His wife Alicja tries to be his Cecil Beaton *grande dame.* He insisted on an English floral garden, tidy flowerbeds round 'the central symbolic tree, a "chimeran graft" of laburnum and broom' (pp. 298–9). Towards the end of the narrative, Saladin, back in human shape and at home, sees on television the very same tree that had been the pride of Otto's garden. The chimeran graft is played off against the walnut tree, the former a symbol of hybridity. Rushdie, however, entertains a doubt and worry regarding hybridity, though it is a major (in his case too) and widely accepted positive today. Saladin, in the end, turns his back on it. Otto turns his back via suicide. Alicja gives up her attempt at integration after Otto's death. She has retained her Jewish self and is only too happy to give it expression again. Significantly, she plants vegetables in Otto's English floral garden. She enters into a happy marriage with an American and moves to California, living there true to her inner self. Moreover, 'chimera' carries the metaphorical meaning 'illusion'. Rushdie leads on the reader into believing that favourable associations envelop the chimeran graft, until the ironic criticism emerges. As in *King Lear*, the events act as a commentary on the words.

Migration has triggered off the revulsion of the indigene from the alien, and this has assumed violent and insidious forms, not necessarily motivated by economic jealousy but exacerbated in times of economic hardship, and especially during a period of crisis which Rushdie believes to be the state of post-imperial Britain:

> I believe that Britain is undergoing a critical phase of its post-colonial period, and this crisis is not simply economic or political. It's a crisis of the whole culture, of the society's entire sense of itself.[25]

The violence in *The Satanic Verses* looks back to the Notting Hill riots of the 1950s, involving working-class West Indians, the racism of the late 1960s of which Enoch Powell is the best-known spokesperson (the text alludes to Powell's notorious 'rivers of blood' speech) and is set in the Thatcherite 1980s when the violence is also directed at the better-off Asians. The violence, by this time, has entered the machinery of the State and distorted the rule of law. At the beginning of the narrative, Saladin is treated by the police, literally, as if he were a brute. Dr Simba is framed by the police for the Granny Ripper murders (the real murderer is a white) because of his black activism, and his death in police custody, though recorded as an accident, is, in fact, murder. 'Gossip changed to rumour as a vehicle of subaltern insurgency' (to use the words of Gayatri Spivak which she applies to something else)[26] as the Granny Ripper/Uhuru Simba affairs work out into a full-scale Brickhall (an allusion here to Brixton) riot – stage-managed, in a way, by the British police. The witch covens among the police can be taken literally and metaphorically, too, as they torment and sacrifice innocents – in the novel, immigrants. Jumpy Joshi and Pamela go to the building occupied by the Brickhall community relations council with the evidence of police witch covens and die in the blaze which engulfs the office when they are inside. The official suggestion is that they are the miscreants, but the author-figure questions the explanation and alleges police complicity and guilt. The Shaandaar Café perishes in a similar act of arson; both Sufyan and Hind die in the blaze.

Saladin and Gibreel are different types. Whereas Saladin is affluent, educated in England, an Anglophile, a radio and television actor, Gibreel is a poor street boy, the son of a tiffin-carrier, an autodidact, who rises to be a millionaire film star. Gibreel's reading of books and newspapers, particularly religious history, resurfaces in his Jahilia dreams. Though the kind of religious movies he acts in are actually called 'mythologicals', the term employed in the novel is 'theologicals', thereby making them 'more intellectual',[27] adding to our sense of Gibreel as having a mind (though not an intellectual) and validating further his religious dreams.

Rushdie reveals:

> Gibreel himself is a mixture of two or three types of Indian movie star. There was in the forties a Muslim actor, a very big star at the time, who did somehow get away with playing major Hindu divinities and because he was so popular it was not a problem. And it was interesting to me that mega-stardom allowed you to cross those otherwise quite fraught religious frontiers. So there was a bit of that in Gibreel. And then there was an element of the big South Indian movie stars, a bit of Rama Rao. And finally

there was a large bit of the biggest movie star in India for the last fifteen or twenty years, Amitabh Bachchan.... There is a famous story about Amitabh. He had an accident on set and almost died. Well, the whole country fell into a state of shock. It was the lead item on the news for weeks: bulletins from the hospital on the hour. Rajiv Gandhi cancelled a trip abroad, came home to sit by his bedside.... Something like the death of a god, almost.[28]

Rushdie makes Gibreel suffer a similar illness with a similar extraordinary impact. Rushdie goes on to to show one way by which he has nevertheless transformed Gibreel into a fictional character: 'mythological movies have not really been a Bombay cinema form. They've...been a South Indian form.'[29] Moreover, 'by mixing up all these people, [Rushdie] was able to use the idea of the Indian movie star as being halfway between the human and the divine'.[30] It gives rise to, and validates, Gibreel's visions of himself as his archangelic namesake and as Azraeel. Gibreel's faith in religion was traditional, deeply ingrained, and in keeping with this intermediate status. He believed that God was taking care of him, and the novel does suggest providential interventions in his life. When both his mother and father died, Babasaheb Mhatre, the General Secretary of the Bombay Tiffin Carriers' Association, adopted him as a son. Then, Babasaheb Mhatre offers him an opportunity in films. His later illness and recovery were both strange. When he emigrates to London, he virtually falls at the feet of the woman he was pursuing, Allie Cone. When he leaves her house and is roaming the streets of London in a demented state, he finds himself on the bonnet of the car of 'Whisky' Sisodia, an Indian film producer. Sisodia recognizes him and takes him back to Allie.

After his mysterious illness, perhaps because of it, Gibreel loses his faith. His openness to the Hindu environment too contributes towards losing his footing in Islam. As Gibreel is not an intellectual, the loss is exhibited on the level of breaking a taboo; Rushdie highlights Gibreel eating pork. Gibreel's loss of faith fractures him: 'the retribution began...a punishment of dreams' (p. 32). Given that his speciality as an actor was playing the roles of deities, it is not surprising that he has a bee in his bonnet about *avatars*. He jilts his mistress, Rekha Merchant, who commits suicide (with her children) as a consequence, and he suffers from guilt (he is haunted by her ghost). Emigration aggravates his disintegration, which develops into a mental illness, paranoid schizophrenia.

He meets Allie Cone at the very moment he breaks faith, conceives an instant love, and pursues her to London, though she had offered no encouragement, because he feels she could give him back faith. The religious overtones of her original name, Alleluia, are significant: she appears a redeemer to Gibreel. Soon after he lands in England, he remains with Rosa Diamond for several days. The episode enacts the Norman Conquest as immigration and takes in other empires, as Rosa relives her past in Argentina. Gibreel shares in her dream and identifies himself as her lover Martin de la Cruz in response to her need. Both Rosa Diamond and, later, Mahound gain control over Gibreel. Gibreel is empathic – to his cost.

Gibreel escapes from Rosa Diamond's clutches and makes his way to London. He is in a neurotic state, but, when all in, he lies in the path of Allie Cone, who takes him to her house. Allie is free of race and class inhibitions (she tells her mother that she does not like even those in her own league). She and Gibreel have sex which turns out to be a mutually satisfying, indeed, great, experience. It is this that attracts Allie to Gibreel. She yearns after transcendental experience: that is why she climbs Everest (the first woman to do so), sees angels there and is haunted by the ghost of Maurice Wilson. Sex, too, provides her with access to this sort of experience. According to Tantric thought, sex brings one into contact with the absolute, the logic being that sex transports one beyond self. In Elizabethan thought, 'to die' also referred to the consummation of the sex act, both absolutes. Thus, thinking from two cultures point in the same direction. It is, surely, significant that when Allie contemplates her sherpa Pemba's warning to her not to attempt Everest again, she felt 'a pang of need so deep that it made her groan aloud, as if in sexual ecstasy or despair' (pp. 303–4).

England changes Saladin's character, but not Gibreel's. In contrast to Saladin's 'conventional cosmopolitan' ten favourite books, movies, female film stars, food, Gibreel's 'top ten of everything came from "back home", and was aggressively low brow. *Mother India, Mr India, Shree Charsawbees*: no Ray, no Mrinal Sen, no Aravindan or Ghatak' (p. 440). Sex is not sufficient to cover up the flaws in the infatuation of Allie and Gibreel. He is pathologically jealous and leaves her when he imagines that he is the archangel. Schizophrenia makes possible the cleavage of identity in Gibreel. In his imagined role as archangel, he wishes to redeem London. Disregarded by the citizens, he is knocked down by Sisodia's car when he tries to halt the rush-hour traffic in a bid for attention. Sisodia, a Dickensian character, not only takes him back to Allie but wishes to exploit him by literally staging a comeback of the film star presumed dead and planning three new 'theologicals' based on the life of Prophet Mohammed. But Gibreel's return is not completed because, halfway through the theatrical performance, he decides to levitate away from the Earls Court stage in his angelic guise. Hovering over London, he pronounces that the trouble with the English is their weather. Whereas Saladin changes his identity to suit London, Gibreel wishes to change London to suit his identity – to tropicalize it.

The author-figure comments:

> Should we even say that these are two fundamentally different *types* of self? Might we not agree that Gibreel, for all his stage-name and performances; in spite of born-again slogans, new beginnings, metamorphoses – has wished to remain, to a large degree, *continuous* – that is, joined to and arising from his past... so that his is still a self which, for our present purposes, we may describe as 'true' ... whereas Saladin Chamcha is a creature of *selected* discontinuities, a *willing* re-invention; his *preferred* revolt against history being what makes him... 'false'? And might we then not go on to say that it is this falsity of self that makes possible in Chamcha a worse and deeper falsity – call this 'evil' – and that this is the truth, the door, that was opened in him by his fall? – While Gibreel... is to be considered 'good' by virtue of *wishing to remain*, for all his vicissitudes, at bottom an untranslated man. (p. 427)

The author-figure archly disclaims this as an 'intentionalist fallacy' but only after giving it due prominence to create an impact on the reader. The text, in fact, validates it. Because Gibreel abandons Saladin when the police confront them at Rosa Diamond's house, thoughts of revenge are born in Saladin. But the evil that prompts Saladin to separate Gibreel from Allie by means of anonymous telephone calls (using his skill at impersonating voices) which exacerbate Gibreel's jealousy, exceeds the provocation. (The anonymous telephone calls recall the anonymous letter sent by Saleem Sinai in *Midnight's Children*, resulting in the killing of Homi Catrack and the shooting of his wife by Commander Sabarmati. At this stage, the relationship of Saladin and Gibreel alludes to that of Iago and Othello; it is a proleptic irony that, when courting Pamela, Saladin had valued *Othello* alone as virtually equal to the complete oeuvre of any other dramatist in any other language.) On the other hand, Gibreel, though he becomes aware that Saladin is the author of the satanic verses that poisoned his relationship with Allie, nevertheless has the grace to save him from being burnt to death in the fire that envelops the Shaandaar Café. Yet the 'untranslated man' is not, in the novel, a pure white ideal. As a film star in India, Gibreel cared nothing for the numerous women with whom he had sex. Rekha Merchant was the only woman to whom he kept coming back, and he drove her to commit suicide (with her children) from the sky-scraper Everest Vilas. Allie suffers the same fate or he pushes her over the roof to her death. (She and Gibreel return to India inde-pendently. Allie had refused to take back Gibreel after the Brickhall fires and he wants to pick up the threads of his film career in India. She comes again to Bombay as a member of an international team of mountaineers on their way to attempt an ascent of the Hidden Peak.) The police suspect Gibreel but he, still unbalanced and his cinematic comeback in India a flop, commits suicide before they arrest him.

The text suggests that there are significances attached to heights/ mountains/Everest. Gibreel and Saladin fall 29,002 feet from the exploding plane – the height of Mount Everest, and their fall is a kind of death. The skyscraper is named after the mountain; Rekha and her children and Allie fall from it to their deaths. Allie longs to make a solo ascent of Everest though warned by Pemba that it would mean her death. The figure of the mountaineer Maurice Wilson who died on Everest, haunts her in London both as an attraction and a warning, and is imagined by Gibreel, as mentioned in his final story, that of Allie (p. 545). Perhaps Allie is harbouring a death-wish (there is a pun on Everest as 'ever-rest'). Pamela's parents both leap together off the top of a high building. The significance of heights is ambiguous. At one point, it represents an 'escape from good and evil', given that in the modern world these are not merely blurred but unclear, in an absolute sense (p. 313). At another, it symbolizes a moral principle, given that Allie sees visions (generated by intense experience) of angels and a cathedral in icefields on Everest. Yet, in its most prominent aspect, it is the focus for the death-wish, a strong drive in human nature.

The number of suicides in the novel is, surely, suggestive. Allie's death is a sort of interrupted suicide, as she was planning to court death by climbing Everest. It is a parallel to her father's suicide (she has inherited his lack of restraint) and her sister Elena's, though Elena was different (confident, proud of her virginity, yet vulnerable inside). Gibreel ends his own life. So do Pamela's parents. All point to a self-destructive tendency in human nature.

Gibreel and Saladin are twinned characters – complementary as well as contrasting figures, their fates intertwined. Rushdie imposes a dependency syndrome on them. Both define themselves against white women. Rushdie draws attention to one of the contrasts:

> In this novel, I've thought of television as the cheaper form, a cruder form [than cinema]. This book contrasts Chamcha, who's a voice-over artist for frozen food commercials, with the gigantic figure of Gibreel. The approximation to divinity that movies offer is not offered by television.[31]

Saladin has no effect on Gibreel, who does not change, but Gibreel does need Saladin as a confidant. On the other hand, Gibreel has an impact on Saladin and, through Gibreel, Saladin finally returns to India and happiness. Gibreel is, indeed, Saladin's *farishta*, his angel.

The immediate cause for Saladin's return to Bombay is the news of his father's impending death from multiple myeloma. Changez Chamchawala is a powerful and appealing figure. When he accompanies his son to London, he wants Saladin to take charge of his purse. Saladin perceives this as harsh because the concern about bills impedes his enjoyment, but this can be viewed from another angle, as giving the son a necessary training. Changez's first wife, Saladin's mother, dies while Saladin resides in London. Changez perpetuates her memory by preserving the original home in its original state and by dressing up the *ayah* in his dead wife's clothes. This, it seems to me, should not be considered grotesque or in bad taste. It recalls Miss Havisham in Dickens's *Great Expectations*, but there is an important difference. Miss Havisham is motivated by loss (her beloved does not turn up for the wedding), and she perpetuates frustration. Changez, too, is motivated by loss (his beloved dies), but he perpetuates happiness, fulfilment. Indeed, Changez is more pleasing than Saladin.

Unlike in *Grimus, Midnight's Children* or *Shame,* the women in *The Satanic Verses* are free of marked oddities of appearance or disposition and are human, even appealing. In *Midnight's Children,* Parvati is a stick figure, her femininity never apparent, any more than Amina's or Padma's. In *Shame,* Rani Harappa is the only normal female figure. In *The Satanic Verses,* Tavleen is in line with the Brass Monkey, Evie Burns and even Sufiya Zinobia, but, in this novel, she is an exception. Saladin's mother, Nasreen, is very much a wife and mother. She is not forceful but is given her place as both. She is very averagely feminine. The *ayah* is devoted to her mistress and master. She replaces her dead mistress without disloyalty, yet with authority. She is not trivialized in portrayal. Rekha Merchant is tough, but has a capacity for feeling. Pamela is vulnerable, and is guilty only of marital infidelity and in extenuating circumstances at that. Like the good usually do in Rushdie's novels before his recent phase, she dies a victim. Allie Cone is a redemptive figure, and she commits suicide or is killed by Gibreel. Mishal and Anahita Sufyan are attractive, natural teenagers, affectionately attached to their immediate kin. Pamela, Allie, Mishal and Anahita are all pleasantly human; even Hind Sufyan and Rosa Diamond are not monsters and Rosa not entirely incredible. The women who inhabit Gibreel's visions, too, offer human interest. Hind, the pagan leader's wife, eats the Prophet's uncle Hamza's heart. She is tough, sexy, faithless. She and the Empress are powerful figures, with something of the Hollywood evil vamp in them. The butterfly girl is a fantasy figure but she, too, is powerful in her own way. The whores are simple and sentimental. Mishal, austere and spirited, exasperates her husband the Zamindar but holds his respect and affection. *The Satanic Verses* offers more female characters than the earlier novels, more fully developed and varied – in keeping with its angle that good and evil can and do coexist.

Zeeny Vakil is the most attractive woman not only in *The Satanic Verses* but in all Rushdie's novels. She is a totally white heroine, too good to be true almost but not quite. Medea in *Grimus* is a comforter, but only physically. She is mindless. Zeeny has a mind – and a humane social conscience, too, and is heroic. She is a fearless doctor who worked with the city's homeless and had gone to Bhopal the moment the news of the disaster broke, and an art critic who propounded a theory about the eclectic hybridized nature of the Indian artistic tradition, illustrated by the Hamza-nama paintings in the Chamchawala collection, as explained in the novel (and elsewhere too) by Rushdie:

> What happened was that the painters were assembled at the Mogul court from all over India, painters working in all the different styles of India ... and they were then required to collaborate ...[32]

Zeeny is the author of a book on 'the confining myth of authenticity, that folkloristic straitjacket which she sought to replace by

an ethic of historically validated eclecticism' (p. 52). This ties up
with Gibreel's song (during his fall from the plane, taken from
the film *Shree 420*) which he translates spontaneously into English:
'O, my shoes are Japanese, These trousers English, if you please.
On my head, red Russian hat; my *heart's Indian for all that*' (p. 5, my
emphasis). Zeeny is politically sincere, anti-nationalist and pro-
cosmopolitan. Indeed, she is identified with India and Rushdie
poetically invests her with the aura of the Earth-mother. Tears
with the colour and consistency of buffalo milk flow from her eyes.
The Indians revere *go-mata* – the cow as mother is tantamount to
a goddess. Zeeny is a redemptive figure – in particular, in respect
of Saladin.

At the end of the narrative, Saladin reintegrates with India. After
long angry decades, he is reconciled with his father and rediscovers
filial fondness. The tragic irony is that this was also the moment of
their final parting, the moment of his father's dying. He resumes his
original name, Salahuddin Chamchawala, and his Urdu comes back
to him, both after a long absence, signifying a return to his original
identity and a new phase in his life. He has finally grown up to real
maturity and has found himself. The re-entry into his life of Zeeny,
given the sort of woman she is, and from whom he learns wisdom
(her address, Sophia – wisdom – College Lane, is suggestive) completes his process of regeneration. He, presumably, lives happily
ever after with her – the only hero of Rushdie's novels to enjoy this
kind of good fortune.

The Satanic Verses is an optimistic book. It is true that Rushdie is
an atheist and God may not exist, but human beings triumph in the
end. Gibreel who is bent on fate and God, cracks up, but Saladin
who lives on the human plane, succeeds. Gibreel as an actor from
a minority (Muslim), playing roles from many religions (including
the majority Hindu), and being accepted, is a positive force during
the opening of the novel; but he disintegrates and falls out of favour
when he attempts a screen comeback on his return to India at the
close. The only prominent and surviving positive is human love,
conceived in the euphoria of marital bliss at this stage of Rushdie's
relationship with Marianne Wiggins. The final impression of the
novel is caught in these lines from Philip Larkin's 'An Arundel
Tomb':

> Our almost-instinct almost true:
> What will survive of us is love.[33]

The emphasis on the redemptive power of love in the novel becomes virtually sentimental at the close; the death-bed reconciliation of father and son is similar in effect. This is in keeping with, and may well have been influenced by, nineteenth-century narrative convention/practice (Dickens is an obvious influence on *The Satanic Verses*; the London of the last phase of the novel mirrors the city Dickens lived in/wrote of) and the happy endings common in Bombay/ Hindi films.

The Satanic Verses is composed of three completely different stories: A. the lives of Saladin and Gibreel; B. the Koranic story rendering the origin of Islam; C. the trek of Ayesha and the villagers towards the sea which, they believe, will open and permit them a passage to Mecca. Rushdie thought that they were three completely different books until he understood, with Bulgakov's *Master and Margarita* as a model, that B and C could be projections of Gibreel's mind.[34] Rushdie thus suggests the basic unifying factor of *The Satanic Verses*, but a result of trying to coalesce three books into one is that certain aspects of *The Satanic Verses* are adumbrated rather than clarified – for instance, the Rosa Diamond story or the significance of heights; a result of something like Shakespeare's problem in *Hamlet*, 'full of some stuff that the writer could not drag to light, contemplate or manipulate into art' (to quote T. S. Eliot).[35]

In *Midnight's Children*, Rushdie is driving himself to be a success and his technique appears at times a showing-off. The novel has sparkle yet, to use Coleridge's terms in the *Biographia Literaria*, it has 'light' but insufficient 'shade'.[36] When Rushdie writes *The Satanic Verses*, he is already at the top and, therefore, he is more relaxed and also ready to be 'as risky' as he could get.[37] He explains:

> *The Satanic Verses* is very big. There are certain kinds of architecture that are dispensed with … since it's so much about transformation I wanted to write it in such a way that the book itself was metamorphosing all the time. Obviously the danger is that the book falls apart.[38]

Rushdie does adopt methods to hold the book together, in addition to the character of Gibreel. Leitmotifs – for instance, the tree, the lamp, the boy on a bike – occur as in the earlier novels. Robert Irwin has observed the 'cross-referenced names and images' which he finds 'a bemusing cat's cradle'.[39] Names are doubled: Hind is the name of Sufyan's enormously fat, grumbling exiled housewife and

of the wife of the ruler of Mecca, promiscuous and queenly; Ayesha
is the name of the butterfly-eating seer and of the Prophet's favourite wife; Mishal is the name of Sufyan's elder daughter as well as of
Mirza Saeed Akhtar's wife; Bilal is the name of the Imam's henchman, a top of the chart pop singer, and of Mahound's supporter,
a freed slave; Cone is the name of the mountain where Mahound
receives his revelations and the surname of Otto and, more significantly, of Alleluia. This may be 'bemusing' to some readers, but is
the result of the crazed mind of Gibreel and, therefore, validated
by the text. Allusions to literary works such as *The Arabian Nights*,
Othello and *The Wizard of Oz* recur but these should not prove
'bemusing' to the literate reader. Milan Kundera has observed that
'the three lines [of the novel] are taken up in sequence in the novel's
nine parts in the following order: A-B-A-C-A-B-A-C-A (incidentally:
in music, a sequence of this kind is called a rondo: the main theme
returns regularly, in alternation with several secondary themes)'.[40]
He adds: 'This is the rhythm of the whole (I note parenthetically the
approximate number of pages): A (90), B (40), A (80), C (40), A (120), B
(40), A (80), C (40), A (40). It can be seen that the B and C parts are all
the same length, which gives the whole a rhythmic regularity.'[41] *The
Satanic Verses* is 'very big', yet integrated, the strands interwoven.

In point of form, *The Satanic Verses* is Rushdie's most innovative and daring novel. *Midnight's Children* was wholly fabulated. In
Shame, the fable was interspersed with a realistic strain introduced
by the novelist/narrator. This trend is developed in *The Satanic
Verses* into a greater variety and range of technique. History which
provided an 'architecture' (to use Rushdie's term) for the whole of
Midnight's Children and *Shame*, is here found only in the short Islamic
sections. *Midnight's Children* and *Shame* are political parables which
do not include diurnal realities. The greater influx of realism in *The
Satanic Verses* permits these realities to a substantial degree. The
narrative (in regard to both character and situation) functions more
on a human plane, giving prominence to feeling. In *Shame*, the relationship of Omar Khayyam Shakil, the repository of Shamelessness,
and Sufiya Zinobia, the repository of Shame, functions on a thematic
rather than human level, whereas in *The Satanic Verses* the involve-
ments of both major characters, Saladin and Gibreel, between each
other and with others, operate on a very human level. It is true
that *The Satanic Verses* is the only novel – before Rushdie's recent
phase – without a character having multiple parents. Gibreel does
have a second father figure, Babasaheb Mhatre, but there is no

element of mystery as in the other novels. The fantasy in *The Satanic Verses*, such as the transformations of Saladin and Gibreel (Rushdie is indebted to Ovid's *Metamorphoses*, 'one of [his] favourite books'[42]) lending Rosa Diamond's 'dream' a material shape, and the 'visionary' aspects of the presentation of the London and Islamic sections, is bolder, unusual, and more varied. Actually, Rushdie blurs the boundaries between fantasy and realism, and, at times, it is difficult to distinguish which mode is operative.

Rushdie's techniques betray the influence of science fiction and the cinema. It is not for nothing that he entered *Grimus* for a sci-fi competition. In *The Satanic Verses*, on Saladin's first flight to London, he read science fiction tales of interplanetary migration: Asimov's *Foundation*, Ray Bradbury's *Martian Chronicles*. Rushdie refers to migrants as 'mutants', distinctively sci-fi terminology. Sci-fi writers often use very innovative styles of writing to simulate thought experiences of time-travellers, aliens and the like; often use concepts of transformations which involve rapid shifts of perspective, scene and so on. Such stylistic effects, found far more often in sci-fi than in mainstream fiction, Joyce apart, could have shaped Rushdie's techniques in *The Satanic Verses*. Rushdie himself reveals that the structure of his novel was influenced partly by the cinematic technique of 'interrupted narratives – flashbacks, dream sequences etc.'[43] The novel is very visual, influenced by the cinema's stress on the image and suits the fact that the novel's two main characters, Saladin and Gibreel, are television and film actors, respectively.

The author as creator appears and intervenes in *Shame* and in *The Satanic Verses*, too, but more playfully and creatively. He appears to Gibreel but does not clarify Gibreel's doubt as to whether he is Ooparvala, 'the Fellow Upstairs', or Neechayvala, 'the Guy from Underneath' (p. 318). He decides not to enlighten Saladin either (p. 409). The devil possesses power but is not a creator. The creator in *The Satanic Verses* creates both Gibreel and Saladin. He claims he is God and, in a sense, he is – as the creator of the novel, not the traditional God of fiction, the omniscient narrator, but a postmodern one. The narrator prevents the reader from getting absorbed into the world of the novel and imparts a Brechtian alienation effect, as in *Shame*, but leaves a sharper sense of the postmodern status of this novel as an art(y)efact. All in all, the narrative of *The Satanic Verses* works on diverse registers, is both puzzling and enlightening, and provides the reader with multiple perspectives.

Five-sevenths of the total number of pages of the novel is taken up by the present-day lives of Saladin and Gibreel, lending weight to the thematics of migration and such issues as hybridity, denationalization and integration, and functions on social, cultural and psychological levels. One seventh of the novel is about the founding of Islam and one seventh about Ayesha's pilgrimage. These episodes are obviously much smaller in bulk, yet arguably the more important ones in terms of their thematics, raising fundamental questions of belief and moral ultimates, and their art going further beyond the conventions of realism.

The satire on Ayatollah Khomeini is brief but hard-hitting. He is projected in the figure of the Imam, an epitome of obscurantism, who proves more of a tyrant than the ruler he deposes. The Empress (the equivalent of the real-life Empress Farah Diba) wishes to control the bodies of the Iranians; he wishes to control their minds as well. That the Empress sits on the throne rather than the Shah (in real life, Reza Pahlevi) is Rushdie's way of suggesting who, in his opinion, wielded the real power in Iran. As in the case of the Widow in *Midnight's Children*, behind the Empress is the figure of the Witch of *Oz*.

Ayesha's pilgrimage acquires a peculiar power deriving from its synthesis of allusions and its basis in reality. It refers to events in the Old Testament (Moses), the life of Mohammed, Gandhi's salt march and other campaigns against the British and the Hawkes Bay case in Pakistan in February 1983.[44] The model for the dream-mansion, Peristan, occupied by Mirza Saeed Akhtar and his wife in Titlipur was an old zamindar's mansion in the depths of rural Bengal in which Satyajit Ray was shooting scenes for *The Home and the World* when Rushdie met him. The model for the giant banyan tree infested by butterflies was seen by Rushdie elsewhere, in southern India, close to Mysore.[45]

Ayesha, a young woman in the village of Titlipur, is strange. She is desirable as well as chaste. She feeds herself only on butterflies and, later, is clothed only in butterflies. She reports to the villagers that the Archangel has spoken to her and that it is his will that they undertake, at once, a pilgrimage to Mecca and that, when they reach the sea, the waves will part and they will walk across the ocean-floor to Mecca. The village council decides to obey the Archangel and the villagers depart. The zamindar, Mirza Saeed Akhtar, remains sceptical but follows the pilgrimage to try and save his wife who has joined it. The villagers enter the sea, but it must not be simply presumed that they were drowned and the pilgrimage interpreted simply as illustrating the delusions and cruelty of fanaticism. Observers testify that they saw the sea parting and, finally, the zamindar, too, does so. It is pointed out that no dead bodies bob up on the sea or are washed ashore. After Ayatollah Khomeini imposed his *fatwa* on Rushdie, the author defended this episode thus: 'I wrote [it] to see if I could understand, by getting inside their skins, people for whom devotion was as great as this.'[46] This is not what the art of the novel conveys. The sequence appears bizarre and weird. It is not like the medieval lyrics or Chaucer, where one can empathize, indeed, share, their faith and devotion to God and the Virgin while reading.

In *The Satanic Verses*, miracles occur. The ending of the Ayesha episode is one such. The safe landing of Saladin and Gibreel from the exploding plane is the first. Saladin, soon after, questions Gibreel: '...and then the waters... *actually*, like in the movies, when Charlton Heston stretched out his staff, so that we could, across the ocean-floor...' (p. 132). When Saladin breaks the news to Mimi Mamoulian over the telephone, she responds: 'Why the waters parted for you and the other guy but closed over the rest?' (p. 259). When Gibreel rescues Saladin from the flaming Shaandaar Café, 'the fire parting before them like the red sea it has become, and the smoke dividing also, like a curtain or a veil; until there lies before them a clear pathway to the door' (p. 468). The miracles are connected by the texture of the language and suggest the ultimate mystery of existence. Lesser miracles reinforce this sense: Pamela's hair becomes snow-white after the shock of seeing Saladin in his altered state; so does her dog; Ayesha's hair too becomes snow-white when she 'meets' the Archangel; Allie and Pemba ascend Everest without oxygen but do not suffer eye or brain damage or death, the normal consequences.

James Harrison observes that 'on a first reading many readers may remain unconvinced that these dream episodes are an integral or essential part of the novel, despite its title'.[47] But they could be so considered if these episodes are interpreted as projections of Gibreel's unbalanced mind, a mind seeking to recover the faith it has lost, and are taken as the explanation for the complete disintegration of his personality. Milan Kundera is right: 'Gibreel Farishta is incomprehensible without the Archangel Gibreel, without Mahound (Mohammed), incomprehensible even without the theocratic Islam of Khomeini or of that fanatical girl who leads the villagers to Mecca... They are all his own potentialities, which sleep within him and which he must battle for his own individuality.'[48] Gibreel had opened the novel with the words, 'To be born again, first you have to die' (p. 3). In a sense, this is true of Saladin: he loses his home and wife, and his job – and his identity. But Gibreel retains his past in the sense of an Islam he can neither believe nor escape. In the Jahilia sequence, he dreams the founding of Islam.

Rushdie himself had chosen to study it as a subject at Cambridge. He explains: 'what seemed to me to be really interesting was that it was the only one of the great world religions that existed as an event inside history'.[49] He has stated that 'almost everything in the dream sequences starts from an historical or quasi-historical basis, though one can't really speak with absolute certainty about that period of Mohammed's life. The records are very partial and ambiguous.'[50] The history is fictionalized – and to suit a dream of a man of Gibreel's character. The text stresses the dream aspect of Gibreel's vision – illusory, distorting, often false, that the dreams are not history. Gibreel is an apostate and so his vision – in any case, a dream – cannot be taken as a valid judgement. Moreover, Gibreel is not an intellectual, a thinker or even socially conscientious.

Jahilia is not a replica of Mecca. Rushdie explains: 'If I had called it Mecca I could not also have made it a city of sand that was threatened by water.... Secondly, the city doesn't look like Mecca; it's a radial city.... It's actually much like New Delhi.... Also, quite a lot of the behaviour in the city, unemployed gangs of youths mugging people and so on, has much more to do with London....'[51] Thus, Jahilia enjoys a wider application and appeal than if it were only a portrayal of Mecca, but the fact remains that it does represent Mecca in the context of the sequence. Jahilia means 'ignorance' and is the name given by the Arabs to the period before Islam. Rushdie's explanation is acceptable: 'The dream-city is called "Jahilia" not to "insult and abuse" Mecca Sharif, but because the dreamer, Gibreel, has been plunged by his broken faith back into the condition the word describes.'[52]

Rushdie argues in respect of Mahound, referring to Mohammed's description of revelation which is incorporated in *The Satanic Verses*:

> He said sometimes he didn't see anything at all, he'd only hear something. Sometimes, he said, it seemed to come from within himself... this is not uncommon as a description of mystical experience.... And one of the reasons he is not called Mohammed is because he's other people too, he's *from* other people too.[53]

Mohammed's experience of revelation is all the more convincing because of what it has in common with that of other mystics, especially given that it is a rare kind of experience, but the fact remains that Mahound stands for Mohammed and no other in the context of the sequence. Rushdie argues likewise that 'the religion of "Submission" both is and is not Islam'.[54] Yet, in the text, it is identifiably Islam and no other.

In depicting the ruler, the Grandee of Jahilia, and his wife, Rushdie modifies history to make it more effective as fiction:

> Abu Sufyan who is the basis for the character Abu Simbel didn't rule the city simply by himself, although he was by far the most powerful figure in it. That was just a simplification. It's not very interesting to dramatize a committee, or a ruling council. It was easier to have different kinds of large operatic figures: the Prophet, the corrupt politician, a kind of Machiavellian, Talleyrand-like figure, and then the absolutist figure of his wife.[55]

Rushdie's use of the place name, Abu Simbel, as a personal name is itself a significant item in his fictionalization and stresses the unreliability of Gibreel's vision – like the use of 'Mahound' as a personal name for Prophet Mohammed.

Rushdie's view of Islam in *The Satanic Verses* is secular and historical. Islam arises from a context. Abu Simbel, Hind and Jahilia itself are corrupt and polytheistic. 'The fortunes of Jahilia were built on the supremacy of sand over water' (p. 102). The opposition of sand and water is important in more ways than one. Jahilia/Mecca was important because of the caravan trails and as a place of pilgrimage. For a long time, it was considered safer to transport goods by land than by sea because of storms. But with the improvements to ships and navigational instruments, the balance tilted the other way. There arose competition not only for trade but for pilgrims too – from a temple in Shaba. Jahilia's answer was to add profanity as an attraction – wine, women and song, and gambling.

Because he was an orphan, Mahound/Mohammed was not protected by the family structure of Jahilia/Mecca. He had been excluded from the ruling council of the city which consisted mainly of the powerful traders – though, as a successful businessman, he merited inclusion. At this time, Mecca was only a third or fourth generation settled city. Mahound, as people did in Mecca, remembers the old nomadic times when the tribes cared for the poorest orphans. He refers passionately to 'this city of gold where people exposed their baby daughters' (p. 118). He is also revealing the change from the matriarchy of old to patriarchy.

After Rushdie had sent Elaine Markson, his literary agent in the United States at that time, the manuscript of *Midnight's Children*, she spoke to him about the possibility of his writing a play about Prophet Mohammed. His reply was: 'it wasn't a good idea because you weren't supposed to portray him'.[56] This caution had left him by the time he embarked on *The Satanic Verses*. He argues:

> Well the point about the book is that there is a view in it that I take – and that is that everything is worth discussing. There are no subjects which are off limits and that includes God, includes prophets.[57]

Amir Taheri expresses the view of devout Muslims:

> The very idea of using the prophet Muhammed as a character in a novel is painful…. The entire Islamic system consists of the so-called *Hodud*, or limits beyond which one should simply not venture.[58]

The Koran does not specifically forbid the portrayal of the Prophet in literature, but this has not been done until Rushdie did it (there have been only some stories of the life of the Prophet). Muslims do not portray the Prophet visually, in terms of art or images. W. J. Weatherby thinks: 'There are no contemporary portraits of him because he feared people would worship them whereas he was only the messenger. And it was the message that should be revered:'[59] But the more cogent reason, in my view, why the Prophet discouraged the making of portraits or images was that the Arab idolators before him worshipped images of gods (in the plural) and he wished to distinguish his message from Allah/God (in the singular) from their beliefs and practices.

The very name by which the Prophet is called in *The Satanic Verses* is part of the controversy. The name is associated with the Crusades, when the Arabs had overrun the Holy Land and Islam was seen as *the* enemy, the Prophet as the Devil. The Oxford English Dictionary explains 'Mahound' as the 'false prophet' Mohammed, in the Middle Ages, often vaguely imagined to be worshipped as a god, and used as a name for the devil.[60] The same dictionary explains 'The Devil' as, in Jewish and Christian theology, the proper appellation of the supreme spirit of evil, the tempter and spiritual enemy of mankind, the foe of God and holiness, otherwise called Satan.[61] A form of the name Mahomet was Baphomet, the alleged name of the idol which the Templars were accused of worshipping.[62] The Templars were a military and religious order, originally occupying a building on the site of Solomon's temple in Jerusalem, founded chiefly for the protection of pilgrims to the Holy Land. They were suppressed in 1312 because of their alleged worship of Baphomet. Mihir Bose observes, 'In the hellish circles of Dante's *Inferno*, "Maometto" is placed only just above Judas and Satan himself. Dante's vivid description of Mohammed's punishment turns the strongest of stomachs even today, and perhaps provides a cautionary reminder of times when cruelty formed a part of Christian culture too.'[63] References to Mahound as a name for the devil abound in Dunbar's *Poems* and occurs in Langland's *Piers Plowman*. Rushdie appears to the devout Muslims to occupy a place in the long line of Western attempts to discredit Islam from the very moment of its birth and his case, added to the rising tide of racism in the West, has rekindled old fears: 'Muslims have reason to think the Crusades are not over yet... the next time there are gas chambers in Europe, there's no doubt who'll be inside them.'[64] 'The gas chambers' provide another 'cautionary reminder of times when cruelty formed a part of Christian culture too' – and the times are very recent.

Rushdie has argued in *The Satanic Verses* itself (p. 93) and elsewhere that his use of Mahound is a part of 'the process of reclaiming language from one's opponents'.[65] This seems to me a willed and unconvincing argument. Moreover, it is beyond the power of Rushdie to turn the tide of history. Yet, in terms of the art of the novel, I see the fact that Mahound is both the Devil and Prophet Mohammed, that both satanic and sacred verses may exist, contributes to establish Rushdie's chief philosophic point – that good and evil are two sides of the same coin, not contraries as usually thought.

In certain ways, Rushdie's portrayal of the Prophet is unexceptionable. He shows how the Prophet went his own way and how he was a reformer. His three chief disciples are Khalid, a water-carrier, Bilal, a slave, and Salman the Persian, a migrant. Thus, Islam is a revolution from the margins. The narrator refers to the disciples as a 'trinity of scum', while Abu Simbel and Baal called them 'that bunch of riffraff' and 'those *goons* – those fucking *clowns*' (p. 101). In this instance, I agree wholly with Rushdie's defence, that 'the scene is a depiction of the early persecution of the believers, and the insults are clearly not [his] but those hurled at the faithful by the ungodly'.[66] As Denis MacErin points out, even Ibu Ishaq, the chief source for the life of the Prophet, puts epithets such as 'fools, blockheads, louts' into the mouths of his Qurayshite enemies.[67]

Rushdie problematizes the Koran and the Muslim identity, individual and collective, which is based on it. The word 'Koran' means 'the Recitation'. Its authority derives from the belief that it is the Word of Allah revealed to the Prophet Mohammed through the intercession of the Angel Gabriel. The Prophet dictates the Word to Salman Al-Farisi, the Persian scribe, because he himself could not read or write. Rushdie defends himself:

> Even the novel's title has been termed blasphemous; but the phrase is not mine. It comes from al-Tabari, one of the canonical Islamic sources.
>
> Muhammad received verses which accepted the three favourite Meccan goddesses as intercessionary agents. The Meccans were delighted. Later, the Archangel Gabriel told Muhammad that these had been 'Satanic verses', falsely inspired by the Devil in disguise and they were removed from the Koran.[68]

But Daniel Pipes comments:

> What Rushdie wrote about Tabari is correct – with one exception. The phrase 'Satanic verses' itself does not come from Tabari.... Further, Muslims know the two abrogated lines, 'These are the exalted birds/And their intercession is desired indeed' not as the Satanic verses incident, but as the *gharaniq* incident. (*Gharaniq* is the word translated here as 'birds'.) In other words, *the phrase 'Satanic verses' is unknown in Arabic* (as well as Persian, Turkish, and the other mother-languages of Muslims). Accordingly, when Muslims hear the phrase 'Satanic verses', it does not register.
>
> Where, then, does the phrase come from? From the orientalist tradition, the Western scholars who study Islam. The phrase was formulated in the West...by far the most important use was by W. Montgomery Watt...[69]

Rushdie recently stated that he came across the Satanic verses incident while studying Islam at Cambridge, with access to scholarship not available, and considered improper, in Muslim countries, and acknowledges Watt himself and other Western scholars like Maxime Rodinson.[70] As suggested above, by using the name 'Mahound', too, he is adopting a part of the orientalist tradition; but, in this case, he claims that he is appropriating and rewriting it.

The Koran existed for some time in a fragmentary form and was not put together and hallowed until sometime after the Prophet's death. Therefore, it is in part the work of ordinary, and fallible, human beings – like any other sacred text. I gather that these 'Satanic verses' suggest either a brief readiness on the part of the Prophet to compromise with the polytheists in power by reintroducing three goddesses, Allat, Manat and Uzza, as subordinate figures, 'daughters of Allah', or, alternatively, an attempt to discredit the Prophet subtly and seemingly mildly by those opposed, but not obviously opposed, to him, early annalists, accepted or rejected by later commentators. Rushdie uses both possibilities for the purposes of his novel.

The Mahound shown as ready to compromise even so deep a principle as monotheism is Gibreel's Mahound, not the historical Mohammed, and it is, as Rushdie sees it, 'a key moment of doubt in [his] dreams'.[71] Mahound appears as a trimmer who is willing to trade his principles to promote his sect – a canny stroke of business. In fact, the text carries a stress on Mahound as a businessman; as hungry for power – over the minds of the Jahilians and/or a seat in the council. But since Mahound is shown as retracting almost then and there – the time lapse is very brief – his agreement to accommodate the three pagan goddesses as Angels and Mediators with Allah, the text emphasizes Mahound's divine inspiration/integrity and, therefore, does not expose the Prophet Mohammed to ignominy. Rushdie could well argue: 'Muhammad's overcoming of temptation does him no dishonour; quite the reverse.'[72] The text has this:

He [Mahound] returns to the city as quickly as he can to *expunge the foul verses* that reek of brimstone and sulphur, *to strike them from the record for ever and ever,* so that *they will survive in just one or two unreliable collections of old traditions* and orthodox interpreters *will try and unwrite their story.* (p. 123, my emphasis)

This works very much in Rushdie's favour; the word 'unreliable' is particularly important. Impressively, in a Jahilia/Mecca where Hind is demanding blood for blood since her brothers have been killed,

Mahound/Mohammed, warned yet fearless, openly revokes the verses accepting Allat, Manat and Uzza as daughters of Allah, the verses he had so recently recited in the tent where the poetry competition was in progress. After all, only two verses were Satanic. It is wrong to assume that Rushdie or the title of the novel is suggesting that the entire Koran was Satanic. The title may, however, suggest that the Koran was not divine revelation but the views of an honest man with a desire to reform religion.

Rushdie humanizes Mohammed as well as Islam. The religion is shown as emerging, not from Allah, but from Mahound who appears a steady, basically honest man. Revelation itself is humanized. Rushdie has stated: 'That paradox.... The fact that the experience of the Prophet which in my view is not faked, is nonetheless not an experience I would have had if I had been standing next to him.'[73] Rushdie here represents not only himself but all ordinary mortals. Rushdie is aware of what he has performed in the novel: 'the point is not whether this is "really" supposed to be Mohammed, or whether the Satanic verses incident "really" happened; the point is to examine what such an event might reveal about what revelation is, about the extent to which the mystic's conscious personality informs and interacts with the mystical event; the point is to try and understand the human event of revelation'.[74] A big blow, surely, to those who see Prophets only as Aeolian harps through which God breathes as sound.

Mahound/Mohammed and Submission/Islam grow in stature as the narrative proceeds. Rushdie notes: 'the book asks centrally two questions about the birth of a big idea.... How do you behave when you're weak, how do you behave when you're strong?'[75] The Satanic verses incident illustrates how Mahound/Submission behaves when he/it is weak. When he/it is strong, he/it only kills a few writers and prostitutes (seeing no difference between these two categories). Rushdie glosses: 'in that opposition between writers and the bearer of a new kind of writing, there was something very important. The people who could not be tolerated were the people who used words in another way.'[76] Mahound/Mohammed and Submission/Islam come through their tests quite well. Rushdie is not disrespectful to the Prophet and Islam, but his view is not that of one of the faithful. His grotesque satire on the crazed evangelism of Eugene Dumsday (his tongue is replaced from his rump and he literally speaks through his arse) stands in marked contrast and shows hostility to religion when it takes such forms. Mahound appears always dignified. Salman the scribe sneers at Mahound when he surreptitiously makes his interpolations and when he narrates the 'Ifk' incident, the alleged infidelity of Ayesha, the youngest and most beloved wife of the Prophet (Rushdie's implication in the text is that the Prophet turned a Nelsonian eye). But the sneering is only that of the scribe, not Rushdie himself, and the Prophet's integrity is unimpaired.

Baal, the satirist, in danger from Mahound's war-leader, Khalid, finds sanctuary with the whores and madam at the *Hijab* ('The Curtain'). The presentation of a brothel as a refuge, like in *Grimus*, has not caused offence, but the prostitutes adopting the names of Mohammed's wives to titillate their clients, certainly, has. It is a common practice to use sacred names for secular things; for instance, innumerable hotels in India are named after Hindu gods and goddesses. But this case is unusual, the practice being extended to the immoral. Rushdie's defence is that he intended to set up an 'opposition between the sacred and profane worlds',[77] but this does not seem to me to operate in the novel. Yet Rushdie's tactic serves other functions. Titillation, true, but the prostitutes become less disorderly. They remain promiscuous sexually but become monogamous and orthodox in their minds. They have a beneficial impact on Baal. He is able to resume writing poetry and this poetry was the sweetest he had ever written.

The question of taste is seldom raised in respect of Rushdie's fiction. Satire via a mentally retarded girl, the dictator's daughter, as in *Shame*, is in bad taste. So is the naming of prostitutes after Mohammed's wives and the naming of the Prophet as Mahound. Rushdie betrays a deep insensitivity to the fact that he will thus bruise the religious susceptibilities of the Muslims and his arguments in his defence reveal that he is unaware of his own insensitivity. Such susceptibilities are perhaps more acute in the case of Muslims than those of the adherents of other religions: Muslims are enjoined to engage in formal worship five times a day; they view the Koran as the direct word of God (not the gospel 'according to' Mark, Matthew and so on). Rushdie's insensitivity is understandable and explicable: he was brought up in a Muslim family, but it was secular; from the age of thirteen until 1988 he had spent almost all his life in Britain – and, in his own formulation, as a 'lapsed Muslim'.[78]

In *The Satanic Verses*, he breaks through the Islamic conceptual framework. On one level, the conflict is between his credo as a writer, complete freedom of expression, and Islam. But he sees it as a part of a wider conflict between literature and religion:

> Between religion and literature, as between politics and literature, there is a linguistically based dispute. But it is not a dispute of simple opposites. Because whereas religion seeks to privilege one language above all others, one set of values above all others, one text above all others, the novel has always been *about* the way in which different languages, values and narratives quarrel, and about the shifting relations between them, which are relations of power. The novel does not seek to establish a privileged language, but it insists upon the freedom to portray and analyse the struggle between the different contestants for such privileges.[79]

Rushdie goes on to locate this conflict and his Bakhtinian view of the novel in the postmodern age:

> This rejection of totalized explanations is the modern condition. And this is where the novel, the form created to discuss the fragmentation of truth, comes in.... The elevation of the quest for the Grail over the Grail itself, the acceptance that all that is solid *has* melted into air, that reality and morality are not givens but imperfect human constructs, is the point from which fiction begins. This is what J-F Lyotard called, in 1979, *La Condition Postmoderne*.[80]

Lyotard defined postmodernism as an 'incredulity towards metanarratives'.[81] By this he means the rejection of all overarching or totalizing modes of thought that tell universalist stories ('metanarratives'), which organize and justify the everyday practice of a plurality of different stories ('narratives'): Christianity, Marxism and Liberalism, for example. Lyotard insists that metanarratives operate through strategies of inclusion and exclusion; they continually attempt to silence other voices, other discourses, in the name of universal principles and general goals. Akbar S. Ahmed, in his *Postmodernism and Islam*, begins from a position close to Lyotard but subsequently insists that the Muslim understanding of the word 'postmodernism' is literal: it is simply 'the period following that of modernism'.[82] He suggests that, in the Muslim world, postmodernism is marked, not by the end of metanarrative, but by its energetic, even militant, resurgence,[83] what the West calls Fundamentalism. Westerners see it as 'reimposed' from above by Ayatollahs,[84] but it is sometimes a deeply personal urge, prompted by religious fervour or a desire to preserve the security provided by traditional belief and custom. Thus, from one perspective, the quarrel over *The Satanic Verses* is between Western postmodernism and the Islamic. *The Satanic Verses* is a defining text of postmodernism in the Western sense.

Fundamentalism is not confined to Muslims. It is found among certain Christian sects and Hindus. It is not necessarily evil but is, arguably, one of the curses of the modern world. Bruce King notes: 'Those who march in protest against Rushdie ... have been told [his novel] was written to order as part of a CIA-Zionist conspiracy to undermine Islam.'[85] It was not necessarily 'written to order'. Rushdie's attitude to Pakistan religious orthodoxy in *Midnight's Children* and *Shame* shows his rebellion against what he sees as the narrow authoritarianism of Islam and it is this vein, in the main, that he fully develops in *The Satanic Verses*. The parameters of his readership extend further. It is Western and subcontinental, as usual, and, in addition, includes the worldwide Muslim constituency. Perhaps the concluding words should be Rushdie's: '*The Satanic Verses* celebrates hybridity, impurity, intermingling, the transformation that comes of new and unexpected combinations of human beings, cultures ... rejoices in mongrelizations and fears the absolutism of the Pure.'[86]

5

Haroun and the Sea of Stories (1990)

Rushdie told Edward Said that *The Satanic Verses* 'would shake up the Muslims',[1] but their reactions exceeded his anticipations. After Viking/Penguin published the novel on 26 September 1988, there occurred Muslim demonstrations and book-burnings throughout Britain, which culminated in a Hyde Park rally on 28 January 1989. But the controversy originated in India, which was the first country to ban it, on 5 October 1988. South Africa proscribed it not long after, on 24 November 1988. Yet what really provoked the until-now silent Ayatollah Khomeini was the death of the faithful: five demonstrators died (dozens were injured) when police opened fire on an anti-Rushdie protest rally in Islamabad on 12 January 1989 and, the following day, one died (more than sixty were injured) in a similar rally in Kashmir; both incidents were shown on Iranian TV. It was only on 14 February 1989 that the Ayatollah imposed his *fatwa*. The full edict runs:

Message on the publication of the apostasian book: Satanic Verses
In the name of God Almighty; there is only one God, to whom we shall all return; I would like to inform all the intrepid Muslims in the world that the author of the book entitled *The Satanic Verses* which has been compiled, printed and published against Islam, the Prophet and the Koran, as well as those publishers who were aware of its contents, have been sentenced to death. I call on all zealous Muslims to execute them quickly, wherever they find them, so that no one will dare to insult the Islamic sanctions. Whoever is killed on this path will be regarded as a martyr, God willing. In addition, anyone who has access to the author of the book, but does not possess the power to execute him, should refer him to the people so that he may be punished for his actions. May God's blessing be on you all.[2]

Khomeini's charge against Rushdie is *kufr*; it covers 'atheism', 'insult to God', 'heresy' and 'apostasy' (that is, breaking with the faith and setting such an example to others).[3] The first phase of Rushdie's life ends. He goes into hiding under the protection of the Special Branch of the British police. Five months later, in July, Marianne Wiggins leaves him.

In September 1991, he emerged from hiding to be honoured by the Writers' Guild of Great Britain for *Haroun and the Sea of Stories.* That the award was made entirely on literary grounds may be doubted, but literary reasons there must have been.

The temporal relationship between *Haroun* and *The Satanic Verses* is important. It throws light on Rushdie's character as well as his preoccupations and values in *Haroun.* Rushdie conceived *Haroun* and began writing it while working on *The Satanic Verses.* W. J. Weatherby notes: 'He had originally planned the story for his young son, Zafar, and he used to read an early version to the boy in serialized form at the boy's bedtime. "It was part of the deal so I could finish *Satanic Verses*", Rushdie once said. "He asked why all my books were for grown-ups and I didn't have an answer." '[4] But it was after May 1989 that the final drafts of *Haroun* were written and the book completed[5] – that is, after *The Satanic Verses* and after the *fatwa.*

In several ways, *Haroun* is close to the heart of Rushdie as man and as writer. He said: 'I began to devise the yarn that eventually became *Haroun,* and felt strongly that if I could strike the right note it should be possible...*to make it of interest to adults as well as children.* The world of books has become a severely categorized and demarcated affair, in which children's fiction is not only a kind of ghetto but one subdivided into writing for a number of different age groups. The cinema, however, has regularly risen above such categories.... But of all the movies, the one that helped me most as I tried to find the right voice for *Haroun* was *The Wizard of Oz*'[6] (my emphasis).

Rushdie's main characters, Rashid Khalifa and Haroun, his son, are introduced *in medias res* from the beginning. Their very names are signs that it will be a story of wonders and fantastic happenings. The names are extracted from that of Haroun-al-Rashid, the fifth Abbasid Caliph (or Khalifa), during whose magnificent reign Baghdad reached its cultural peak, and whose court is associated with the tales of *The Arabian Nights.* Their origin suggests that these two characters can be regarded, from one perspective, as two aspects of a single role: the father as the creator of artistic works and the son as the preserver of these works. This reflects Rushdie's own relation to Anis, father and storyteller, underlined by the fact that 'Rashid' alludes to the writer's own name too. Moreover, the connection to *The Arabian Nights* (unmistakable when the reader learns that the houseboat in which Rashid and Haroun are to stay on Lake Dull is called *Arabian Nights Plus One*) intimates another dimension in the story: the context in which Rushdie was placed while writing it, under a death threat. As Foucault has observed, 'the motivation, as well as the theme and the pretext of Arabian narratives – such as *The Thousand and One Nights*...was the eluding of death'.[7]

The simplicity of *Haroun* is, then, deceptive. Rather, it is complex and multi-layered. Medieval allegory, as in *Piers Plowman* or Dante, operates on three levels – the literal narrative, the moral and the spiritual or mystic. Spenser's *Faerie Queene* works on the levels of the fairy story, the political and the moral. Swift's *A Tale of a Tub* (1704) is a comic religious allegory. *The Lord of the Rings* (1954–55) by J. R. R. Tolkien, a cult figure in the 1970s, functions as a literal story, on a moral level as the epic confrontation between Good and Evil, and on a political level, as a self-glorifying account of little England defeating Hitler. Rushdie, self-consciously postmodern, appears to hark back to medieval, later and recent allegory, and he substitutes his own levels – children's story, the political, the mystique of art and the personal.

As appropriate in a children's story, the hero is a child, Haroun. Read at this level, the book is an entertaining mix of fantasy and the everyday world, with such characters as the reckless bus driver, politicians, the (harmless) gangsters and the flying bird. The immediate starting point of the story is a domestic catastrophe. Haroun loses his mother, Soraya. Mr Sengupta, who lives upstairs, seduces her. Rashid Khalifa's livelihood and motivation for living was in his gift for storytelling, and Sengupta makes Soraya lose faith in him by undermining his position as storyteller. Sengupta is the first to ask the most important question in the book: 'What's the use of stories that aren't even true?'[8] Rushdie's portrayal of Sengupta and his wife is important: 'Mr Sengupta was a clerk at the offices of the City Corporation and he was as sticky-thin and whiny-voiced and mingy as his wife Oneeta was generous and loud and wobbly-fat' (p. 19). Western cartoon presentation is basic to Rushdie's technique in the book and Rushdie's sympathies are suggested clearly. Sengupta hated stories and storytellers, and has no imagination; this in itself is a significant criticism of the man. The key question he puts to Soraya is italicized soon after and Rushdie adds that Haroun was haunted by what he considered 'the terrible question'.

Haroun is eleven years old, so is Rushdie's son, Zafar. Soraya elopes at eleven a.m. and Rashid smashes all the clocks in the house, which thus remain halted at eleven, an episode recalling James Thurber's story 'The 13 Clocks'. Eleven is an interesting number because it consists of a doubling of the same digit and it is the first of such numbers. It becomes a sort of magic number because Haroun finds that thereafter he cannot concentrate on anything for more than eleven minutes. Faced with the elopement and his father's pathetic response, Haroun angrily asked Rashid Sengupta's question (p. 22). Haroun is penitent as he recalls this soon after (p. 27), but the damage has been done. Rashid loses his ability to tell stories. (From one perspective, *Haroun* is about writer's block and the freeing of the imagination.) The shortcomings of his parents compel the son to try to rectify matters. The influence of *The Wizard of Oz* is potent here and a parallel to the film evident. Rushdie wrote: '*The Wizard of Oz* is a film whose driving force is the inadequacy of adults, even of good adults, and how the weakness of grown-ups forces children to take control of their own destinies.'[9]

One of the answers to the central question of the book is given by the politicians. They found that Rashid's stories were useful, not despite their falseness, but because of it. The action of the story takes place near election time and the politicians need Rashid's help to win votes. 'Nobody ever believed anything a politico said, even though they pretended as hard as they could that they were telling the truth. (In fact, this was how everyone knew they were lying.) But everyone had complete faith in Rashid, because he always admitted that everything he told them was completely untrue and made up out of his own head' (p. 20). The suggestion, then, is that one of the uses of the storyteller is as a propagandist.

In the very first sentence of the book, the name of the country in which the story occurs is stated – Alifbay, important because it comes from the Hindustani word for 'alphabet'. It puts the focus on language and writing. Soon after the reader is told that Haroun often thought of Rashid as a Juggler 'because his stories were really lots of different tales juggled together, and Rashid kept them going in a sort of dizzy whirl' (p. 16). Haroun recalls this metaphor for storytelling when he witnesses Blabbermouth's marvellous juggling: 'You keep a lot of different tales in the air, and juggle them up and down, and if you're good you don't drop any' (p. 109). This seems to apply to Rushdie's own technique in *Haroun*; it is not inapposite to compare it to Shakespeare's handling of a multiplicity of characters and plot-lines in *King Lear* or Conrad's in *Nostromo*. The final reference to juggling, literal and metaphorical, is the mesmerizing performance of the Chupwala ambassador (p. 182). When, as a one-man suicide squad, he juggles as a cover so he can hurl a bomb at Prince Bolo and General Kitab of the Guppees, the deceptive and destructive possibilities of art are suggested.

When Rashid Khalifa is invited to perform by politicos from the Town of G and the nearby Valley of K, he fails. He and Haroun then board a bus to the Valley of K. To give the two a view of the Valley before sunset, the bus driver, Butt, drives his vehicle at increasingly breakneck speed, which paradoxically increases with the climb. He punctuates his speech with 'but', a pun on his name, and the colloquial expression 'no problem', ironical in view of the hair-raising speed and dangers the passengers are subjected to. The Valley of K is a fictionalized version of Kashmir and Rashid explains to Haroun its other names – 'Kache-Mer', which means 'the place that hides a Sea' (French: *cache* – hiding place; *mer* – sea; significant, in that in Rushdie's book it conceals the Sea of Stories) and 'Kosh-Mar', a word for 'nightmare' (French: *cauchemar* – nightmare; significant, in that Haroun's and Rashid's experiences in Kashmir can be so described).

In the Valley of K, Rashid meets Buttoo, the leader of the ruling party of the Valley on whose behalf he had agreed to appear. The similarity in name between Butt and Buttoo pairs them off as comic characters and stresses the contrast between their natures, the former coarse and sincere, the latter slick and insincere. The satire on Buttoo goes beyond the personal: 'During the five-minute walk to the shore of the Dull Lake, Haroun began to feel distinctly uneasy. Mr Buttoo and his party (which now included Rashid and Haroun) were permanently surrounded by exactly one hundred and one heavily armed soldiers; and such ordinary people as Haroun noticed on the street wore extremely hostile expressions' (p. 42). Lake Dull is the ironic (in view of the interesting things that occur there) fictionalized name for Kashmir's legendary Lake Dal. Buttoo appears an unpopular tyrant, dependent on military support. The closeness of his name to Bhutto, the real-life Pakistani politician and prime minister, makes Rushdie's immediate target obvious (many Western readers have perceived Zulfikar Ali Bhutto and Zia ul-Haq through Rushdie's Iskander Harappa and Raza Hyder in *Shame*). Buttoo tells

Rashid: 'My enemies *hire cheap fellows* to stuff the people's ears with *bad stories* about me .... You will tell happy stories, *praising* stories, and the people will believe you ... and *vote for me*' (p. 47, my emphasis). The role of storyteller as propagandist is thus confirmed.

The title and concept of Rushdie's novel are derived from those of the Kashmir poet Somadeva's eleventh-century compilation of tales, the *Katha-Sarit-Sagara* or 'The Ocean of the Streams of Story', which is actually mentioned in Rushdie's text (p. 51). The *Katha-Sarit-Sagara* is a literary version by Somadeva of a lost Prakrit work, the *Brhadkatha* (that is, folk tales). Rushdie explains:

> the stories were held here in fluid form, they retained the ability to change, to become new versions of themselves, to join with other stories and so become yet other stories; so that unlike a library of books, the Ocean of the Streams of Story was much more than a storeroom of yarns. It was not dead but alive .... Nothing comes from nothing, no story comes from nowhere; new stories are born from old – it is the new combinations that make them new. (pp. 72, 86)

This concept of creativity, linked to India, is nevertheless postmodern. From the notion of a 'Sea of Stories' (Rushdie's title) one could expect a story within a story or connections between stories. This is precisely what transpires.

The Ocean of the Streams of Story originated in Kashmir and it is, therefore, logical that Rushdie adopts the Valley of K as a setting in his novel. This also ties up with the personal level of the novel because Kashmir was Rushdie's ancestral home. During Haroun's and Rashid's first night on the fantastic houseboat on Lake Dull, Haroun discovers the Water Genie, Iff, disconnecting Rashid's Story Water supply. Rashid has cancelled his subscription by a P2C2E, a Process Too Complicated to Explain, a gimmick originating in a similar anagram which names a robot in the film *Star Wars*. Haroun manages to grab Iff's Disconnecting Tool and refuses to return it until Iff takes him to Gup City to meet the Walrus, the Grand Comptroller (he recalls Lewis Carroll's 'The Walrus and the Carpenter' in *Through the Looking Glass*), and get the problem solved. Iff acts as Butt's counterpart in fantasy-land, as suggested by his very name. Haroun and Iff travel to the earth's second moon, Kahani, on the back of a mechanical bird, a Hoopoe, who merges into Butt, suggested by their physical resemblance and by the bird's adoption of the bus driver's name. As in *Grimus*, Rushdie alludes ironically to Farid-ud-din 'Attar's twelfth-century Sufi text, *The Conference of Birds*, an allegory of man's Way to perfection. There the hoopoe leads the other birds to their spiritual goal, only thirty surviving, just as the bird, mechanical in Rushdie's novel, carries Haroun on his less arduous venture, at first artistic, and with no loss of life (it remains to be seen whether this shall be true in the real world for Rushdie).

Significantly, the moon is called Kahani, which means 'story': it is the location for the Ocean of the Streams of Story, and the setting for another story with more of 'storybook things' (p. 79). From a domestic tragedy, Haroun is now catapulted into a crisis involving a whole nation and, incidentally, the 'fairy tale' romance of Prince Bolo and Princess Batcheat. Kahani comprises the lands of Gup and Chup, divided by a Twilight Strip. 'Chup' means 'quiet' and 'Gup' means 'gossip'. Their names, it turns out, are perfectly appropriate. Chup was always dark – the darkness of evil, the darkness of (deliberately imposed) ignorance, and its inhabitants were deprived of speech. Its leader was the Cultmaster, significantly and ominously named Khattam-Shud (meaning 'completely finished', 'over and done with'). He is the arch villain. He is first mentioned by Rashid when Haroun and he are relieved to find themselves enjoying the sight of the sun setting over the Valley of K: 'Khattam-Shud is the Arch-Enemy of all Stories, even of Language itself. He is the Prince of Silence and the Foe of Speech' (p. 39). These words carry weight and are repeated by Iff when introducing Haroun to the Land of Chup (p. 79). But Khattam-Shud has grown worse: 'In the old days the Cultmaster, Khattam-Shud, preached hatred only towards stories and fancies and dreams; but now he has become more severe, and opposes Speech for any reason at all. In Chup City the schools and law-courts and theatres are all closed now, unable to operate because of the Silence Laws' (p. 101). He has moved beyond censorship to a repression of student protest, the rule of law and protest theatre. Khattam-Shud can be credibly interpreted as an image of Ayatollah Khomeini.

Salman Rushdie regards Tolkien's *The Lord of the Rings* as a 'great fantasy',[10] and it functions as an intertext. Both *The Lord of the Rings* and *Haroun* have a line of action in common – the quest. Frodo Baggins, a Hobbit, a man and some dwarfs set out to destroy the Ring and defeat the Dark Lord, Sauron; Haroun, a mortal, a genie, a Floating Gardener and a machine set out to defeat the Lord of Darkness and Silence, Khattam-Shud. The Mali (Gardener) represents the imagination in a Coleridgean sense – trimming and keeping art in control. The symbol of Khattam-Shud is the sign of the Zipped Lips, a parallel to the sign of Mordor carved on the decapitated heads of enemies, 'the foul token of the Lidless Eye'.[11] *The Lord of the Rings*, however, is essentially serious, even grim in the telling, fascinating for anyone over thirteen, perhaps too frightening for children. *Haroun* is very openly comic; it lacks something of the seriousness of childhood which makes *Alice* so good for children. Perhaps the non-serious tone of *Haroun* suits the children of today; *Alice* was for Victorian girls, after all, yet there are similarities.

For example, when Khattam-Shud explains his motivation to Haroun:

> 'But why do you hate stories so much?', Haroun blurted, feeling stunned. 'Stories are fun.'
>
> 'The world, however, is not for Fun', Khattam-Shud replied. 'The world is for Controlling.'
>
> 'Which world?', Haroun made himself ask.
>
> 'Your world, my world, all worlds', came the reply. 'They are all there to be Ruled. And inside every single story, inside every Stream in the Ocean, there lies a world, a story-world, that I cannot Rule at all. And that is the reason why.' (p. 161)

This opposition between the politician, especially one of an autocratic cast of mind, and the writer is not new, but traditional. It is significant that Haroun's little emergency weapon is the Bite-a-Lite. When he did bite it, 'the light that poured out from his mouth was as bright as the sun!' (p. 165). It is suggested that the mouth is the source of illumination – the medium for free speech, argument and discussion.

The portrayal of Khattam-Shud and the Chupwalas is as the antinomy of conventional villains:

> As for the Chupwalas ... how ordinary they were, and how monotonous was the work they had been given .... Mindless routine jobs ... boring ... weaselly, scrawny, snivelling clerical types ... up to nothing less than the destruction of the Ocean of the Streams of Story itself! 'How weird', Haroun said to Iff, 'that the worst things of all can look so *normal* and, well, *dull*.' (p. 152)

It is suggested that routine and dullness are anti-creative. Haroun's observation of the Chupwalas as 'weaselly, scrawny, snivelling clerical types' had, in fact, been made earlier (p. 148), and is virtually repeated by Prince Bolo as he tactlessly insults the Chupwala ambassador (p. 166). This is only one instance of the recurrent phrases that run through the book. These have been, probably, prompted by the fact that recurrent phrases are a great joy to children – for instance, in 'Three Little Pigs', 'I'll huff and I'll puff and I'll blow your house down', 'Not by the hair on my chinny, chin, chin', or in 'Goldilocks', 'Who's been eating/sitting/sleeping', etc. The Chupwalas, it is emphasized, are unimpressive. So is their leader: 'a skinny, scrawny, measly, weaselly, snivelling clerical type, exactly like all the others' (p. 153). The cardinal difference between him and his followers is that he talks a great deal despite the cult of silence. Iff remarks: 'the Grand Panjandrum himself does exactly what he wants to forbid everyone else to do' (p. 154). This is one of the hallmarks of a dictator. Yet Khattam-Shud's voice, though clear, is dull and inflectionless, 'a voice nobody would ever have remembered' (p. 153). Thus, even his single distinguishing trait is devoid of distinction.

Chup is the opposite of the enlightened Gup, with its books and free speech and clear daylight at every hour. Haroun thinks:

> 'Gup is bright and Chup is dark. Gup is warm and Chup is freezing cold. Gup is all chattering and noise, whereas Chup is silent as a shadow. Guppees love Stories, and Speech; Chupwalas, it seems, hate these things just as strongly.' It was a war between Love (of the Ocean, or the Princess) and Death (which was what Cultmaster Khattam-Shud had in mind for the Ocean, and for the Princess, too). (p. 125)

This is a compact summary, but Haroun goes on to think that the contrast between Gup and Chup and the issues are not as simple as set out above:

> the dance of the Shadow Warrior showed him that silence had its own grace and beauty (just as speech could be graceless and ugly); and that Action could be as noble as Words; and that the creatures of darkness could be as lovely as the children of light. (p. 125)

The immediate reference seems to be to Mudra the Shadow Warrior. He employs the Language of Gesture and the suggestion is that actions speak louder than words. This passage is meant to be profound and evidently Rushdie thinks it of thematic value, since it does not advance the storyline, nor is it entertaining to adult or child. But the complexity is not worked out further and the main contrast between Gup and Chup remains a simple cartoon-style one between white and black.

When Haroun arrives at Gup, he does so at a time when the country is in a state of crisis and in a state of war. The Chupwalas were not merely poisoning the Ocean of the Streams of Story but were trying to block the Wellspring, its very Source, with a giant Plug, and so permanently kill creativity. The Ocean of Stories and the Wellspring is a metaphor for art and the imagination. There is no completely original writer as such. There is a common stock of experiences and methods which an individual recasts, refashions, reinvents. This ultimately leads to, in Rushdie's words, 'that will-o'-the-wisp of (post) modern critical theory – the authorless text',[12] an extension of the modernist view, articulated by T. S. Eliot in 'Tradition and the Individual Talent': 'The poet...must be aware that the mind of Europe – the mind of his own country – a mind which he learns in time to be much more important than his own private mind – is a mind which changes, and that this change is a development which abandons nothing *en route*, which does not superannuate either Shakespeare, or Homer or the rock drawing of the Magdelanian draughtsmen!'[13]

The Chupwalas had captured Prince Bolo's fiancée, Princess Batcheat, and were planning to sew up her mouth and sacrifice her to their idol, Bezaban, who, significantly, has no tongue. In his portrayal of the romance of Bolo and Batcheat, Rushdie satirizes the hero and heroine of conventional romance: the phrase that distinguishes Bolo is 'dashing but a little foolish', while what distinguishes Batcheat is her ugliness and execrable singing. Rushdie's satire also touches on the monarchs of today, at least, those still left; he implicates them as he repeats Iff's – and the Guppees' – view expressed with reference to Bolo: 'it's not as if we really let our crowned heads do anything very important around here' (pp. 104, 193). When the Page Blabbermouth leads Haroun to his room on his first night at Gup, he accidentally knocks off the page's cap and discovers the page to be a girl. Blabbermouth explains: 'You think it's *easy* for a girl to get a job like this? Don't you know girls have to *fool people* every *day* of their *lives* if they want to get *anywhere*?' (p. 107). Here Rushdie expresses the grievances of feminists. Blabbermouth's resemblance to romantic girls disguised as pages (in Shakespeare and Sir Walter Scott) indicates that the sea of stories is timeless and joins East with West. Haroun develops a soft spot for Blabbermouth but it is to Mudra that she responds, an incipient romantic interest in the book.

It is an immense advantage to the Guppees that Mudra, the Champion Warrior of Chup, considered by most Chupwalas to be second in authority only to Khattam-Shud, has become disgusted with the increasing cruelty and fanaticism of the Cult of Bezaban, has broken off relations with Khattam-Shud and is willing to join them. His Abhinaya (Language of Gesture) is interpreted by Rashid who has reached Kahani through his own magic. Mudra explains that in the Land of Chup, Shadows are considered the equals of the people to whom they are joined and enjoy a semi-independent existence. There are possibilities of diversity and conflict as well as unity between Self and Shadow, a version of the twinned characters typical of Rushdie's novels (Saleem and Shiva in *Midnight's Children*, Iskander and Raza in *Shame*, Saladin and Gibreel in *The Satanic Verses*), which reflect divisions within himself arising out of the 'accidents in [his] life'.[14] It is Khattam-Shud's distinction that he alone of the Chupwalas has separated himself completely from his Shadow and can be in two places at once. But Mudra adds: 'this new, doubled Khattam-Shud, this man-shadow and shadow-man, has had a very harmful effect on the friendships between Chupwalas and their Shadows.... It is a sad time when a Chupwala cannot even trust his own Shadow' (pp. 133–4). The suggestion is that mistrust is an ingredient of totalitarianism. During the crisis, Khattam-Shud's Shadow is in the Old Zone, supervising the poisoning of the Ocean and the plugging of the Wellspring, while the Self is in Chup City in command over the fate of Princess Batcheat.

Haroun leads his small party to cope with the situation in the Old Zone. General Kitab (Book) leads the army of Gup, consisting of Pages organized into a Library, to rescue Batcheat. As the army gathers, the emphasis is on noisy argument and contradiction (even of General Kitab who takes it in good part):

'What an army!' Haroun mused. 'If any soldiers behave like this on Earth, they'd be court-martialled...'

'But but but what is the point of giving persons Freedom of Speech', declaimed Butt the Hoopoe, 'if you then say they must not utilize the same? And is not the Power of Speech the greatest Power of all?' (p. 119)

Haroun's, and the reader's, misgivings are allayed. 'The Pages of Gup, now that they *had talked through everything so fully*,... remained united, supported each other... and in general looked like a force with a common purpose. All those arguments... created powerful bonds of fellowship' (pp. 184–5, my emphasis). On the other hand, the Chupwalas' habits of secrecy made them suspicious and distrustful; they stabbed one another in the back, mutinied, and, finally, ran away. Seemingly muddled and inefficient democracy triumphs over a state that represses freedom of speech.

Yet it detracts from the triumph that it is partially brought about by a *deus ex machina*. When Haroun and his party are getting the worst of the battle with the Shadow Khattam-Shud and the Shadow Chupwalas in their Shadow Poison Ship, Haroun finds the small bottle of *Wishwater* in his pocket, he drinks it and his wish that the moon Kahani revolve is granted. When the sun shines on the Old Zone, the Shadows all melt and Haroun is able to save the Ocean. In Chup City, it is true the army of Gup defeated the Chupwalas, but then the sun shines on it, the ice world melts, the Colossus of Bezaban falls and its huge head crushes Khattam-Shud's Self. Light uncovers what lies concealed, overcomes Darkness, evil and obscurantism. The vanquishing of Khattam-Shud is presented in pure cartoon style. The story loses impressiveness and force because Khattam-Shud and the Chupwalas are always denied dignity; threat and menace are lacking because Khattam-Shud is pettifogging and the Chupwalas clumsy. The allegory is simple and some of the ideas thrown out (for instance, regarding creative writing) lose focus.

It is finally revealed that the story the reader has been reading is, in fact, one of Rashid's own tales. This is a pleasant surprise and imparts a sense of a neat and circular structure, and also incorporates an interesting ambiguity: the reader is left uncertain – is Haroun's journey only a dream; or a trip into the imagination? The conclusion underlines the importance of the messages from the fantasy world. In the supposedly less unreal, primary world, Rashid's tale of the Union of Zipped Lips and the fact that the Chupwalas hated Khattam-Shud, their ruler, and become free of him, propels the people of K to get rid of their unpopular leader, Buttoo. The intellectual/artist appears as a potential social reformer, the storyteller as opposed to tyranny. The main link between the two worlds of the novel had been suggested earlier when Khattam-Shud asked the central question of the novel, 'what's the use of stories that aren't even true?' and so Haroun sees him as a double of Mr Sengupta (p. 155).

Stories, however fantastic, are conceptually true; the writer, the value and power of the imagination are vindicated in the novel. On a different plane, the episode in *The Satanic Verses* which outraged the Muslims is presented as dream, but the guise of fiction has been of no use to Rushdie, given the consequences. The central question of *Haroun* is put naively, as appropriate to a children's story, but the implied answers are deep and serious.

There are other links between the two worlds of the novel: the repetition and similarity of names (But the bus driver and the Hoopoe, Buttoo the politician; Kahani is the name of the second moon and, it turns out at the end, also of the sad city in Alifbay introduced at the beginning) and resemblances between the two Butts and the two floating gardens. These do not merely hint at a mirror world of the kind found in *Alice* but suggest the relevance of the secondary fantasy world to the primary 'real' world beyond the novel. (It is not insignificant that Butt is the maiden name of Rushdie's mother and Soraya the name both of Rashid's wife and the beautiful, childless first wife of the Shah whom Khomeini deposed.) And, of course, the structural link between the two worlds of the novel is the humour.

Rushdie dedicated *Midnight's Children* to his son, Zafar, not only as a sign of a bond of affection but also to Zafar as an inheritor of India's legacy. *Haroun* begins:

> Z embla, Zenda, Xanadu:
> A ll our dream-worlds may come true.
> F airy lands are fearsome too.
> A s I wander far from view
> R ead, and bring me home to you.

In this dedication, in the form of an acrostic, it is the bond of affection that is important – indeed, all-important in the context of the marital and other difficulties of the twice divorced, sentenced-to-death Rushdie. In his interview with James Fenton, he said: 'I was a very lucky man to have that son. And I'm a lucky man to have that promise [made to the son to write a children's book]. Because I needed something bigger than what was happening to me to bring me back to the typewriter. The only thing that could be bigger was a promise to a child.'[15]

In the Ocean in Kahani are the Plentimaw Fishes, Goopy and Bagha. Their names 'don't mean anything special, but they are also the names of the two goofy heroes of a movie by Satyajit Ray. The movie characters are not fishes, but they are pretty fishy' (p. 217). In the book, ironically, Goopy and Bagha are not 'fishy' at all, in the metaphorical sense, though they are so in a literal sense. It is important to observe that they are faithful partners for life and that their doggerel in rhyme is not only humorous but an expression of perfect union. (The film, *Goopy and Bagha*, is a fantasy, and 'is, in Bengal, as well loved as *The Wizard of Oz* is here'.[16]) At the conclusion, Prince Bolo and Princess Batcheat are reunited; Soraya, who had eloped with Sengupta, returns to Rashid and Haroun, and domestic harmony is restored. In one of its dimensions, *Haroun* is an assertion of family values.

A happy ending is a convention in a children's story, but what the reader finds in *Haroun* is more than mere convention. The conclusion is happier than that of *The Satanic Verses* and of a different texture. He told Fenton: 'Actually it's very hard to write a happy ending that feels right... *actually,* it was lovely to write... sometimes in life, things do turn out okay, and it's wrong of writers to deny this fact'[17] (Fenton's emphasis). It is a sign of Rushdie's strength of character that he has written his most cheerful book when he was placed in such difficult circumstances. For, while on one level, *Haroun* reads as a covert critique of Iran and those Muslims who support her stand on *The Satanic Verses*, the book shows Rushdie to be optimistic about the eventual outcome. As he wrote a year later: 'There is evidence that reason is slowly replacing anger at the centre of the debate, that understanding may slowly be putting out the fires of hatred. That process must be encouraged, and I will certainly continue to do my bit.'[18] *Haroun*, in a sense, is one such contribution: it is both an escape from grim reality (like *The Wizard of Oz* was before the Second World War or 'The 13 Clocks' to Thurber[19]) and a presentation of it, and communicates a promise of hope.

In *Haroun*, there is much broad simple fun, yet, all in all, the humour is not only entertaining but also positive and life-enhancing. Rushdie's style is less flamboyant than in his earlier novels, but the sheer verbal exuberance remains. There are the rhymes of the Plentimaw Fish and those connected with the K bus; the pun when Haroun muses: 'there are really Plentimaw Fish in the Sea, just as old Snooty Buttoo said' (p. 84); Batcheat's song:

> He won't play polo,
> He can't fly solo,
> Oo-wee but I love him true,

Our love will grow-lo,
I'll never let him go-lo,
Got those waiting-for-my-Bolo
Blues

(p. 187)

– a parody of blues lyrics. Rushdie's use of the spoken idiom in dialogue is more than merely spicy: in the opening pages, Rashid pleads: 'What to do son, storytelling is the only work I know' (p. 22); Oneeta Sengupta, abandoned by her husband, wails, 'O! O! What is to become?' Rushdie uses Indian English at moments of intensity such as these as well as at normal times. In a sense, the Empire is writing back. Rashid incorporates Continental lingo too in his speech: 'In the Valley of K, I will be terrifico, magnifique' (p. 26), while General Kitab, a parody of the Sandhurst military man, adopts a British type of slang: 'Dash it all, will you be quiet: Spots and fogs' (p. 130). Really, Rushdie employs an eclectic, international kind of language in his dialogue which enhances the universality of the novel's appeal and relevance. The Land of Khattam-Shud represents what the Soviet Union and China meant to the West during the Cold War and, more recently, what Iran under Khomeini meant, and, essentially, what dictatorial regimes throughout history have meant.

The element of allegory in *Haroun* compared to that of *Midnight's Children* and *Shame* is less particularized in place and time, but more referential than *Grimus*. J. R. R. Tolkien wrote in his 'Foreword' to *The Lord of the Rings*: 'I think that many confuse "applicability" with "allegory"; but the one resides in the freedom of the reader, and the other in the purposed domination of the author.'[20] *Haroun* is 'applicable' rather than 'allegorical', in Tolkien's sense. Paul Griffiths, reviewing *Haroun* immediately after publication, observed: 'It is a great assertion of the imagination: of the writer's imagination necessarily ... but also of the reader's in laying hold of the iridescent story sea.'[21] He is right to suggest the necessity of response and interpretation, but he is blind to the book's limitations, a common blindness.[22] Admittedly, its success is difficult to judge. As an effervescent, readable and entertaining story, both children and adults are likely to enjoy it. Its play of ideas regarding freedom, the artist and creativity is beyond children, will certainly interest adults, but I have reservations in respect to their articulation.

Rushdie's imagination continues to be connected to India. He spent the early, perhaps most impressionable, years of his life there and it is natural that he should turn to it for a children's book. With the valley of Kashmir and Lake Dal as a setting, with Goopy and Bagha (both the characters and the influence of the film), with Indian characters and Indian English, with names having meanings in Urdu, it is, above all, the way in which the references to the *Katha-Sarit-Sagara* are woven into the fabric of its meaning that makes India more than just a setting for the novel.

From another perspective, *Haroun* is impeccably Western. Its mode is the fairy tale. True enough it alludes to *The Arabian Nights*, but it does also to *Alice in Wonderland* and *Through the Looking Glass*. The cartoon is basic to its technique. The use of generic names is part of the Western tradition of comedy and allegory. Western film, especially *The Wizard of Oz*, is an important influence. The ocean is not only Indian as such but, in the real world, a body of water uniting (and separating) lands – it is international. The implied attitudes to censorship and democracy reflect Rushdie's faith in Western liberal democracy which he has held from *Grimus* onwards.

Haroun lies in the central line of Rushdie's development as a writer. Its continuities with *Midnight's Children*, *Shame* and *The Satanic Verses* are clear. They have in common an interest in wonders and fantastic occurrences, and an opposition to dogmatic exclusiveness (the Chupwalas are rigid believers/ideologists who exclude much). Rushdie's identity remains part-Indian, part-Western, both partial and plural at once; only such a writer could have produced *Haroun*. A modest achievement, in my view, yet remarkable in that it was attempted, given the circumstances in which Rushdie was placed.

6

East, West (1994)

In a highly publicized event, on Christmas Eve 1990, Rushdie, at a meeting with six Muslim scholars, re-embraced Islam. The general attitude towards this can be summed up in the words Rashid Khalifa tells Prince Bolo, in answer as to why he, unarmed, dressed in a nightshirt and half-dead with cold, did not try to rescue Princess Batcheat from the Chupwalas: 'some people prefer good sense to heroism' (p. 104). Soon after, Rushdie said that he 'felt a good deal safer' and also added: 'What I know of Islam is that tolerance, compassion and love are at its very heart.'[1] This is very true of the Sufi view. There is a danger of homogenizing Western and Muslim points of view; setting up crude binaries, the West versus Islam; and constructing a monolithic Muslim identity. But the fact remains that there are two broad points of view discernible, the Western liberal (complete freedom of expression) and the devout Islamic, and their continuing conflict can be explained in terms of Lyotard's differend:

> As distinguished from litigation, a differend would be a case of conflict, between (at least) two parties, that cannot be equitably resolved for lack of a rule of judgment applicable to both arguments. One side's legitimacy does not imply the other's lack of legitimacy. However, applying a single rule of judgment to both in order to settle their differend as though it were merely a litigation would wrong (at least) one of them (and both of them if neither side admits this rule).[2]

The conflict is compounded by being entangled in national and international politics. Khomeini's motives were, probably, mixed. Within Iran, his edict was a method of uniting competing factions, the pragmatists (like Ali Akbar Hashemi Rafsanjani, then the Speaker, and Ali Akbar Velayati, then the Foreign Minister) who were advocating better relations with the West, and the radicals who believed that mending ties with the West was proceeding too far and too rapidly. In the West, Fundamentalism has replaced Communism as a bogey and the Rushdie case has become a means of consolidating power by isolating and demonizing the Muslims. In 1992, Rushdie again renounced Islam, feeling betrayed that the six Muslim scholars who 'agreed that [*The Satanic Verses*] had no insulting motives.... "Now we will launch a world-wide campaign... to explain that there has been a great mistake", broke that promise'.[3] The result is that, though Khomeini was dead, Rushdie's plight remained the same.

Yet Rushdie has never wavered in what he has always seen as a vocation – being a writer. In 1994, he brought out a new book *East, West*, a collection of stories. Six of the nine stories in the volume had been published earlier and at different times. The 'acknowledgements' mention this but do not give the dates – perhaps, a deliberate piece of obfuscation. In any case, since Rushdie has revised the stories, it is difficult to place them in the line of his development as a writer. But the fact is that the three stories of the first section, 'East', were written first; those of the second section, 'West', later and those of the last section, 'East, West', are new and written last of all. Though not preplanned, they fall into a pattern, a kind of journey and development of their own. Rushdie has written two or three other stories but has excluded them from this collection because they do not fit in.

The stories in the first section, titled 'East', are set in this region, specifically, India and Pakistan. In 'Good Advice is Rarer than Rubies', a would-be immigrant rejects life in the West in favour of that in the East. Miss Rehana is one of the 'Tuesday women' who come to the Consulate to get visas or permits to go to England. They are exploited by an old man, an 'advice wallah', Muhammad Ali, who intercepts them, frightens them, and then offers to get them the necessary permission through a contact of his at the Consulate. Relieved and grateful, they would often pay him five hundred rupees or give him a gold bracelet for his pains. Then they would go away. Muhammad Ali always selected women who lived hundreds of miles away, so that, when they found out that they had been gulled, they were too far away and it was too late anyway. Yet impulsiveness makes Muhammad Ali give free and honest advice to the spirited young Rehana and even offer her the ultimate prize, a stolen passport. But Rehana refuses the passport and deliberately bungles her interview at the Consulate. Her motives are suggested. Her husband-to-be is more than twenty years her senior and now sounds like a stranger when he telephones her from England. She returns to continue her life as an *ayah* to 'three good boys [who] would have been sad to see [her] leave'.[4] Immigration is a dream totally desirable to many, but not to independent, hard-headed Rehana. What is the ultimate explanation of the narrative as to why the East is better/more desirable than the West? It seems to lie in the impulsive warmth of even casual encounters. The story is vigorous and successful.

So is the next one, 'The Free Radio'. It projects self-deception as an aid to happiness – through its central character, Ramani, the young handsome rickshaw-wallah. He falls in love with a thief's widow, attractive, but probably ten years his senior, with five children alive and two dead, and totally improvident. The narrator of the story is a 'mister teacher sahib retired', an elder who observes and passes judgement on the town's affairs. In his opinion, Ramani's love for the widow is folly, and he a victim of her designs. The central metaphor of the story, Ramani's burden, is made real as he carries his beloved and her children in his rickshaw. The widow will marry Ramani only on condition that she will bear no more children. So he decides to undergo a vasectomy and also expects the government to reward him with a free transistor radio. He did not know that this incentive had been withdrawn long ago and, while waiting in hope, makes do by holding an imaginary radio to his ear, mimicking broadcasts. He then decides to go off to Bombay with his wife and ready-made family – to become a film star. He sends back to the narrator, via a professional letter-writer, accounts of his success and affluence, but the elder knows that these are delusions. Ramani's strong imagination is an adequate substitute for the realization of his dreams. It is easy to sympathize with the charming Ramani, but Rushdie evokes sympathy for the narrator too, vinegary as he is. There is much truth in his views and he does care about Ramani – and Ramani is attached to him, judging by the way he continues to keep in touch.

The concluding story of this section, 'The Prophet's Hair', set in Kashmir, is more complex. It is characterized by a fast-moving sardonic narration, with fantastic events, and starts with mystery and suspense – all evoking curiosity, wonderment and 'whatnextism' as in *The Arabian Nights*. In the ancient mode, such stories had a happy ending; in the modern, the reverse. In fact, its detachment of tone, cynical flavour and rapidity of incident recall Robert Louis Stevenson's *The New Arabian Nights*, the adventures of Prince Florizel of Bohemia, incognito. In the very first line, Rushdie emphasizes the modernity of his story via the date, the year 19—.

In the 1960s, there was an actual sensational incident when a relic, the Prophet's hair, was stolen from a mosque in Kashmir and then found, authenticated by the thieves and the holy men of the place, and returned to the shrine. Rushdie thinks of the thieves panicking, getting rid of the hair and, then, a *second* purloining taking place – before the final restoration. This gives his imagination the space (between two historical moments) to create a story. In his story, the second theft is committed by a wealthy moneylender, Hashim – not for the hair's religious value, he claims, but to add to his collection of memorabilia. Under the influence of the stolen relic, the polite, comfort-inducing secularism in the family is replaced by the harsh-ness and arbitrary violence of Fundamentalism. Hashim becomes truthful, to the detriment of the family's peace of mind. He had ear-lier encouraged in his daughter, Huma, a spirit of independence, but he now accuses her of lasciviousness because she goes about without a veil and demands that she enter purdah immediately. He begins to pray daily for the first time in his life. All books save the Koran (which he compels his family to study) are burned. He attempts to cut off the right hand for 'theft', in the case of a defaulting debtor. He assaults his wife, son Atta and daughter. Atta and Huma decide to employ a professional burglar to steal the relic from their father. On the night of the burglary, Atta screams and dies. Hashim, awak-ened and with sword in hand, unknowingly thrusts it through his daughter and then, remorse-stricken, turns it upon himself. His wife is driven mad by the carnage. The burglar is killed. Under the influ-ence of the relic, his sons whose legs he had smashed at birth so that they could earn a living as beggars, are restored to health but are ruined because their earning powers are reduced by 75 per cent.

The hair of the Prophet (its authenticity is never questioned), therefore, does much evil and very little good. The trend of the story is risky. The *fatwa* has not scared away Rushdie from Islamic subjects. The ending is like that of a Jacobean tragedy. Rushdie had referred to this relic in *Midnight's Children*.

The stories of the 'West' section focus on three icons of Western culture – *Hamlet*, *The Wizard of Oz* and Christopher Columbus, respectively. 'Yorick', in which the jester has married an older, foul-breathed Ophelia, is a clever little squib hurled at *Hamlet*. Rushdie's word-play here parallels Yorick's and, indeed, that of Shakespeare and the Elizabethans. 'At the Auction of the Ruby Slippers' has more substance. The ruby slippers are those worn by Dorothy in *The Wizard of Oz* to escape the Wicked Witch of the West and return home to Auntie Em. In Rushdie's story, the sequinned slippers are placed in a bullet-proof case at the centre of a nightmare society.

The narrative is set in the future but written in the present tense, so that it is clearly speaking of contemporary tendencies and, incidentally, of the author's own predicament. The society reveres the ruby slippers because of 'their powers of reverse metamorphosis, their affirmation of a lost state of normalcy in which we have almost ceased to believe and to which the slippers promise us we can return' (p. 92). There is nostalgia for the lost world of the 1940s. The contrast between the naive certainties then and our sophisticated layered knowledge now is central. Then no one questioned the line between 'fiction' and 'reality'. Now even the narrator's beloved Gale is 'not entirely a real person. The real Gale has become confused with my re-imagining of her' (p. 96). Possession of the slippers promises the wearer the ultimate dream of the migrant, a safe journey home, but the narrator notes: ' "Home" has become such a scattered, damaged, various concept in our present travails' (p. 93). The Fundamentalists have openly declared that they are interested in buying the magic slippers only in order to burn them – 'and this is not, in the view of the liberal auctioneers, a reprehensible programme. What price tolerance if the intolerant are not tolerated also?' (p. 92). Perhaps the most frightening warning of the story is that, in this society, everything may be auctioned, bought and sold, everything turned into commodities – human achievements (the Taj Mahal, the Statue of Liberty, the Sphinx), nature (the Alps), human desires (such as 'home'), human souls, human beings, indeed, any living thing ('cat, dog, woman, child' [p. 103]) – a development from *The Satanic Verses* where Saladin and Mimi as 'ethnic' performers are placed on this level in today's world.

'Christopher Columbus and Queen Isabella of Spain Consummate Their Relationship (*Santa Fé*, AD 1492)' is a curiously powerful story. The mode is pure narration but not, as in the traditional sense, a sequence of events – rather, a sequence as in cinema, cutting from pictures of Columbus, giving not only his appearance and behaviour but his aspirations and frustrations, to more cryptic, purely externalized portrayals of Isabella. When she lets him braid her hair and toy with her breasts (titillation by hope), then banishes him to the piggeries or condemns him to wash lavatories, the account is, surely, not realistic but symbolic. But Columbus continues to demand

'Consummation' from Isabella (Ferdinand is necessarily banished to the margins with a phrase). The panorama of history – Isabella's victories over the Moors, the defeat of the ex-Sultan Boabdil, her banishing of the Moors – is vivid and potent. Colombus's ride away from the court is dramatic. Finally, Isabella feels she must support his voyage to the West and feels linked to him 'for ever with bonds harder to dissolve than those of any mortal love, the harsh and deifying ties of history' (p. 117), while 'He [then] stands up, like a requited lover' (p. 119) and decides to return to the court. The suggestive, metaphorical prose makes a strong finale.

The final section of the collection, titled 'East, West', brings together East and West, and focuses on crossings between them. In 'The Harmony of the Spheres', the writer Eliot Crane suffers from paranoid schizophrenia, the same mental illness as Gibreel Farishta. Eliot and his wife Lucy Evans move from Cambridge to the Welsh Marches for relief, like Gibreel and Allie Cone move from London to Durisdeer, a tiny village in Scotland. Both Eliot and Gibreel commit suicide – by shooting themselves. Eliot and Lucy are friends of an Indian couple, Khan and Mala. The East/West crossing takes the form of two inter-racial liaisons: Eliot-Mala and Khan-Lucy. Whereas Eliot seems aware of his wife's affair, Mala's confession of her infidelity to the unsuspecting Khan provides the surprise ending in what is a conventional story.

'Chekov and Zulu' is about how the forces of history impinge on personal lives, the boyhood to manhood companionship of an Indian (Chekov) and a Sikh (Zulu). As boyhood friends, they share interests, especially an interest in science fiction. Their enthusiasm for Star Trek is particularly important: it gives them their nicknames (Chekov and Zulu represent an Indianization of the Star Trek characters Check-off and Sulu) and lends the story its central metaphor. (Rushdie's own interest in science fiction has been evident from *Grimus* onwards.) Chekov and Zulu are virtually blood brothers though different types: Chekov displays bookish excellence, Zulu athletic prowess. They continue their friendship in England as 'diplonauts', exploring new worlds and new civilizations, like the cosmonauts of Star Trek – Chekov now Acting Deputy High Commissioner and Zulu an intelligence officer. But the recent schism in India, Hindu-Sikh, gets between them. The massacre of Sikhs after Indira Gandhi's assassination (in November 1984 by her Sikh bodyguards), with no real effort on the part of the central government and Hindus to contain it, alienates Zulu from both.

True to his profession, he does hand over to Chekov information regarding Sikh extremists. Then, true to his conscience, he resigns from service. He expects Chekov to follow suit, but Chekov is smug with regard to the massacre. Zulu tells him: 'I am a security wallah. Terrorists of *all* sorts are my foes. But not, apparently, in certain circumstances, yours' (p. 169, my emphasis). Zulu returns to India and sets up a private security service. Chekov, too, returns to India, rises in government service but is killed in the Rajiv Gandhi explosion. The terrorism, in this instance, is not by those in contact with the West or returning from there, but home-made. The irony is that Chekov is politically and socially fairly high-up but killed, whereas Zulu is politically of no consequence and socially lower, yet survives, indeed, flourishes. A part of the message of the story is orthodox: the morally better person is also the more fortunate. Chekov and Zulu can be friends now only after death. Chekov at death has a momentary vision, not of what might have been, but of their earlier togetherness. Schism in India, prominent at Partition, continues to bedevil the political scene, and is central to Rushdie's vision in *The Moor's Last Sigh*. This story possesses an emotional depth deriving from the importance of the problem of divisions in India. As for East/West crossing in this story, it is present: Chekov and Zulu are Indians/ Easterners in England/the West; their lives in the West are influenced by India/the East, and they return from West to East. The crossing is part of the context of the story, not its thematics.

In 'The Courter', the crossing furnishes both the context of the story and its thematics. Rushdie is at his most tender. As Rushdie confesses, the story is closely wedded to autobiography: 'how he had, like his hero ... been joined by his parents in London for a time in the 60s; how his parents had brought over his *ayah* ... who had struck up a friendship with the porter at the flats where they lived; how he had based the porter on a different man, the office boy at the advertising agency where he worked in the 70s'.[5]

In the story, the *ayah* is called 'Certainly-Mary' because she never says a simple 'yes' or 'no', but always 'O-yes-certainly' or 'no-certainly-not'. When she crosses to the West, she is able to cope with it. The young children take to her and the sixteen-year-old narrator very much so (he feels let down when she departs). She strikes up a relationship with the porter – on her own terms (no 'monkey business' at her age – she was sixty and unmarried). The porter, a widower, is known to the children of the family as Mixed-Up, but his real name is Mecir and he hails from Eastern Europe. He has been a chess grandmaster and teaches Mary the game. In fact, they use their games of chess as the language of love. Their East–West relationship is a kind of courtly dance. On the other hand, the two maharajahs in the same block engage in illicit sex – their kind of East–West relationship. The Indian narrator's amorous longing (for Western girls) is typical of the young. There is a contrast between age and youth – in love. But the narrator acquires an adult importance when he confesses that he has ropes pulling him both Eastwards and Westwards, and he refuses to choose, wishes to be free to respond to both East and West. Rushdie confesses: 'In that sense, he is quite like me.'[6]

Yet Mary as an Indian/Easterner is not at home as such in the West. This is suggested at the level of language: she has difficulty with the 'p' in English (that is why she refers to the porter as the courter, giving the story its suggestive title) but not in her vernacular. Rushdie claims that 'the story is about language',[7] but language does not figure as a theme; rather, it suggests the mismatch of cultures. Mary acquires heart trouble but this baffles the doctors who find nothing wrong with her physically. She diagnoses the cause as homesickness and insists on returning to India. She is, indeed, proved right. She is cured by India and lives thirty years longer. Mary in this story, Rehana in 'Good Advice is Rarer than Rubies' and Saladin in *The Satanic Verses*, all find their native land necessary to their happiness. Rushdie's view of hybridity is critical and complex, not a simple paean to it.

Rushdie said: 'when I started thinking of calling the stories *East, West*, the most important part of the title was the comma. Because it seems to me that I am that comma – or at least that I live in the comma.'[8] The hyphen had represented the earlier Salman Rushdie, the earlier version of hybridity. The comma indicates a change in perspective – an understanding of separate but connected worlds. Thus, *East, West* marks a new development in Rushdie's literary career. As the stories move from 'East' to 'West' and, then, to 'East, West', a structure enclosing them, emerges. There is a neatness, even a circularity, to it as both Rehana, the heroine of the first story, and Mary, the heroine of the last, affirm the importance of the same bent, the Eastern part of the inheritance. The stories show a continuity with Rushdie's preceding novels and *The Moor's Last Sigh* in that they use earlier and later elements, but these are part of essentially new works, on a much smaller scale and on a lighter note. The vein of feeling which Rushdie opened up in *The Satanic Verses* and continued in *Haroun* where it assumed a simple form and is stated rather than emerges from the narrative, is evident in *East, West* and leads on to *The Moor's Last Sigh*. The stories are written in a variety of modes: 'At the Auction of the Ruby Slippers' is in the mode of 'magic realism'; 'The Prophet's Hair' has the quality of a fairy tale; 'Christopher Columbus and Queen Isabella' is cinematic and symbolic. But most of them are in a realist mode – 'Good Advice is Rarer than Rubies', 'The Free Radio', 'The Harmony of the Spheres', 'Chekov and Zulu' and 'The Courter'. Hermione Lee accused Rushdie of 'unreadability' in her review of *The Satanic Verses*[9] and he has been bothered by 'the fact that it became rather fashionable to say that my writing was unreadable'.[10] In *East, West*, Rushdie is showing the reading public that he is able to write 'readable' prose and also in the realist mode, if he wishes to – and that this is an ability he has always had, given that six of the stories were written earlier and at different times. The achievement of *East, West* is modest but significant.

7
The Moor's Last Sigh (1995)

Rushdie has spoken of 'the incredible psychic and physical disruption of the early period' after the *fatwa* and the fact that 'for a few years [he] didn't have the capacity, the singleness of purpose, to attempt a large piece of architecture'.[1] That is why *The Moor's Last Sigh* (1995) is his first novel in seven years. But it underwent a much longer period of gestation, beginning with his visit, in his undergraduate days, to the Alhambra Palace at Granada, Moorish Spain's red fort, mirrored in those of Mogul India at Delhi and Agra. The famous sigh, to which the title refers, was breathed in 1492 by Muhammad XI (Boabdil), the last sultan of Andalusia, looking back at Alhambra and bidding farewell to his kingdom, ending Arab-Islamic dominance in Iberia. Moorish Spain was important to Rushdie as an example of multiculturalism, the Muslims, Catholics and Jews co-existing. Yet 1492 was also the year when the Jews were offered the choice of baptism or expulsion. It was Spain's fissiparous hour. Thus, a phase of Spanish history provides a defining metaphor for India, the subject of Rushdie's novel. In addition, 1492 was the year when Columbus, financed by Boabdil's royal conquerors, Ferdinand and Isabella, sailed forth to seek a new route to the East. It was left to Vasco da Gama to find one in 1497.

The Moor's Last Sigh is not a historical novel. The Iberian story is linked to a narrative of twentieth-century India – not only metaphorically. The protagonist-narrator, Moraes Zogoiby, is descended, on his mother's side, from an illegitimate offspring of the Portuguese Vasco da Gama, and, on his father's side, from an ejected Jew who slept with the exiled Boabdil. Tom Shone observes that 'for the first 100 pages you can't see his childhood for the family trees',[2] but 'the family trees' are important.

Rushdie's main concern is with present-day India, but the novel has a historical panorama of almost a century. He uses the past not only to show the evolution of history but to highlight what has befallen contemporary India. The drama begins with Moraes's great-grandparents, the da Gamas. Francisco is a wealthy spice

131

exporter of Cochin (Kerala). He is presented as a real positive – a progressive in politics (a nationalist during the Raj) and in the arts. A patron of the arts, he tells his wife, Epifania: 'Old beauty is not enough. Old palaces, old behaviour, old gods. These days the world is full of questions, and there are new ways to be beautiful' (pp. 16–7) – anticipating postmodernism and articulating Rushdie's credo. Epifania was for 'England, God, philistinism, the old ways' (p. 18) and develops into a vicious matriarch. They have two sons, Aires and Camoens. Aires follows his mother's views; he acquires a British bulldog which, to irritate Camoens, he names Jawaharlal – after Nehru. In India, there is a saying that one gives a dog the name of a person one despises. Aires is a homosexual, and on his wedding-night there occurs the escape/escapade when he wears his wife's wedding dress and goes away with a partner, nicknamed Prince Henry the Navigator. Camoens takes after his father: he is a nationalist and undergoes imprisonment. But he is a passive positive, constantly criticized for inaction. He bears the name of the Portuguese poet who wrote *The Lusiad*, an epic of Portuguese discovery/conquest in the East, of Western subjugation and the roots of the colonial enterprise. Camoens writes copiously (on the subject of nationalism) but never publishes a word.

Francisco commits suicide and leaves his estate to his sons. But Epifania writes off the sons and decides to run the family business with Aires's wife, Carmen, as her lieutenant. She invites her clan, the Menezes, to Cochin and Carmen retaliates by inviting hers, the Lobos. Commerce spawns greed which results in violence and cruelty. The clans quarrel, torch the spice gardens, and even tie human beings to trees with barbed wire and burn them. But Rushdie's treatment of commerce is not simplified. It is shown to have a good side to it: it makes possible the contact and interaction of cultures and nations, and hybridization. This is suggested by the references to Vasco da Gama, Prince Henry the Navigator (he opened the sea ways to the East by funding and sending ships round the Cape of Good Hope) and Columbus.

There is no simple contrast between past and present in the novel. Life in Cochin in the early years of this century was more spacious and relaxed than in present-day Bombay, but the violence and cruelty then was no less than today (later we witness Abraham's violence and ruthlessness) – as in T. S. Eliot's *The Waste Land*, the love of Elizabeth and Leicester is more glamorous than that of the typist and the clerk but both are equally sterile. There is a human deficiency embedded in the course of history, whether of Rushdie's India or Eliot's England.

Camoens's wife, Isabella (Belle), steps into the breach, demarcates the family property, and tells Epifania and Carmen: 'As for the chapel along with ivory teeth and Ganesha gods, you are welcome to it. On our side we have no plans to collect elephants or to pray.'[3] Aires's hobby was collecting carved tusks and Ganesha images which Belle hates and her daughter, Aurora, dumps in the river. Belle is secular; cash and religion is the rot that settles on the new India. It is Belle who saves the family business.

Aurora is the sole heir to it. She falls in love at first sight with Abraham Zogoiby – a lowly employee (the godown duty manager), 20 years her senior, poor, inarticulate and, most important, a Jew. His mother, Flory, a vivid, perhaps visionary, character, is the caretaker of the *Jewish synogogue* in *Cochin*, especially of its blue ceramic tiles from *Canton*, which are true to fact and, fictively, portray histories personal and general. The focus in the novel is thus on the minutest minorities in India – the Portuguese Catholics and Jews of Cochin, and the novel asserts that they too are an integral part of India so as to bring out how diverse and multicultural India is. There was a Jewish strand in *The Satanic Verses.* Perhaps the Jews interest Rushdie because until the 1940s they were perforce a migrant race, with no country of their own, until Israel was wrenched from Palestine. The stress on the Jews in India activates a memory of Hitler's Germany and places the problems of minorities on a broader historical basis than a merely Indian one. Flory reads in the tiles of the synogogue a prophecy of the atomic bomb and Hiroshima occurs soon after. In *Midnight's Children*, Emerald rushes through the streets without a dupatta to Major Zulfikar on the same day that 'a weapon such as the world had never seen was being dropped on yellow people in Japan' (p. 61). Rushdie suggests that human self-destructiveness is global and frightening.

Aurora and Abraham are not deterred by the barriers to their union. Aurora is not the central character of the novel but is its focus. She suffers from sleeplessness, like Omar Khayyam Shakil and Gibreel Farishta. Omar is a would-be poet; Gibreel an actor and imaginative, even overimaginative; Aurora an artist. Insomnia is thus associated with social perceptiveness. Aurora grows into a giant public figure, the great beauty at the centre of the national-ist movement and a leading artist. For such a figure, Cochin was too confining. She and Abraham moved to Bombay. Their house is named 'Elephanta', which is appropriate to both in different ways. The reference to the Elephanta caves is apposite to Aurora the artist, while the allusion to the Elephant-headed God, Ganesh, the patron deity of commerce, suits Abraham, given that this is his field of professional activity (in the open and underground). In *Midnight's Children*, Ganesh was projected in his aspect of the god of wisdom. Ganesh is the scribe who writes down the *Mahabharata* as well as the scribe who takes down accounts. In *The Moor's Last Sigh*, Ganesh even appears as a symbol of brutality and corruption (the concomitants of commerce). From another aspect, Aurora's name for her house is ironic: she dances her defiance and contempt for religious fervour and Fundamentalism which Ganesh Chaturthi represents.

Abraham develops a Jekyll-and-Hyde personality. He is a deferential servitor in his marital and public role, an efficient planter and exporter of spices, and, at the same time, an underworld boss – a supplier of girls from southern temples for work as devadasis/prostitutes in the city of Bombay, a dealer in narcotics under the guise of talcum powder and a trafficker in arms. In modern Bombay, commerce and corruption go hand in hand; indeed, there is virtually no difference between the two. Here Bombay synecdochically stands for India.

Abraham, though a total monster of evil, is also human. It is true that he is responsible for the killing of his wife, Aurora, and his daughter, Mynah, who takes him to court for criminal activities, though he escapes. But he orders the murder of Aurora not for anything connected with commerce but because of the sexual jealousy aroused by her promiscuousness. He does have affection for his son, Moraes.

Aurora, as a mother, is worse than negligent. She belittles her daughters and son: Christina, Inamorata, Philomina and Moraes are nicknamed Ina, Minnie, Mynah and Moor. The daughters represent three tendencies, three possible faces of Eve – the superficial glamorous (Ina), the religious (Minnie becomes a nun) and the activist (Mynah campaigns for a radical feminist group, WWSTP – which stands for We Will Smash This Prison but is interpreted by its detractors as Women Who Sleep Together Probably). But Aurora cares for her son. He is a more complex figure than her daughters. He is the subject of her painting; the daughters have no place. When he sits as her model, he is more than just a model; he is an object of affection as well. These sessions are mutually fructifying. Yet Aurora's love is more in the Moor's mind than in her actions; there is a touch of the Oedipal. In India, 'the idea of the mother is associated with the idea of the nation'.[4] The myth of Mother India is most famously expressed by the film of that name, starring Nargis as Mother India: 'the nation was invented as a village woman who triumphed over horrible hardships'[5] – a long-suffering, noble, heroic, sentimentalized figure. Through Aurora, Rushdie projects an alternative vision of India-as-mother – a mother of cities, heartless and lovable, brilliant and dark, multiple and lonely. Nargis, in fact, makes an appearance at an Aurora soirée and they clash; Moraes sees Aurora as a version of Nargis (p. 219) – the connection and contrast between 'Nargis' and 'Aurora' are clear.

Moraes's parents are important. Characteristically for a major Rushdie character, he has multiple parents and there is an element of mystery about his birth. His father could have been Abraham Zogoiby (in which case his period of gestation would have been four and a half months) or Jawaharlal Nehru (in which case his gestation would have been nine months). The subtext has it that both are, probably, his fathers and that there has been a kind of conglomerate gestation. He seems to have inherited traits from both – from Abraham, ruthlessness; from Nehru, secularism.

The Moor's Last Sigh is a sequel to *Midnight's Children*, written from a different perspective. Its main concern is with the phase of history after *Midnight's Children*, but it begins at the same point. In *Midnight's Children*, a Muslim family experience was at the centre. Though *The Moor's Last Sigh* takes an Arab-Muslim (Spanish) moment of history as a defining metaphor, there are almost no Muslim characters. It is also different in that its settings include South India and Spain, while Bombay is common to both novels. Like Saleem, Moraes is born late in the narrative. But in the case of Moraes, it is his death that is presented first, at the opening of *The Moor's Last Sigh*, and also at the close, and thus frames the narrative. Saleem's physical and psychic peculiarities, an extra large nose and telepathic and olfactory powers, find their equivalents in Moraes's deformed but power-packed arm and pace of living. That Moraes lives, and declines, at twice the normal pace is a metaphor for the change that has come over life in the present. The links between *Midnight's Children* and *The Moor's Last Sigh* include references in the latter novel to Cyrus Dubash, Lord Khusro Khusrovani Bhagwan; the Sabarmati affair; and Braganza Brand lime and mango pickles; the major link is Aadam Sinai. Zeeny Vakil and the big Chamchawala house of *The Satanic Verses* reappear in *The Moor's Last Sigh*. All this shows Rushdie's coherent and changing vision, governed by current events. Moreover, whatever its affinities to, and connections with, Rushdie's earlier novels, *The Moor's Last Sigh* is an artefact *sui generis*.

Neither the Jewish nor the Christian authorities in Cochin will solemnize the marriage of Abraham and Aurora. Moraes was raised 'neither as Catholic nor as Jew...a jewholic-anonymous, a cathjew nut' (p. 104) – a hybrid. At 'Elephanta', since both Aurora and Abraham were so engrossed in their work that they had little time for Moraes, he was often left with only the ayah and the chowkidar for company. An ayah is not the mother, yet is an important formative figure. Moraes's ayah is significantly named Jaya He – the refrain of the Indian national anthem. She introduces him to the diversity of India, as suggested in the anthem itself:

Thy name rouses the hearts of Punjab, Sind, Gujarat and Maratha
Of the Dravida and Orissa and Bengal...[6]

(But she is not idealized or sentimentalized. She is tough, dishonest and a trouble-maker.) The chowkidar's (her husband, Lambajan) influence is different. He teaches Moraes how to use his strength – his club-like arm – and solely for destructive purposes. In his role as the Hammer, he uses it to serve the chauvinists, the Hindu fundamentalists. Lambajan introduces him to the narrowness of India.

The text refers to Macaulay's minute which launched English education and Western knowledge in India.[7] Rushdie's focus in the novel is on the English-educated. He is conscious of the mass of the people and they are present in both *Midnight's Children* (for instance, the slum scenes) and *The Moor's Last Sigh*. But he does not enter into their lives. Moraes in jail has only a glimpse of the life outside his circle; he has been taken there by the police without any voice or willingness in the decision. In the course of liberal-secular Aurora's efforts to be a socialist, she makes an incursion into a naval strike, but she is of no help or use to the strikers and injures one of their representatives, Lambajan, by running over his leg in her car. He is then supported/patronized by Aurora who installs him as her chowkidar. He seems comic – and loyal. Yet, like all the people, the blue-collar sons of the soil, he is *terra incognita* to the liberals like Aurora. Secretly, Lambajan has his own aspirations for the country – and is an effective and enthusiastic supporter of Mainduck. Rushdie has this measure of understanding.

After Aurora had established herself as a major artist in India and a star of Bombay society, Vasco Miranda, an improvident painter from Goa, knocks at her door. She offers him refuge – a studio and a free run of the house, despite Abraham's opposition. She treats him virtually as if he were a court jester, while he harbours love–hate feelings in regard to her. His first assignment is to paint the nursery in her house. This does provide warmth and security to Moraes and his sisters, and proves a nurturing activity. Vasco proceeds to achieve great success in a different vein – as a purveyor of commercialized art to the West. He is the spurious artist, as opposed to Aurora, the genuine artist.

When Ina was three months old and Aurora was pregnant again, Abraham, proud husband and father, requests Vasco to make a portrait of Aurora and Ina. When Vasco unveils the finished portrait, Abraham finds that Vasco had ignored Ina and depicted Aurora as sitting cross-legged on a chipkali (a lizard – Aurora's 'signature' on her subversive records of the Bombay naval strike) with a bared breast. Abraham rejects the portrait and Vasco paints over it a new work, *The Moor's Last Sigh*, a self-portrait of the artist as Boabdil. Aurora later made a picture with the same title. She proceeds to paint a Moor sequence. When Alhambra leaves Spain and appears on Malabar Hill in Aurora's paintings, it is a key moment in the narrative – a blending of West and East, a definition of the East in terms of a Western metaphor. After declaring:

Before the Emergency we were Indians. After it, we were Christian Jews. (p. 235; to Rushdie, the Emergency is a watershed in Indian history)

and directly before the first entrance of Uma Sarasvati, Moraes records:

There was turmoil in Paradise. Ina died, after her funeral Aurora ... painted a Moor painting in which *the line between land and sea had ceased to be a permeable frontier.* Now she painted it as a harshly-delineated zig-zag *crack*, into which the land was pouring along with the ocean ... the office-workers ... and ... the barefoot lovers ... *were screaming as the sand beneath their feet sucked them down towards the fissure* ... Marine Drive itself *distorted* ... was being *pulled towards the void* And in his palace on the hill, the *harlequin Moor looked down at the tragedy, impotent, sighing, and old before his time.*

Dead Ina stood ... by his side, the pre-Nashville Ina ... (pp. 235–6, my emphasis)

Up to this point, there has been an insistence on Moraes as living in Paradise – perhaps, the illusory Paradiso of Ignorance (before eating of Knowledge). Ina had simply been desperately in love with her pop-singer husband and dies of love. In her earlier Moor pictures, Aurora had created 'a romantic myth of the plural, hybrid nation' (p. 227) and, in them, the land and the sea had been a fluid frontier. Now, for the first time in Aurora's series of paintings, the reader is informed of the breaking-up of this concept of nationhood. In the 'Moor in exile' sequence, the most important work of Aurora's later years,

> she abandoned not only the hill-palace and sea-shore motifs of the earlier pictures, but also the notion of 'pure' painting itself ... elements of collage ... became the most dominant features ... The unifying narrator/narrated figure of the Moor was usually still present, but was increasingly characterized as jetsam, and located in an environment of broken and discarded objects ...
> When the Moor did reappear it was in a highly fabulated milieu, a kind of human rag-and-bone yard ...
> And the Moor-figure ... sank into immorality ... crime. He appeared to lose his previous metaphorical role as a unifier of opposites, a standard-bearer of pluralism, ceasing to stand as a symbol – however approximate – of the new nation, and being transformed, instead, into a semi-allegorical figure of decay. (pp. 301–3)

The sequence is appropriate to this phase of the narrative. Moraes's actions are dictated by outside economic and political circumstances as he is 'Mainduck' Fielding's henchman. The shabby, squalid, sordid setting is appropriate to Rushdie's portrayal of the activities of politicians among the urban proletariat and the rural poverty fringe. Moraes does deteriorate and the reader later finds that Aurora knows of her son's life with Fielding. Moraes forfeits his earlier metaphorical status. Rushdie seems aware of the limitations imposed by the allegorical mode. He adds the resources of poetry: Aurora's paintings are expanding images.

Moraes's affair with Uma is tempestuous. She is everybody's darling at first and seems to know exactly how to play up to each individual, changing her personality to suit the other's. Only Aurora is unimpressed. Uma is always pitted against her – as artists and as characters. Uma's art is religious, Aurora's Western-derived and expressionistic. Uma is seductive, false, insidious. Aurora is honest, aggressive.

Aurora employs the famous private detective, Dom Minto, to investigate Uma. Uma's account of her background and deeds differs from Dom Minto's and Mynah's who, according to Uma, was a lesbian. Minto's information is so well documented and Mynah's word so obviously genuine that even Moraes realizes that Uma's version is false. The case of Uma perfectly fits the Hindu idea of Maya which is that one sees reality through a veil. Moraes does see Uma through a veil. It is stripped away partly by Minto and partly by Mynah. But he is in the grip of love, the only love open to him in his deformed state.

Uma's calculating nature has a deeper dimension. It is not directed to a profitable end, even to herself. She is not merely bad but mad, a dislocated personality; not merely destructive but self-destructive. She gives Aurora a tape of the love-making between herself and Moraes but it includes reference to incest that revolts Aurora. Aurora had earlier twitted Nargis ('Mother India') on this score. Aurora disinherits Moraes and banishes him from home. Uma gains nothing. She then offers Moraes two tablets as if this were a suicide pact of lovers. It turns out that one was a harmless lozenge; she swallows the poisonous one (unable to distinguish between them when they fall on the floor after a slapstick collision of heads). In the end, her calculations prove self-destructive; she, in effect, kills herself.

When Abraham transfers to Moraes the tape which Uma had given Aurora, Moraes is forced into understanding Uma's character. When he calls himself 'O fool! O thrice-assed dolt!' and Uma 'O most false! O foully false and falsely foul!' (p. 320), he is alluding to *Othello*. Rushdie is using pastiche, a favoured resource of postmodernism, to identify the two deluded Moors and Uma, the plural betrayer of mother, father and son, as Iago, the betrayer of Roderigo, Cassio and Othello; and to suggest that Uma's malevolence (like Iago's) is motiveless. The change in Uma's image from angel to devil reflects the alteration in Rushdie's view of Marianne Wiggins. He now thinks she is 'the worst' of his four loves and their marriage 'a very bad mistake'.[8]

In *The Moor's Last Sigh*, love is a positive value, though not put across as strongly as in *The Satanic Verses*. Uma's love is stripped of all its pretensions and Moraes's love for her is wrongly conceived, but a positive impression remains. Moraes's attachment to Aurora and his family is permanent. He does not wish to free himself from his family and is upset when he is rejected over the Uma affair. His trip to Spain at the close of the novel is undertaken as a quest for revenge on Vasco on his mother's behalf.

The police enter the death-scene with Uma and arrest Moraes on a charge of narcotics smuggling, suspecting his involvement in Abraham's nefarious businesses. Moraes is taken to Bombay Central jail – Inferno. Rushdie employs a *deus ex machina*, the faithful unconsidered old retainer, Lambajan, to rescue Moraes and introduce him to Raman Fielding, Lambajan's leader. Fielding is one of the founders of Mumbai's Axis, named after the mother-goddess of Bombay. What 'Bombay' stands for is different from what 'Mumbai' does. Fielding is a fictionalized equivalent of Bal Thackeray, who is behind the Shiv Sena (an organization named after the army of a seventeenth-century Maharati warrior) coalition government in Maharashtra. Rushdie alters his appearance and name in a contrary vein. Thackeray is light-skinned and slender; Fielding is dark and paunchy. Thackeray is a Maharati name. Rushdie plays upon a coincidence of his sharing the surname of the Victorian novelist William Makepeace Thackeray. Rushdie switches English novelists, calling him after a different, earlier writer, Fielding. But the resemblances are telling. Like Bal Thackeray, Fielding is a vicious cartoonist with pretensions to being an artist; his 'signature' was a frog which resulted in his nickname Mainduck. As in real life, the cartoonist raises himself out of lower-middle-class obscurity by hiring his thuggish followers as strike-breakers. He builds a political empire by uniting regional and religious (Hindu) nationalism, not averse to strong-arm methods and links with Bombay's underworld. Rushdie's criticism of Fielding is political, not religious. He sees Fielding's cry for Hindu solidarity as a means of securing power.

As narrator, Moraes is a sensitive recording consciousness – sensitive as a seismograph recording the shocks that run through the Indian body politic: the brutalization of the Indian psyche, the corruption, the violence, the chauvinism and so on. He registers the two major events which shape Rushdie's vision in the novel – the Sikh massacre in 1984 and the destruction of the Babri Masjid mosque at Ayodhya by Hindu zealots on 6 December 1992, which Camoens foresaw as the coming of the Battering Ram. V. S. Naipaul's *India: A Million Mutinies Now* (1990) which stops at the edge of Rushdie's

main period, is virtually a kind of blueprint for *The Moor's Last Sigh.*
Rushdie's response to Bosnia-Herzegovina is relevant:

> There is a Sarajevo of the mind, an imagined Sarajevo whose
> ruination and torment exiles us all. That Sarajevo represents
> something like an ideal; a city in which the values of pluralism,
> tolerance and coexistence have created a unique and resilient
> culture. In that Sarajevo there actually exists that secularist
> Islam for which so many people are fighting elsewhere in the
> world.[9]

Granada, Bombay and Sarajevo come together in Rushdie's mind
as centres of multiculturalism/secular Islam, centres under siege.
Bosnia-Herzegovina has been in the forefront of news in recent
years. The citizens of Britain feel particularly close to occurrences
there. The First World War began in Sarajevo. Rushdie observes:
'as Susan Sontag has said, Sarajevo is where the twentieth century
began, and where, with terrible symmetry, it is ending'.[10] This is part
of the impetus behind *The Moor's Last Sigh.*

In 1987, the fortieth anniversary of Independence, Aurora falls
to her death while dancing her annual dance against the gods.
Abraham informs Moraes that she was dead before she fell – murdered on the instructions of Fielding. The ruthless side to Moraes
makes him kill Fielding in revenge. He and Abraham unite, but
when Abraham reveals the plans of his greatest enterprise, the
financing and secret manufacture of large-scale nuclear weaponry
for certain oil-rich countries and their ideological allies, Moraes
draws the line and identifies himself as a Jew. He does not reject
hybridity but is making a point to suit this specific context. Moraes
counts himself as one of Jehovah's people whereas he is implying
that Abraham is not one because of his evil; that Abraham, though
racially a Jew, is not morally so. Rushdie is also showing that he is
against anti-Semitism.

The criminal-religious/political can be destroyed by human agencies. Fielding is killed by Moraes; his set-up and henchmen suffer.
But the criminal-entrepreneurial is more deadly and can only be
destroyed by itself. Abraham, by telephone, can cause explosions
in Bombay, yet his own Tower can perish only by his own hand. It
is destroyed in an explosion of evil. Still, there is no evidence that
Abraham himself is killed in the explosion. The tendency he represents is impossible to eradicate.

Aadam, the elephant-eared hope of *Midnight's Children*, is, in this novel, a black joke. A computed money-crazy yuppie, he is a very contemporary figure. He is connected to the shop worship of Ganesh and Gaja-Lakshmi, and rises so fast in the criminal-entrepreneurial empire of Abraham that he ends up as Abraham's heir. He is no longer Sinai ('The Promised Land') nor the neutral Braganza, but the unfortunate *El-zogoybi*. He is involved in the complete collapse of Abraham's empire and embodies the failure of his generation. Abraham's surname suggests his ultimate fate and that of those connected to him. It is a characteristic of the postmodern novel to name characters in the vein of the satiric tradition.

Rushdie presents his version of Mother India through Aurora and Miss India through Nadia Wadia – companion figures. Nadia recalls the Beauty Queen-cum-medical student Sushmita Sen. Abraham and Fielding spy on each other, spar, both attempt and fail to get Nadia. Thus, Rushdie is metaphorically suggesting depressing developments in post-Emergency India: black money, organized crime and big business are in conflict with chauvinistic fanatic religion – for political power. Nadia was serious-minded; she had hoped to, yet never made it to medical college. Her reign as Miss India and Miss World ends. At eighteen, she was 'a has-been, broke, rudderless, adrift' (p. 345). In these difficult circumstances, she and her widowed mother receive from Abraham the offer of a luxury apartment and a stipend. She accepts but does not wish to compromise her integrity. She only agrees to appear on the commercials of Abraham's enterprise, Siodicorp, and be Moraes's fiancée in name. On the morning of the Bombay explosions, Sammy Hazaré, an ex-henchman of Fielding with a crush on Nadia, slashes her face with a cutlass. The disfigured Nadia is interviewed on television:

> And yet her beauty was so touching, her courage so evident, *that in a way she looked even lovelier than before...* she spoke directly into... *every viewer's heart*. 'So I asked myself, Nadia Wadia, is it the end for you? ... What pagalpan (madness), what nonsense ... The city will survive... Better days will come. Now I am saying it every day. Nadia Wadia, the future beckons. Hearken to its call.' (pp. 376–7, my emphasis)

Rushdie betrays a soft spot as in *The Satanic Verses*. Nadia is invariably presented as moral, spunky, dignified, and so her message carries weight. Her Bombay dialect blends with Rushdie's own voice. She generates optimism.

Moraes leaves for the Spanish village of Benengeli to reclaim from Vasco the best part of what remained of his mother, her paintings, which Vasco has stolen. Vasco, spurned by Aurora, morally deteriorated, had retreated there. Benengeli has, appropriately, an Arab sound to it and alludes to the fictitious Arab (Moorish) historian whom Cervantes claims as his source for the story of Don Quixote. Just as Cervantes was relating illusion to life, so is Rushdie in this phase of his novel, the most fantasized phase. The whole journey to Benengeli has the atmosphere of phantasmagoria and sets the tone.

The dog Jawaharlal – perhaps a development from the imaginary dog in *The Jaguar Smile* (p. 105) – was first alive in the day of Camoens and Aires, and was a symbol of Nehru's vision of a secular democratic India. The dog dies and is stuffed, suggesting ideals cherished but never realized – stifled by Indira's Emergency, then by the rising tide of realpolitik and corruption. The stuffed dog is retained by Godfather, Abraham, and gifted to Moraes. That Moraes takes it with him to Spain suggests the importance of the ideals. In Benengeli, he pulls the stuffed dog on wheels amidst real dogs, imparting the absurdity of a Shaggy Dog story yet heightening the significance of the mascot. But he leaves it behind with Vasco's housekeepers when he proceeds to Vasco's folly, suggesting that he is entering a dimension of evil where no ideals, even dead ones, matter. Jawaharlal ends up as 'just another abandoned Andalusian dog' (in a broom-cupboard in a foreign land [p. 407]). Rushdie plays with the title of Buñuel's film *Un Chien Andalou* (1928).[11] Jawaharlal's position in the narrative is marginal but not inconsequential.

The art of *The Moor's Last Sigh* is curiously mixed. The characters are not such as we find in orthodox novels, but tendencies or representatives of tendencies. The only character as such is Uma, but she too illustrates tendencies. She reveals exploitative tendencies, found in spheres such as politics and commerce, in her own fields and thereby suggests how widespread these are. She is exploitative in art: she exploits religion. She is exploitative in personal and sex relations. She makes a marriage of convenience to an old man and leaves him when he is paralysed. Moraes is a victim of hers and, like Fielding or Abraham, she is not averse to murder. There are traces of the comic book in the characterization – Abraham, Fielding and Vasco (in the last phase) as villains, Uma as the seductive villainess, Moraes as the Hammer. Fielding's henchmen are monsters. Rushdie has been influenced not only by *The Arabian Nights* but also by the *New Arabian Nights*. His prose continues to be 'readable'. Noteworthy is the scintillating wordplay which refracts and illuminates ideas. The pace of the narrative is fast. *The Moor's Last Sigh* is a parable as an 'entertainment', in the Graham Greene sense.

The inhabitants of Benengeli on the streets seem as if in Limbo (the Dante parallel is continued). Moraes stays in the house of Felicitas, who seems tough, realistic, practical, and Renegada, who seems mollifying, sentimental. Felicitas and Renegada are lesbians but whether they are half-sisters or not is uncertain despite their professions. They are reassuring, ambiguous and sinister by turns. As housekeepers of Vasco, they have entry to his fortress and take Moraes there disguised as a woman, like Raza and Omar at the close of *Shame* and Gibreel during his comeback on the Earls Court stage in *The Satanic Verses* – suggesting helplessness, lack of control of their own fate.

Vasco's deterioration has continued to the point that he is now totally evil. He holds Moraes responsible for the wrongdoings, as he sees them, of Aurora and Abraham, and makes a prisoner of Moraes. He shows Moraes the palimpsest (J. M. Coetzee points out Rushdie's use of 'palimpsesting' as a device in the novel[12]) through which Aurora reveals that her murderer is not Fielding but Abraham. After administering this shock to Moraes, he makes a Scheherazade out of Moraes. He has to recount the saga of the Zogoibys and as long as his tale holds Vasco's interest, he would be permitted to live. Thus, it transpires that this is how the narrative came to be written – the overall convention.

Moraes has the company of a fellow prisoner, a Japanese restorer of paintings, named Aoi Ue – after the bride of Genji in the famous eleventh-century Japanese novel *The Tale of Genji* by Lady Murasaki Shikibu. Her task is to remove the top layer of Vasco's *Moor* painting, leaving intact the Aurora portrait underneath. J. M. Coetzee thinks that in the case of Aoi, Rushdie is ignoring 'elementary rules of fiction, like not introducing new characters in the last pages'.[13] But this does not seem to me unjustified or odd in the context of the novel: Aoi has a place in its scheme. She offers Moraes comfort and security, which he has hitherto not known, and reveals decency and heroism too. She embodies positive potentialities in life. She offers Moraes the chance to be heroic, to try and save her from death at Vasco's hands, but he fails. Moraes himself is saved because Vasco dies in an explosion of evil – like Sufiya in *Shame* and Krook in Dickens's *Bleak House*.

Moraes is, appropriately, connected to Luther. He nails the truth (his life story) on a door for the public to see/read. He escapes to a graveyard above Vasco's Alhambra. Boabdil's sigh is echoed in the asthma of Abraham and Moraes. In Benengeli, Moraes's asthma fares better; but in the last scene, his 'lungs no longer do [his] bidding' (p. 433). Moraes is connected to Christ too (recalling Oskar in *The Tin Drum*). He awaits death at the same age, as Christ, thirty-six, and, presumably, will experience resurrection. Moraes is also connected to Arthur in Avalon and Barbarossa in his cave – who will awaken to lead conquering armies. Moraes's death is presented as a sleep, to be followed by a resurrection or wakening to a brighter day – optimism at the close of the novel. Moraes's values, like those of Christ, Arthur and Barbarossa, are not, in the end, negated.

The general trend and content of the novel suggest a closure of possibilities. But Nadia Wadia and the conclusion suggest that there is room for optimism. So does the vitality of the novel's rhythm. So does the teeming multifariousness of India, which seemed to E. M. Forster, in *A Passage to India*, a 'muddle', something negative. Yet, the central spirit of the novel is as the title suggests: it is an elegy – for lost ideals, for Bombay, for India, for home, and, ultimately, for Rushdie himself.

8

The Ground Beneath Her Feet (1999)

Rushdie's 'plague years'[1] under the *fatwa* ended when the Iranian Government publicly declared on 24 September 1998 that it did not intend to pursue the death sentence and disassociated itself from the bounty placed on his head. Though the death threat was not wholly removed – the Government possessed no power to annul the *fatwa* imposed by a religious leader, while the hardliners remained adamant and a fresh bounty of £20,000 was offered, Rushdie was able to re-enter public life.

When he was writing his next novel, *The Ground Beneath Her Feet* (1999), Rushdie continued to reside in London but 'summered' in New York. In 1999, he decided to migrate to the United States. He believed that Britain treated him in an unfeeling way.[2] Rushdie contrasts the attitudes of the American press and the British in regard to the *fatwa*: '...Americans saw the issue as I did, as one in which an old, taken-for-granted freedom had become a life-and-death affair...'. In Britain, it seems to be about a man who has to be saved from the consequences of his own actions.'[3] 'In interviews, Rushdie has shown awareness of the reluctance of the British public to warm to him... he complained he was sick of being called arrogant.... "In certain sectors of Britain there was a prejudice because I am an immigrant." '[4] America appealed to him more because it was essentially a migrant civilization and Rushdie was just another migrant.[5] The American response to him was characterized by warmth, even by the highest politicians, and in regard to the *fatwa* President Clinton and the Administration supported him in 1994, before Tony Blair and his government did, in 1998. America's response may be explained in terms of the Arab–American divide, especially since Iran rejected the pro-American Shah Reza Pahlevi and installed Ayatollah Khomeini, but what is important is not the explanation but the kind of relationship that existed between Rushdie and America. New York, 'a kind of community of displaced persons' like

Bombay,[6] seemed more vibrant and friendlier than London, and, indeed, to him 'the beating heart of the visible world'.[7] He stated: 'I've now moved into understanding the world from the kind of positions Americans think about things. I'm constantly shocked by the relatively alien mindset with which I'm confronted [in Britain] and with which I used to be completely at home.'[8]

'The triangle of cities'[9] – Bombay, London and New York – supplies the structure for Rushdie's life to date and for *The Ground Beneath Her Feet*. Indeed, Rushdie has conceived his narrative in terms of triangles. In regard to its theme, he asserts: 'What you have is a triangle at whose corners are art represented by music, love and death.'[10] The novel is, certainly, dominated by these three overwhelming forces, but their conception in terms of a triangle is a part of Rushdie's intention which may not be shared by the reader, given that these forces are not necessarily or causally connected. 'The love triangle'[11] of Ormus, Vina and Rai is pervasive.

Rushdie was aware that he had written 'a global novel...a novel which was intercontinental...a novel of our age'.[12] Its embryo is found in earlier works. Globalization does not enter *The Moor's Last Sigh*, but it points forward to its central position in *The Ground Beneath Her Feet* and *Fury* (2001) through forces in common: the rapacious commercial acquisitiveness (driving an individual's, Abraham's, lawless and devious commercial empire) and the development from the muted operations of multinationals to the state-sponsored international ingestion of capitalism. Moreover, the continuous presence of Spain in *The Moor's Last Sigh* suggests that its issues set in India are not confined to one region and this anticipates the emergence of globalization. Though *Midnight's Children*, for all its dark tragedy, ends on a note of hope, *The Moor's Last Sigh*, though not totally pessimistic, virtually marks the end of hope due to relentless commercialism and thereby points to a negative aspect of globalization, which is depicted in *The Ground Beneath Her Feet* and *Fury*. *The Moor's Last Sigh* moves outwards from India towards the West (Spain), pointing forward to *The Ground Beneath Her Feet* which also moves outwards from India (further) towards the West (Britain and America).

Rushdie responds to urgent contemporary pressures. His novels expand their scope but, at the same time, lessen in tautness and intensity. This slackening of cohesiveness and force robs us of the fencer's grace, precision and sharpness that marked his work from *Midnight's Children* to *The Moor's Last Sigh*. However, if the critic's search reveals less to marvel at and Rushdie seems more fallible on

the plains than the peak, there is more than enough to arouse interest and questioning.

Rushdie's first fiction to depict the ambiguities of America's
dominance in the context of globalization, its lure and its power,
is the short story 'The Firebird's Nest' (1997) – a magic-realist,
modern-day fable. Mr Maharaj attempts to exploit his American
woman to bring fertility (via rain) and capital, to be a regenerating
force for his drought-stricken land. She does bring rain but it clears
the region not only of 'its horrors, its archaic tragedies' but also of
'life'.[13] It seems as if an ancient and decaying country needs capital,
but the intrusion of Western capital is strangling. Miss America, the
intended victim of the firebird who turns out to be Mr Maharaj,
becomes the victor; she kills the firebird and makes a profit out of
it (she carries away their child to America), illustrating the ruthless,
self-serving power of America. India can destroy the liberal ally of
America, Miss Maharaj, Mr Maharaj's sister who befriends Miss
America and is burned, but not America itself.

Globalization involves 'the *intensification* of worldwide social relations which link distant localities' (my emphasis).[14] Some theorists
argue that globalization is an exclusively late twentieth-century
phenomenon, brought about by the internationalization of economics, politics and culture, and engineered by postmodern consumer
capitalism. Others trace the origins of globalization far back: to
such inventions as the steam engine, the telephone, the printing
press, ocean-going ships; to the emergence of language and even
the earliest migration of our African ancestors.[15] Rushdie draws
attention to these distant beginnings. The parallels that William
Methwold and Darius Cama find between the myths of ancient
Greece and the Sanskrit myths of India testify to a linguistic connection crossing national boundaries. But Rushdie is also aware that
the 'intensification' of global contacts is a distinctive characteristic
of the contemporary world, propelled by the unprecedented rapidity of communications and new technologies. He illustrates it in *The
Ground Beneath Her Feet* most notably by the rise of pop music, *the
art form of the twentieth century, the only specific and new form
connected with the era from the late 1940s to the 1990s, the half-a-
century timespan of the novel.*[16] As Rushdie points out, rock and
roll 'was the world's first globalized cultural phenomenon, when the
world was not yet globalized'.[17] Globalization, then, in its aspect of
mass culture is a central theme in *The Ground Beneath Her Feet* and
Fury. Furthermore, in *The Ground Beneath Her Feet,* pop music is not

only an exemplar of cultural globalization but a metonym of globalization itself. The intensification of migration (via commercial air travel) and media diffusion in the post-war period, are also related phenomena that are crucial to the narrative.

Midnight's Children and *Shame* dealt with countries of the Indian subcontinent. Even *The Moor's Last Sigh* is essentially set in India; Spain is marginal and not portrayed as a real land but as phantasmagoria. Only *The Satanic Verses* focused on two countries, Britain and India (the Middle East being a mental projection). Rushdie's later novels, *The Ground Beneath Her Feet*, *Fury*, *Shalimar the Clown* and *The Enchantress of Florence* mark a departure in that his perspective becomes global. In *The Ground Beneath Her Feet*, the global reach is reinforced by references to myths, legends and histories of places in the East and the West. Furthermore, triggered off by Gunter Grass, Rushdie had presented the portrait, not of individuals or groups, but of entire nations in *Midnight's Children* and *Shame*, and of people caught between nations and cultures/civilizations in *The Satanic Verses*, but now his focus widens to take in eras, how changes of period affect human emotion. Time rather than place is the dominant factor in guiding Rushdie's structure and locations. *The Ground Beneath Her Feet* moves from India when the British were an imperial power to the swinging London of the 1960s and flower power, to later developments in America as the new imperial power and fount of pop culture. It was written during a period of personal stability in Rushdie's life, happy with his partner, later wife, Elizabeth West, and having a son by her.

It is a groundbreaking novel. The use of magic realism to express through images ideas that cannot be articulated as forcefully through orthodox realism, is already a characteristic technique of Rushdie. What is a departure is the presentation of popular culture as the central focus of a literary novel – the explosion of popular culture as a global phenomenon affecting values and lifestyles and applying this occurrence in the 1960s to contemporary life; the startling juxtaposition of ancient Greek mythology (especially the Orpheus/Eurydice myth) and popular culture; and the conception of the global novel. Through the reference to Gluck's opera *Orfeo and Euridice* (1762), to Greek myth and Dante, Rushdie reveals the roots and background of an era which flowers/deteriorates into a highly commercialized, highly publicized pop culture. It is an attempt to capture in 1999 what impinges of twenty centuries and provides an alternative history of the aesthetics of the millennium centred on the core concerns of the writer.

The date of publication of *The Ground Beneath Her Feet* is important: 1999, the last year of the millennium, a vantage point from which to contemplate it. It is not simply that Rushdie, perhaps, felt that he was the only writer big enough to immortalize it – to delineate, analyse and celebrate it, but that the change of centuries is thematically a salient factor in this choice of timing. He focuses on key aspects of the millennium – pop music, photography and drugs, one of the defining ingredients of flower power and pop culture (of course, drugs of various sorts have been in use since ancient times, but these became prominent in the lifestyle of the young in the 1960s and continued to be more widespread since). Given that Rushdie is attempting to write an epic and we in the modern world are the epigoni, the nearest to the heroes and heroines of old are the pop stars and they are a little weird. The pop stars, Ormus and Vina, are figures inflated by genius and publicity, and dominate an era. Rushdie adopts a technique that attempts to make them almost mythical, as Elvis Presley has become.

Elvis Presley (1935–77) is still very much in public thought and this explains why Rushdie thinks of him as the phenomenon of the age, a definite marker of the crazes of the time and the way the passage of time and change affect the world. References to him and his agent occur prominently. In portraying Ormus, Rushdie recalls Elvis. Ormus has a stillborn twin. So has Elvis. Elvis's manager, Colonel Tom Parker, was dominating and virtually ran Elvis's life. Ormus has Mull Standish as a deft but unobtrusive agent. There are also straight resemblances between Ormus and Elvis – their guitar-playing and 'pelvis-swivelling',[18] for instance – and allusions to songs. The presentation of the last phase of Ormus's life includes a replay of allegations made in respect of Elvis – that he is neglected, fleeced and on drugs. Vina, 'a kind of diva figure',[19] matches his stature.

The Ground Beneath Her Feet moves in four distinct phases. It starts with a bang, an earthquake in which Vina dies; followed by a less intense retrospective account; then a retelling of Vina's death; and finally, after Ormus's death, a movement forward in time to narrate Rai and Mira's relationship. The Orpheus–Eurydice mythic strand runs through the whole narrative as an attempt to give it weight and *gravitas*, and as a binding thread, and more importantly, it contributes to meaning and links with the key thematic points – music, love and death. All the phases are crowded with incidents which mirror our crowded era. The over-crowdedness is not a failure of Rushdie's art but a part of his conception. The developments in the Victorian age did not crack the sides of the imagination, but the twentieth century was a period of explosive evolution. Rushdie's design in this novel is ambitious and, whatever the criticism, design there is. *Midnight's Children* shattered the form of the novel and critics/ readers responded. The question is whether, in this case, Rushdie's concept and design work.

The earthquake in the novel occurs on 14 February 1989, the date of the announcement of the *fatwa* on Rushdie by Ayatollah Khomeini, a death sentence. The date 14 February is St Valentine's Day, a date signifying love. Thus, the date of the earthquake brings together the binaries of death and love, and thereby underlines Rushdie's theme of love that crosses the boundaries of death. The earthquake stretches from South America and so suggests the general instability of the period. It is not only an event that takes place literally but also the central metaphor of the novel, underscored by the title. Rushdie needs Vina to be in the underworld not only for the purposes of his plot but also to articulate the love theme and pursue the Orpheus–Eurydice parallel. The earthquake is a metaphor for the possibility of sudden and violent upheaval, and, above all, for the seismic cultural changes (institutions, beliefs, standpoints undergoing upheavals, transformation and destruction) – a world visibly changing before our eyes. The exuberant metanarrative states: 'The abnormal, the extreme, the operatic, the unnatural: these rule. There is no such thing as normal life ... to defend us against us the big bad wolf of *change*' (p. 500, my emphasis). 'Change' is a key note of the novel. A millennium novel is a new note struck, celebrating the inevitability and necessity of change. Rushdie claims that the earthquake is symbolic of 'the earthquakes that happen inside people's lives, inside their emotional lives.'[20] But no upheavals as such are *felt* by the reader except during the opening scene when Vina, after the breakdown in her career, tries to reconstruct it, unpromisingly attempting to stage a comeback, not from a major cultural centre such as New York, but from a distant town, Guadalajara.

The opening scene starts with and focuses on Vina, but there is considerable space devoted to Rai as well. He is the narrator and a suitable choice it is – for one thing, by virtue of his profession. Photography is essentially a twentieth-century art – like pop music. As a photographer, Rai is a voyeur and a witness. A photographer records and immortalizes; time passes but the camera traps a moment of time; in a photograph, time is fixed. Rai's pictures fix the time of the millennium and immortalize it. Rushdie places an emphasis on the pitiless single-mindedness of the chronicler. During the earthquake scene, Rai is frantically photographing all its oddities, not thinking of the casualties. One would expect him to be emotionally shattered by the loss of his long-time love, Vina, whom he has slept with, but this kind of feeling is lost in the professional instinct. The human aspects and human sympathy are drowned in the urge to record a striking event. Rai's mindset is, probably, quite typical of professional photographers. Kevin Carter, who won the 1994 Pulitzer Prize for Feature Photography with his picture – epitomizing the Sudan famine – of a toddler crawling towards an United Nations food camp with a vulture sitting a little behind, waiting for her to die (Carter left the scene without helping her), once said during a shoot: 'I had to think visually. I am zooming in on a tight shot of a dead guy and a splash of red.... But inside something is screaming, "My God." But it is time to work. Deal with the rest later.'[21]

Andrew Teverson thinks: 'the narrator...uses his medium as a "way of understanding the world" (p. 210) and in part because the novel's subjects, celebrities, live their lives under the gaze of the camera.'[22] But photography is not used as a way of understanding the world. Moreover, Rai is not a photographer of celebrities, like, say, Cecil Beaton. He is a news and investigative photographer. He makes his reputation by exposing Piloo Doodhwala's scam in regard to wholly fictitious goats, which is based on Laloo Prasad Yadav's involvement in Bihar's 'Fodder Scam' with wholly fictitious cattle (Piloo and his wife, Golmatol, originate from Yadav and his wife, Rubri Devi).[23] Rai's exposure is done with photographs not his own but with those of another photographer murdered during his investigation. Rai says: 'Piloo Doodhwala had his scam; and as you see, I had mine. He made four million dollars. I just made my name' (p. 245). Stephen Morton thinks that Rushdie is suggesting that 'Rai is a fraud or a fake',[24] but I feel it stresses Rai's wry honesty (after all, he cheats no rival except a corpse, and he does give the dead photographer the credit in his narration). The reader needs to believe in Rai's honesty if he is to accept his narration as 'true'.

As a travelling photo-journalist, Rai is able in his role of narrator to reflect on the immediate narrative as well as on the world and the period he inhabits. His global value is illustrated in the way he permits Rushdie to bring in Vietnam – 'Where the soldiers had failed, U.S. values – that is greenbacks, set to music – had triumphed' (p. 441) – and connect it to his central concerns. Globalization, both in its military and cultural aspects, is powered by American capitalism; its military aspect may fail but its cultural aspect is more insidious and less resistible. Rai is also a device which enables Rushdie to consider 'the nature of representation'.[25] There is a hint that photography and writing are parallel arts, that the cameraman is an allegorical equivalent of the author: both chronicle and focus (professional photography is not mere straight recording). Rai is important as a character too. He is a positive figure because his feet are planted on the ground. Therefore, it is easy for the reader to relate to his narration. Moreover, he is less egoistic than Ormus and Vina. His character retains human proportions.

Rushdie's first declared intention in the novel is to celebrate parents, 'the first superstars of our lives'.[26] But the finished novel does not bear out this intention. It is not true of Rai in relation to his parents. The first interaction between V. V. and Ameer Merchant when they come to the nursing home to visit Lady Spenta Cama and, in common, bring Kashmiri honey as a gift, shows complete harmony though they are strangers. Their original love and Rai's childhood happiness disappear when their interests diverge. V. V. continues to be interested in Bombay's past (which for him is rich and leisurely), recalling Omar's subterranean exploration of Pakistan's past and prehistory in *Shame*. Ameer succumbs to the encroaching commercialism (an aspect of globalization) in Bombay and is transformed by it. They are characters of human proportions, with definite personalities, and their changing relationship is a touching story by itself.

Darius and Spenta Cama make no impact on their children. They are idiosyncratic, Dickensian characters. Darius, like Saladin Chamcha, suffers from a heavy colonial cringe. He is one type of native: he is, and wants to be, a brown sahib. He makes a companion of the Britisher, William Methwold, a symbol in *Midnight's Children* but here a symbol humanized. In his case, Rushdie employs his technique of reusing old colonial metaphors as a mode of criticism. The apex of Darius's dreams is Methwold's classical mansion in England, which he can never gain but ends up occupied by dysfunctional gentle wrecks. Darius sins against the values he idolizes. He is a success career-wise and is knighted, but his professional achievement as a lawyer is based on a falsehood (he had not qualified as a barrister in England as he claimed and was reputed to be). Darius and Methwold have interests in common, but Methwold is relentless in his cutting of Darius when he discovers the fraud. Spenta (named after Amesha Spentas, the angels in ancient Parsi mythology) is traditional, totally obsessed with religion and engaged in social service – altogether, a more worthy character. Methwold accepts her totally out of recognition of Spenta's essential integrity. He accepts the fact that a person can be totally native yet respectworthy. Rushdie demonstrates how (in this case) East and West can meet in ordinary life.

Ormus is connected with three siblings, two of them more fantastic than himself. Virus, silenced by a cricket ball, is seen by Spenta voyaging in a spiritual realm. Cyrus is an inventive serial killer. Rushdie's tone of humour in presenting him undercuts the seriousness. His killings do not feel like murder but seem a parlour trick. To Rushdie, he is 'a fabulous character...a heroic figure...a philosopher',[27] but he is merely a sensational figure, a superficial imitation of Dostoevsky. On the level of plot, Cyrus is needed to dispose of Darius. Gayomart is a kind of ghost who communicates with Ormus after death.

Ormus and Vina of the later generation are mega celebrities. Rushdie himself is a (literary) celebrity and writes of global celebrities with insider's knowledge. *Midnight's Children* was an instant success and ensured a readership for *Shame*. He was famous before the *fatwa*, but the *fatwa* made him the world's most famous – and most controversial – writer. In Martin Amis's quip, Rushdie 'had vanished into the front page'.[28]

Ormus is a songwriter and singer. He claims to be the 'secret originator' and 'prime innovator' (p. 89) of rock music. Anshuman A. Mondal interprets: 'it is a postcolonializing gesture that decentres the West by ascribing to one of its most hegemonic cultural forms an origin outside the West'.[29] Stephen Morton agrees: '*The Ground Beneath Her Feet* challenges the global dominance of American popular culture by suggesting that rock-and-roll was invented in Mumbai.'[30] According to the novel, it was not Ormus's genius that created the music; it was the result of a ghostly communion with Gayomart (it is not that 'Rushdie imagines all the great songs of twentieth century Western pop music have been first invented by Gayomart', as Shaul Bassi claims,[31] but that Gayomart appears to have a foreknowledge of American pop as if he had an auditory second sight, 'a hearer' like a seer – and a conveyor) though it was Ormus who was skilled enough to catch audience interest. This is a completely incredible fantasy, meant to be a part of the element of Rushdie's humorous complicity with the reader. The novel does

make it clear that pop music is an American-led global cultural phenomenon. It is an American band (The Five Pennies of Red Nichols)
on tour in Bombay that discovers the talents of Ormus and Vina;
at that time, they were stars while Ormus and Vina were not. VTO
became famous only after they performed in America. And pop
music pre-exists in the USA before VTO is dreamed of.

Rock and roll gathered momentum partly because of its personalities. Elvis Presley captivated his audience by his personality and his
voice. Ormus and Vina belong to a later generation. The music was
established when they started their careers. Christopher Rollason
and Andrew Teverson agree that 'the musical work of VTO never
seems interesting enough to persuade readers that it is anything
other than a rather banal, run-of-the-mill, stadium rock band'.[32] This
may be true (though it is interesting, for instance, that Ormus anticipates Bob Dylan's 'Blowin' in the wind' with 'The ganja is growing
in the tin' (p. 141) – whereby Rushdie is cynically undercutting the
revolutionary fervour and exhilaration of flower power by placing
the stress on drugs). But what matters more is that Ormus and Vina
became idols and thereby VTO became famous. Personalities count
more than the music. And the final result is that the personalities
survive the death of the persons; so does their music.

The meteoric rise of Ormus and Vina to stardom is typical of their
profession. But rock stars are generally prone to crash and burn, and
suffer premature death, as exemplified by Elvis Presley. Ormus and
Vina, however, do not conform to this trend. Their singing partner-
ship is falling apart at the end, but both are over the hill by this time.
They are not young when they die. Yet Ormus's murder by a Vina
impersonator is very much of a piece with the killing of John Lennon.
The enormity of 'the scale of the worldwide response to [Vina's] death'
(p. 479) was suggested by that to Princess Diana's death.[33] It is not
simple 'hyperbole' as interpreted by Anshuman Mondal,[34] but based
on reality. Like Bob Geldof, Vina has campaigned against famine, for
the alleviation of the Third World's debt and the like (p. 478). After
death, she becomes a symbol of freedom, equity and redemption.
The loves and songs of Ormus and Vina become a transcendental
unifying force, Vina a divinity. Mondal takes exception mostly to the
claim that 'all over the globe Vina's adoring constituency has acquired
a taste for collective action and *radical* change' (pp. 486–7, emphasis
Mondal's). He thinks 'celebrity culture does not possess a radical
political potential'.[35] Princess Diana campaigned not only to eradicate the stigma attached to AIDS victims but also to eliminate the

use of landmines in military conflicts – with notable success. Rushdie rightly regarded pop music as an expression for the young of 'a kind of rebellious spirit'[36] and as a vehicle for political protest. He said: 'When I was protesting against the Vietnam War in England, the music was protesting against the Vietnam War.'[37] Talking to Václav Havel, Rushdie discovered that the Velvet Underground/rock music was an inspiration for the Velvet Revolution in Czechoslovakia.[38] Music has the potential for igniting radical change. Thus, the impact of Ormus and Vina is not only rendered in the mode of inflation in which they are always presented, but also relates to aspects of reality. The names and reputations of Ormus and Vina live on after their deaths – as in the case of Elvis Presley. This is especially so in the case of Vina's music because something of her quality as an artist survives in Mira. Rushdie also links art with twentieth-century technology; both Ormus and Vina continue to sing, on television: 'I [Rail] thought they were supposed to be *dead*, but in real life they're just going to go on singing' (p. 575, Rushdie's emphasis). Significantly, these are the last – positive – words of the novel. The immortality of art becomes a central theme of *The Ground Beneath Her Feet*. It is reinforced by the Orpheus–Eurydice motif. The key attribute of Orpheus is that he was a musician. The myth is relocated and modernized.

The names, Vina Apsara and Ormus Cama, carry meanings which suit their respective characters and the themes articulated through them. Vina (also spelt 'veena') is the name of an Indian musical instrument, symbolic of music itself. Apsara is a heavenly nymph seductive to hermits in Eastern mythology. Vina incorporates submerged allusions to Venus, the goddess of love, and 'Vine' – Dionysiac intoxication. Vina Apsara, then, signifies a goddess of music and of love. The name Ormus is linked with Apollo. Ormus (Hormuz) alludes to Ahura Mazda, God of Light. Apollo is the sun-god, patron of poetry and music. Kama is the god of love. Ormus Cama, then, signifies the god of music and of love. (The pop singer, adored, worshipped, capable of promoting ecstasy and frenzy among her/his fans, is a kind of goddess/god of music anyway.) The love of Ormus and Vina grows strong rapidly. They find seemingly odd reasons for not being together, but their love does not need physical togetherness or sex, being of the kind John Donne celebrated in 'A Valediction: forbidding mourning':

> But we by a love, so much refin'd,
>   That our selves know not what it is,
> Inter-assured of the mind,

Care less, eyes, lips, and hands to miss.

It is their love that entirely and endlessly drives them on. But to some extent, it proves self-destructive and leads to strains and rupture. Yet theirs is a love that even transcends death. Ormus's love is such that he seeks Vina even after her death, goes into the Underworld and brings back a substitute; he adopts a mimic Vina who is both Vina and not Vina. The immortality of love, too, is a central theme of the novel.

Rushdie also projects a negative conclusion to art and love, which connects with the sad finale of the original Orpheus–Eurydice myth. Indeed, Rushdie supplies and stresses the whole theme:

> Death is more than love or is it. Art is more than love or is it. Love is more than death and art, or not. This is the subject. This is the subject. This is it. (p. 202)

He repeats it thrice, emphasized further by the slangy variation – a thread to which all the beads can cling, dramatic and sublime enough to give weight to a magnum opus. Rushdie relates this crux of the novel to the myth:

> Is the failure of Orpheus to rescue her [Eurydice] a token of the inevitable fate of love (it dies); or of the weakness of art (it can't raise the dead)... (p. 499)

Love challenges death. Delighting in the Indian and Greek version, Rushdie punnily makes Vina refer to 'Mousie' – actually Rati, wife of Kama (it was the woman who brought love back from the dead). 'A figure recalling... Rati twice gets Ormus to come back to life.'[39] Death defeats love. Vina cannot return from the world of the dead because this is not possible even with the aid of art. Ormus accepts the finality of death, concedes his irreversible defeat and makes an agonizing comeback to reality. Rushdie's meditation on art and love is, ultimately, about the destiny of the human being.

The reader heads for an optimistic conclusion despite the disintegrating world, full of bleak change and crazy confusion, tragi-ridiculous, projected until then. It belongs to the Rai–Mira relationship, less flamboyant but more fulfilling than the Ormus–Vina; the reader relates more easily to it because it is of a commonplace kind – domestic, middle class, but not an anti-climax because it is the bread-and-butter of life which humanity cannot do without.

Mira's child, Tara (meaning 'star' in Hug-me, p. 521), is a bright spot, a symbol of the renewal of hope, like the child in Lawrence Durrell's *Alexandria Quartet*. Rai was the pet name given by Vina to her 'back-door man', but his real name was Umeed, (significantly) meaning hope. Mira, who is so wholesome, succeeds Vina as his love, and their affair is fairy-tale. Thus, the novel ends on a life-affirming note.

In regard to gender issues, Rushdie has come a long way from the portrayal of Bird-Dog in *Grimus*. Vina and Mira represent two aspects in the development of women. They are rather like the two Catherines in Emily Brontë's *Wuthering Heights*. Vina, like the first Catherine, is more charismatic, passionate and vulnerable. Mira is more of a positive figure: though a risk-taker and daring, she is more stable, more in command of herself. Vina belongs to the 1960s when there was a movement towards free sex, psychedelic drugs and music. She is fearless and unlimited by convention. Rushdie has consciously tried to provide motivation for her faithlessness in love in terms of her sordid, appalling origins and feeling betrayed by Rai's mother,[40] but it really does not click. Vina's private life remains the commonplace of behaviour in her formative period and the commonplace of pop stars and the like. She also does have needs of her own. She later moves to a positive kind of feminism (conscious after her arrival in America), and her own efforts to liberate women are convincing as an expression of her free thinking and aggressiveness. She is associated with the most powerful female Egyptian pharaoh, Hatshepsut. Known for sporting a false beard and dressing like a man, as demanded by royal rites, Hatshepsut ruled for twenty-one years (1479–58 BC), after the death of her husband and half-brother, Tuthmosis II, as both male and female pharaoh. Vina too breaks down the barriers between women and men, and enjoys autonomy. Her successor is Mira, a single mother and also fearless. She is appealing in the way she relates to her child, her ability to look after herself and use weapons, and her progress from Vina impersona-tion to reach stardom herself, finally fulfilling her destiny. Her name too is suggestive. Mira (spelt like the Latin adjective) means 'marvel', and she is, indeed, a mira-cle. Rushdie's view of women has become increasingly liberal. He presents positively, and approves of, the liberated woman.

Rushdie's epigraph taken from the fifth of Rilke's *Sonnets to Orpheus* (1922) is the key to the second overall theme of the novel – the vatic mission of the artist. Viktoria Tchernichova writes: 'On the basis of intertextual links perceivable between the *Sonnets to*

Orpheus and *The Ground Beneath Her Feet*, it is possible to shift the narrative discourse of the novel from the Greek version of Orpheus's myth towards a discourse concentrated on art and the figure of the artist.[41] Actually, one need not exclude the other. Rushdie employs both Greek myth and Rilke. According to Rilke, all poets are Orpheus's metamorphoses; only a single spirit exists, which reappears in individuals; song/art is important, not the name of the individual artist. This notion underscores the seriousness of art and the importance of art's continuity as a principle that helps to cross frontiers between different worlds. Orpheus also represents aspects of the power of poetry/art, earlier clearly underlined in *The Jaguar Smile* and *Shame*, aspects which made Shelley dub the poet as 'unacknowledged legislator' and inspired the Georgian O'Shaughnessy's claim 'We are The Music-Makers' and Auden's assertion of the poet's special responsibility in 'In Memory of W. B. Yeats'. In this light, Ormus is the fleeting contemporary metamorphosis of Orpheus.

Ormus was born with a small purplish bruise on his left eyelid, 'a sign marking in the world of myth, those who are in contact with the world of the dead, which causes an alteration in his sight, and a special quality in his gaze; this spot is thus a physical anomaly that underlines his special vision'.[42] Thus, he has the potential to be a seer, a visionary. His contact with Gayomart is involuntary; it happens to him. Perhaps in the Gayomart connection, Rushdie shows how the creative artist has access to a different dimension. Since Gayomart is dead and a ghost, Ormus-Orpheus enters, or is on the edge of, the Underworld. The artist's vision can, and does, give him a glimpse of the future, guides him to see potential developments – even see and, perhaps, influence future socio-political trends. Ormus possesses the gift of seeing alternative realities, no less real than the realities around us. On the plane from India to the West, he crosses a 'membrane' and there also occurs the impinging of another world/dimension on Ormus's sight/mind. It is involuntary, it happens, just as the contact with Gayomart does. Maria, a beautiful sexy young girl, enters his world. After the accident in England, he finds Gayomart leaving his mind, the purplish bruise fades, but 'alternative universes have begun to spiral out from his eyeballs in rainbow-coloured corkscrews of otherness' (p. 307). He is now equipped with a similar ability to see beyond the existent phenomena (that is, what others see) and view alternative realities. But Ormus, recalling Omar Khayyam Shakil in *Shame*, does not use his gift, betrays his own power, and abdicates his responsibility, as suggested by his wearing an eye patch (to avoid seeing).

The novel offers the possibilities of parallel worlds. There is the real world. Then there is the world of the novel which diverges from it by including deliberate distortions of historical facts (as in *Midnight's Children*) such as an earthquake which occurs on the West coast of Mexico on 14 February 1989, and the jamming of Lee Harvey Oswald's rifle at the crucial moment, and thereby make the reader more alert, more suspicious. There is Ormus's inner world and also the Maria dimension. Parallel worlds are a stock idea in/since science fiction. Rushdie's constant references to science fiction and fantasy serve to alert the reader to a need to break out of the daily round of thought, to perceive the possibility of plural, parallel realities – potential ways of living. Also, if myths recall human linkage to the past – most classical allusions come up in the consciousness of Anglophone Indians (the Cama home is Apollo Bunder, Rai's is Villa Thracia, his father plans to build a cinema to be called Orpheum), suggesting the influence of colonialism and hybrid minds – sci-fi invokes now-ness. Science fiction is prominent in the text because it is a distinctively twentieth-century genre (though its origins lie in the nineteenth century and even earlier), like rock music, and, of course, because Rushdie fancies science fiction (*Grimus* was entered for a science fiction competition), though to him it is a tool, not an art form as it is to Heinlein and Arthur C. Clark.

In *The Ground Beneath Her Feet*, Rushdie seems to be working on will rather than inspiration. In *Midnight's Children, Shame* and *The Moor's Last Sigh*, he wrote on concerns that hounded his mind; *The Satanic Verses* involved the very stuff of his life. In the case of *The Ground Beneath Her Feet*, he had to find a subject to write about and resurrects an idea born in 1991.[43] There was no pressure behind it to fire his imagination. But it did give him the scope to write an epic, and the space to engage in experimentation with technique, play and playfulness,[44] and indulge in some pontificating. The novel is portentous. The Orpheus–Eurydice motif, pronounced and overworked though it is, nevertheless does not bind the narrative sufficiently to save it from being sprawling and unwieldy due to the fact that two divergent strands, which the author pursues, do not coalesce. The treatment of the Vina–Ormus grand passion is strained, inflated, ineffectual, and serves as commentary and criticism, unlike the positive treatment of the Rai–Mira teaming. Crisper but rarely dazzling or startlingly new is the satire at the expense of intellectual and artistic fads and fashions, including the significant volte-face by Marco Sangria and Remy Auxerre who eulogize VTO as musically reconciling the Apollonian with the Dionysiac element and promote their international success, then accuse them of artistic decay when they go political. Rushdie's technique in trying to make Ormus and Vina mega, almost mythical, celebrities is deliberate, but it seems a mistaken choice because it does not elicit sympathy for them and the effort results in a case of overkill. It is mainly Rai and the Rai sections that hold the reader's interest. Bombast may be used for the purpose of ironic undercutting. Maybe human aspiration in love/art are shown in all their height and overblown intensity to provoke a smile, at the thought of their inevitable limitation/defeat. Maybe there is an appeal against the restrictions of view and attitude imposed by monologic thinking. Ultimately the novel with its relentless input of distracting information is too much for the mind to take in – like our era.

The Ground Beneath Her Feet remains an important novel. It is 'a kind of evocation of an age' (to apply Rushdie's comment on *Fury*), and if, as Rushdie thinks, 'you look at the Jazz Age through Fitzgerald',[45] you look at the Age of Rock through Rushdie. Further, the equation, with Orpheus, the keynote struck by the Rilke epigraph, lead to profound intimations, which constitute the raison d'être of the novel. The man who wrote *Midnight's Children* had to try to match *himself* once more.

9
Fury (2001)

In *Fury*, Rushdie's earlier tendency to present countries per se is present in the projection of Fiji, but the new desire to focus on eras predominates. His time frame here is the late twentieth to twenty-first centuries, the contemporary period. He emphasizes different aspects of globalization: the overriding force of commercialism, and the proliferation and dispersion of products. Specific attention is directed at the intellectual, the author and art.

Cambridge, representing the best of British academia, is regarded as provincial and stultifying. Dubdub, one type of intellectual in the modern world, tries to escape by joining the glamour act of literary criticism and travelling on the international academic circuit. But 'the more he became a Personality, the less like a person he felt',[1] and he retreats back into traditional academe, Cambridge, believing he could set up house with Perry Pincus and thereby showing his innocence. He gets depressed, cuts his wrists, but Perry is not 'the nurse type' (p. 25). They part, both victims of the culture industry.

Malik Solanka – the protagonist of the novel – historian of ideas, despairs of academic life, resigns his position at Cambridge, and pursues a different path. Originally driven by fury in pre-Mumbai Bombay because he is sexually abused by his stepfather, he now breaks off into a creative fury. He plunges into television and develops a series of popular history-of-philosophy programmes for the BBC – *The Adventures of Little Brain*. These were meant to enlighten, to disseminate knowledge. Rushdie deals with a radical change: in the past, the author retained his/her personality and had a say, but now the market controls the author. Solanka's creation becomes an enormous success but his individuality is eclipsed and it goes out of his control when it becomes a commodity. When he gives Little Brain over to the representatives of commercialism, Little Brain is devoured, regurgitated and proliferates, seemingly without end, into different areas as vapid products – transformed into a money-making monster.[2] To Sarah Brouilette, the very name, Little Brain, 'connotes her intelligence and inquisitiveness',[3] But considering

162

A. A. Milne's Pooh – 'I am a bear of very *little brain*', the name is ambiguous and, thereby, fits the changes in the status of the doll – from middle-brow to low-brow. When his creation was moving out of his control, Solanka could have stopped it or, at least, tried to resist the process. He, however, surrenders to the flow; he continues to receive royalties. Solanka is a representative figure as a present-day creator.

Solanka is strangled by the success of Little Brain and sees no future in Britain except as its creator. The pent-up fury thereby gathered in him is reflected when he stands over his sleeping wife and son with a knife – though he bore his wife no animus and loved his child. His real feeling for his wife and son overcomes his fury. He realizes that the world he wants to destroy is the world of Little Brain. Therefore, he proceeds to stab the doll he had concealed in his cupboard at home (after asking Eleanor to get rid of the dolls) because of his lingering attachment to Little Brain as the source of his success. He takes the damaged doll to America, unconsciously hoping that it will be possible to heal his world there. He subscribes to the view that America is 'the land of self-creation' (p. 79). Solanka is haunted by the knife scene where he had shown himself capable of irrational, unnamed rage. As such, he is also capable of a rage that can result in the random killing of the three American girls; his chaotic, groping, confused condition could have resulted in his becoming a serial killer in a fugue. He is haunted by this thought too. He goes to America partly to be distant from the knife scene. Thus, the inner self is a major concern of the novel. 'Fury' becomes important in this area. It appears partly as the product of modern urban life – like road rage (shown by the taxi driver), a new syndrome.

Short phases of *Fury* are set in Britain, India and Fiji, but it is the novel in which Rushdie confronts America most directly and in the most sustained way. He compares Europe and America. Europe is finished in both senses of the word – polished and dying. He calls Tony Blair 'Tony Ozymandias' (p. 256). Via Shelley's poem, he refers to an extinct Empire (Ozymandias was 'king of kings') like Britain's to confirm at the end of the novel Solanka's sense of Britain as being of yesterday compared to America as being of today and dynamic. This explains his main motivation (like Rushdie's own) in moving there. The novel opens, in America, with a ferment of money, success and frenetic activity, the pursuit of luxury and satisfaction of appetite. In Dickens, money can be dull, sordid; but here money is glamour, power and can savour of high intellect too. Solanka is

aware, and critical, of American consumerist excess but this does
not obstruct him living in and with it. He is not guiltless but in a
position of passive complicity.

More seriously, over-opulence has led to decadence. It is stressed
that the three murdered American girls and their partners, the
murderers, are rich. The girls are totally idle, not economically
liberated. They and their partners are driven by sexual fury, by
insatiable appetites. The women end up as trophies, not women, and
the men as hunters; the scalping is a sign of these. This episode is
included, not for sensationalism, but to make a serious point. There
is something perverse and warped about the killing, and the rendering implies a condemnation of the decadence eroding American
society.

Jack Rhinehart, an African-American, was a respected, radical
journalist, but he had been corrupted by glamour and wealth, and
lost his integrity. He gave up visiting war zones, and began to write
instead lucrative profiles of the super-powerful, super-famous and
super-rich, becoming their 'home nigger' (pp. 57–8) and severing
links with his black community. Rushdie characterizes Rhinehart as
a male chauvinist (Rushdie is critical of the male chauvinist angle
in this novel as he is of the patriarchal in *Shame*), only interested
in his own satisfaction and disrespectful of women, ignoring their
rights and needs. Women were, to him, mere sex objects. This leads
to the kinks that are his undoing. Through the fact that he shows no
kinky tendencies while Neela Mahendra is his lover, it is hinted that
his perversities are not compulsive. In fact, the kinky sex appears
to be inspired by a snobbish urge to belong to the spoilt rich white
boys' club, to be part of an exclusive group. Rhinehart's ghastly
involvement in the S and M Club as well as his admiration for the
doings of the white brats and his desire for solidarity as revealed by
this, is punished by his fate. Rushdie, being a coloured man though
armoured in Western culture, would be keenly aware of the kind
of predicament into which coloured men in America could fall. His
portrayal of Rhinehart is admonitory.

An ambivalent attitude to the USA is common to immigrants – an
acceptance of the opportunities America offers (primarily, money-
making in the case of the working class such as the Urdu-speaking
taxi-driver, a synthetic fundamentalist; other things too in the case
of people such as Solanka) and damning America (as the taxi-
driver and, apparently, Solanka do in regard to American foreign
policy in the Middle East). Rushdie's feelings, too, are divided: while

criticizing the country, he is also pro-American. As newly settled in America and not absorbed by 'the melting pot', he tries to define/analyse what strikes him about America in a fresh and keen way. Unfortunately, the novel reflects on, rather than reflects, America.

Fury reveals that Rushdie has matured further along liberal, discriminating lines in dealing with gender politics. Critics have found it difficult 'to figure out' why Solanka 'should be such a babe magnet'.[4] There is nothing particularly attractive about him. He seems an unhappy underdog. Yet he is extremely kind and loving to women, though he reveals a queer streak in dumping them: he is unable to commit himself totally to an emotional experience, probably because of his past (sexual abuse by stepfather, unsupportive mother).

Yet, in the case of his first wife, Sarah Jane Lear, he has a cause for rejecting her. She deteriorates from academic pursuits to commercial success; she is later shown as horribly rapacious. Actually, she is introduced in such stick figure form that the reader does not *see* the decline. Her engagement with literature is not the personalized, bold and emotional involvement with it suggested by Eleanor Masters's reading of *Othello*, so that the development from stick figure to caricature is slapdash. Sarah's decision to enter the advertising profession is symptomatic of the keynote of the contemporary world (in Rushdie's view in *Fury*): 'It was a horrible thought in that era [the 1970s] – nakedly capitalist. Selling things was *low*. Now everyone – eminent writers, great painters, architects, politicians – wanted to be in on the act... . Everybody, as well as everything, was for sale' (p. 33, Rushdie's italics).

Solanka does appeal to Eleanor who is a home-maker and caring. She has every chance of being a liberated woman, but remains old-fashioned (she makes love only when ovulating) and Solanka is not satisfied. Theirs is not a free and equal interchange of desire.

Rushdie distinguishes between the genuinely liberated women such as Mila and Neela and the mimic such as Perry. Perry thinks of herself as sexually completely liberated, but she is partly a poseur. She knows how to sell her assets in both senses of the word. A literary groupie, her speciality in teaching in a college is selling the work of famous critics and writers she has slept with. Solanka does not come up to her expectations in regard to sex.

The relationship of Solanka and Mila is motivated. As a young girl, Mila had been thrilled by Little Brain and, therefore, its creator meant a great deal to her. Moreover, both Mila's admiration for her father and her incestuous relationship with him would lie behind her relationship with Solanka. She dresses like Little Brain and is seductive. Solanka's relationship with her is a surrogate for an incestuous relationship. Solanka makes love to her but stops short of completing the sex act – although he goes all the way with Neela.

Mila is an intellectual with strong, definite ideals. She thinks she has the potential to be Solanka's Muse and acknowledges the fact that she is his Muse in regard to his second creation, this time in cyberspace. She persuades him: '... you don't lose control ... you have a better vehicle ... the financial upside is very, very strong ... . The whole concept of ownership as far as ideas is so different now, it's so much more cooperative ... . You're still the magician, but let everyone else play with the wands sometimes' (p. 178). Solanka achieves success, on a commercial level, with his second product marketed by Mila's company, and his concepts colour politics even in a place as distant as Lilliput-Blefuscu. (New technologies intensify globalization, and are impelled commercially.) But in this instance, the theme is static, not developed. The whole Galileo 1 and Puppet Kings episode remains fugitive and smoky. The Puppet Kings' costumes are appropriated by the Filibistani Resistance as political totems, but their motivation is obscure; in this

> Theatre of Masks, the original, the man with no mask, was perceived as the mask's imitator: the creation was real while the creator was the counterfeit! It was as though he were present at the death of God and the god who had died was himself. (p. 239)

This seems froth and bubble, difficult to relate to or even understand. Indeed, the projection of Solanka's ideas into Fijian politics is limp and ineffectual.

Solanka dumps Mila on being attracted to Neela – sexually. Solanka at fifty-five is Rushdie's age and Neela is a projection (down to the scar on her arm) based on Rushdie's partner, Padma Lakshmi, to whom the novel is dedicated. There is complicity between the author and the reader as Rushdie offers Padma a bouquet in public. The stunning beauty of Neela may be partly jokey as a compliment to Padma, who has dazzled Rushdie, but his dwelling on its extraordinary quality and impact appears farcical. Neela is attracted to Solanka because he is the opposite of her partner, Jack Rhinehart, not a male chauvinist but one who treats women with respect. Yet Neela is interested in Solanka only in so far as he does not affect her involvement with Fiji, her homeland. Neela's surname, Mahendra, recalls Mahendra Pal Chaudhry, the first Indo-Fijian Prime Minister of Fiji. It reflects the urge of Rushdie to connect the fictional politics of Lilliput-Blefuscu with the actual politics of Fiji, and is a small prod to the reader to do so. The sharp, if remote, struggle between the descendants of the Indian indentured labourers brought into Fiji by the British colonizers (the 'Indo-Lillies') and the native Fijians (the 'Elbees') may have caught Rushdie's imagination because of his and Padma's Indian origins (she is from Chennai), and the substantial coverage in the US media at the time of the novel's composition (which prompted Rushdie to write a column in *The New York Times*, 'June 2000: Fiji'). But from a longer perspective, *Fury* marks the re-emergence of Rushdie's earlier interest in and experimentation with fictional settings that 'not quite'[5] resemble actual countries and their political situations – which he had displayed in *Shame*.

Neela is totally tied up with the politics of Lilliput-Blefuscu. The Indo-Lilly representative, Babur, who comes to New York to head a demonstration, appears a Hollywood style barbarian master and Neela is overwhelmed by him. She conceives a passion for him and they become lovers – which Solanka resents. She follows Babur to Fiji and wishes to make her planned documentary there. Her situation at the beginning is ambiguous. In the meanwhile, Babur, gaining confidence, has taken control of the Indo-Lilly resistance movement and becomes, like Marlowe's Tamburlaine, a crazed tyrant; Neela plays up to him as a slave. The historical Babur established a great empire in four years (1526–30) and was a vigorous warrior, an epitome of fitness. The name is appropriate for the fictional Babur because he possessed a manliness – which attracts Neela sexually. More importantly, by assuming the name, Babur, the Indo-Lilly leader suggests the seeds of egoism and egotism within him (he sees himself as the centre of things so that his desire becomes not so much to help his people but to project his own image) – which finally leads him, apparently, to cross the border of sanity.

'Lilliput-Blefuscu' is selected not merely to show Rushdie's knowledge. Characteristically, his allusions are far-flung but purposive. Just as Gulliver realizes the overweening ambition of the Emperor of Lilliput and does not wish to be the cause of making the free and brave people of Blefuscu slaves of the Emperor in Swift's *Gulliver's Travels*, so Neela wants neither the Indo-Lillies nor the Elbees to be under the fascist megalomaniac, Babur. Neela's liberalism overrides her nationalism (reflecting Rushdie's own position in *Imaginary*

Homelands). In the interest of freedom of speech and thought, Neela has to betray the Indo-Lillies and help 'the bad guys [in the eyes of Neela and Rushdie, but not necessarily the reader's] win' (p. 253), feeling herself a traitor and sacrificing her own life in the process. The conclusion is that the status quo in Lilliput-Blefuscu will return. Speaking in terms of art, it is amazing that Rushdie after his Nicaraguan experience (recorded in *The Jaguar Smile*) should make such a woolly mess of the Filibistani Resistance Movement and war. Neela remains a paper doll. Neither her sensual beauty nor heroism is ever conveyed.

Neela is totally liberated, sexually, and aggressive. She involves herself in a political campaign with military activity. In Lilliput-Blefuscu, she manages the release of the hostages and Solanka with deftness and efficiency. Mila, too, is enormously effectual. Both enjoy sex. Mila even seems to have enjoyed perverse sex. She seems to have seduced her father rather than the other way round. Mila has relationships with Solanka and Eddie at the same time. Neela has her evening games and Solanka too. Both Neela and Mila are capable of satisfying desire. Their images as professionals are impressive. Altogether, they are striking contrast to the self-indulgent, hedonistic and unproductive sex objects and victims of the S and M Club. Rushdie accepts strong feminist tendencies.

Solanka has lost Mila and Neela, and is in a dreadful state at the end. He 'had withdrawn from the world' (p. 258), but takes an outing to Kenwood, stimulated by a desire to see his son, Asmaan. Eleanor, now with Morgen as her partner, tries to cut him from his son. Yet Solanka is not downbeat as he shrieks on the bouncy slope of the fairground: 'Look at me, Asmaan! I'm bouncing very well! I'm bouncing higher and higher!' (p. 259). *Fury* concludes on this optimistic, positive note, as Solanka asserts his rights over his son and is set to recover.

The Ground Beneath Her Feet was Rushdie's last burst of self-display; he was erudite and high-brow. He employed magic realism though it was going out of fashion because of his sensitivity to the bygone era which he was harvesting, and it suited that age. In *Fury*, there is no magic realism. Rushdie is sensitive to the new era too, the turn-of-the-century contemporary world which is his subject, and chooses a technique which he thinks suits it – 'a kind of hyperrealism'.[6] He packs in 'factual details about modern life', topical references, which are natural and inevitable in any work that seeks to evoke a sense of the period in which it is set. In *Fury*, these are 'overloaded'.[7] Stylistically too, *Fury* is a departure, but this is not necessarily a virtue. It is totally lacking in the characteristic Rushdie exuberance and sparkle. The language tends to operate on the level of statement rather than work evocatively. In *Fury, Shalimar the Clown* and *The Enchantress of Florence*, Rushdie's style becomes more accessible and, thereby, he seems to be trying to appeal to a wider audience. Like Shakespeare, he wants to enlist the groundlings too.

As a novel, *Fury* neither works nor coheres in its portrayal of a period. It did not, however, go 'out of date' after 9/11, at the very moment of its publication, as Rushdie claimed.[8] Security fears have altered the American scene, but the target of Rushdie's satire – the irresistible, commercial power of USA that shapes, or distorts, people willy-nilly – remained seemingly intact, at least, until late 2008. Indeed, his rendering presages the crisis of neo-liberal capitalism into which the Western world was rapidly heading. *Fury* represents a trough in Rushdie's writing career. Perhaps, his mind was overloaded at this time – adjusting to America and coping with the complexities of his private life (still married to Elizabeth West and attached to their son, while having a relationship with Padma Lakshmi). Some explanation is needed for the failure of imagination that undermines the novel. The biographical reason, though conjectural, goes part of the way.[9]

10
Shalimar the Clown (2005)

Rushdie's private life becomes less problematic. His marriage to Elizabeth West is dissolved in 2003 and he marries Padma Lakshmi in 2004. Kashmir, one of the focal points of *Shalimar the Clown* (2005), was his family's ancestral home; the region was familiar to him in boyhood and was, for him, a lost paradise. Submerged in his unconscious, it emerges throughout his career – most notably, in *Midnight's Children, Haroun* and *Shalimar*. These circumstances facilitate an artistic recovery in *Shalimar*. Rushdie's perspective remains global. Here he focuses on a different aspect of globalization (only touched on earlier) – politics. His vision spans India, Europe and America.

Shalimar is a clown by profession. Character-wise, he is rather obtuse, not acute or inspired – but not comic. He is a peasant and remains somewhat a peasant despite his overseas experiences, many of these occurring among terrorists rather than in stable or sophisticated society. Shalimar, the name of the great Mogul garden of Kashmir, conjures up the pristine condition of the region. It means 'abode of joy', and this appears ironical when the idyll is shattered.

The personal story of Shalimar, Boonyi, Max and India takes on socio-political ramifications. Shalimar and Boonyi, despite being physically attractive, are not appealing to the reader, unlike Romeo and Juliet who intrude on the consciousness because of Rushdie's epigraph 'A plague on both your houses', though he is referring to the Indo-Pakistani dispute over Kashmir. Rushdie appears to keep Shalimar devoid of personality or individuality. The reader is informed of his traits and skills, but he remains a cipher. Shalimar's reflexes are superb, whether he is engaged in tightrope-walking or killing, in whatever he does physically, and his will is steel-like. He has a superhuman force, but is not glamorized – possibly a blueprint for a terrorist pure and simple. His emotions are kept rudimentary. He lives on his feelings, and his relationship with Boonyi is the root of his happiness. When she goes away with Max, her betrayal is, to him, a terrible act. He feels empty and, on the rebound, he vows revenge as he had sworn to her after their first love-making. Rushdie refers to Shalimar at this stage as 'a gentle young man'.[1] 'Gentle' seems hardly an appropriate epithet when Shalimar appears to possess an inbuilt ferocity.

On the other hand, Boonyi has more of a personality and individuality as her egoism and egotism emerge as a part of a distinctive temperament. She is, at first, intoxicated by Shalimar's physical attractiveness (young, handsome, athletic) and by the sexual urge (strong, in her case) that comes with youth. Her narcissism induces her to see the world entirely in her own terms. It disposes her to imagine that she can cut a figure in the outside world and influences her to visualize horizons which make Shalimar seem confining. She finds Kashmir claustrophobic; this is a reflection of her make-up and is not to be interpreted as a criticism of Kashmir. She thinks that Max will open the doors of the world to her. She makes overtures to him and he, true to form, is ready to respond. She is totally responsible for her own disaster, though her faults are expiated by her suffering, particularly over the loss of her daughter. Boonyi, as an ambitious would-be artist, is among the pivotal figures of artists in Rushdie's fiction (Gibreel, Saladin, Aurora, Vina, Ormus, Solanka).

Kashmir (the presence of villages is exceptional in Rushdie's oeuvre) is presented as a paradise physically (a generally accepted view) and culturally. There is an emphasis on its tolerance and friendliness, so much so that it appears a model of hybridity in the real world. Though Shalimar is a Muslim and Boonyi a Hindu, their initially illicit love affair is eventually condoned by their families and community. Shalimar's father, the sarpanch Abdullah Noman's peroration at the meeting of the panchayat that 'at the heart of Kashmiri culture there was a common bond that transcended all other differences',[2] and the clinching comment of Boonyi's father Pandit Pyrelal Kaul – 'To defend their love is to defend what is finest in ourselves' (p. 110) – strike a false, sermonizing note, too much a definition of a concept of multiculturalism and too inspirational and anachronistic in 1965. Pre-war Strasbourg is the other model of hybridity presented in the novel. Both models are destroyed. From another perspective, Kashmir and Strasbourg are both oppressed. America, the liberator in the Second World War, is the oppressor in Asia. From still another perspective, all the three settings, though different and distinctive, are alike: 'Everywhere was a mirror of everywhere else. Executions, police brutality, explosions, riots: Los Angeles was beginning to look like wartime Strasbourg; like Kashmir' (p. 355). The global perspective yields both positive and negative aspects.

Max Ophuls is polished, articulate, witty, irresistible and seemingly an expert in every field – a glamorized, cinematic hero. His adventures during the Resistance are redolent of the fiction of the Second World War. But the pages about his connection with the sexily sadistic female Nazi known as the Panther include serious suggestions. Nazism seems to go beyond the political, and liberates perversity, latent aggression and unconscious psychopathic urges. More important is the Alsace question (like the Kashmir question) – should it belong to Germany or France or be autonomous? Indeed, Rushdie is exploring the roots of the present in the Second World War and its aftermath. Having been a courageous and honoured fighter in France, Max's abilities are acknowledged by his ambassadorial appointment in India. He is open to every experience and totally responsive to the experience of the moment. He has enjoyed a stream of lovers and Boonyi, too, attracts him, at first, sexually. Yet Boonyi is, to him, not totally a sex object and this suggests a residual element of the idealism that inspired his activity in the Resistance. His feelings for Boonyi influence his articulation of foreign policy: 'He began to object, in private session and in public speeches, to the militarization of the Kashmir valley, and when the word *oppressors* passed his lips for the first time the bubble of his popularity finally burst' (p. 197, Rushdie's italics). The exposé of his liaison with Boonyi, which followed, led to the termination of his ambassadorship.

The liaison begins with 'the treaty of their affiliation' (p. 172) and the political overtones of the language signify the beginnings of the allegorical dimension it acquires. Boonyi, as a representative of Kashmir, is consumerist, distorted, degraded and, finally, abandoned to misery by Max, the agent of the US. America is interested in its empire; it attempts to control regions abroad and then creates a total mess (as in Kashmir, and in Vietnam, Afghanistan and the Philippines, which enter the novel peripherally).

The motivation for Shalimar becoming an international terrorist is provided as in a realist novel. He possesses the revolutionary fervour of youth and awakens to the fact of oppression: 'the enemies we never see, the ones who pull the strings' (p. 248). His hate for Max, whom he has never seen, appears to transfer itself to the neo-colonialists who create the scenario. Moreover, Max is an American, and America, trying to impose its power over them, is considered *the* enemy by the Muslims. From another perspective, Shalimar's suppressed violence seems to be given license by Boonyi's infidelity. He becomes a deft exterminator before he brutally decapitates her. During, and after, his training as a terrorist, he gets a physical kick out of murder (he prefers the knife to the gun), but he has no identification with a specific cause except Kashmir.

Rushdie touches on the grievances driving terrorists to *jihad* (in Kashmir, the intrusion of India is resented and feared as a harbinger of annexation), the procedures and psychology of terrorists such as the brainwashing of recruits, and includes a fine touch when Shalimar is given a pep shot before his murder assignment in North Africa (without implying that he lacks courage). Rushdie depicts a (presumably representative) terrorist camp: he sees Muslims united and in the same place, but coming from different localities due to diverse problems (all created by infidels, mainly). Rushdie tries to convey the sensation of how terrorism functions. *Shalimar* is written after 9/11, but Rushdie was aware of terrorism earlier. (He knew of the Tamil terrorist organization, the Liberation Tigers of Tamil Eelam (LTTE), and the Indian involvement in its conflict with the government of Sri Lanka. The murder of Rajiv Gandhi by the LTTE in 1991 enters *East, West*.) Rushdie has suffered under the *fatwa* imposed by Islamic fundamentalists and is now, understandably, more critical of the Muslims, though he is not anti-Muslim in a blatant way. He not only shows that terrorism is a wrong-headed approach to further a cause but presents the *jihadists* as ardent, fanatical, ferocious. Maulana Bulbul Fakh, a fundamentalist, portrayed as a robot, is non-thinking but possesses the power to drive people. 'F(orward) C(amp)-22 was bursting at the seams with men with *the snarling, spittle-flecked* manner of attack *dogs* straining to be unleashed' (p. 273, my emphasis). This is hardly a dignified image for fighters. Rushdie thus even belittles Islamic terrorism. The stress on Muslim fundamentalism and its brutality caters to the fear in the West – augmented by the use of Samuel P. Huntington's 'Clash of Civilizations' theory[3] – of an Islamic movement perceived as increasingly powerful and anti-Western.

The Jaguar Smile represents the first important stage in Rushdie's evolving attitude to America. *The Ground Beneath Her Feet* and *Fury* mark further stages; they are not influenced by *The Jaguar Smile* and their concerns are different. *Shalimar* embodies still another stage. There is an allegorical parallel between Max's career and developments in the US. America was a defender of the oppressed in the Second World War, but it is later drawn into a different role: manipulating rather than defending the world. Max begins as an idealist and a buoyant, optimistic man of action in the Second World War.

He later fights the good fight for Uncle Sam: counter-terrorism's secret manipulator with arms, negotiations, cash. *Shalimar* makes us aware of the American commitment in Afghanistan; Rushdie makes a deliberate mistake and anachronistically inserts the Taliban into the 1980s. In 2002, Rushdie argued: 'America did in Afghanistan, what had to be done, and did it well.'[4] In November 2002, he supports the US-led invasion of Iraq.[5] But by the time he writes *Shalimar*, he has become more balanced, having witnessed more of the results of American foreign policy. His attitude to US interference in Islamic conflicts is now influenced by a perception of the short-sightedness and irresponsibility of American policies.

Shalimar embraces terrorism without surrendering his private agenda. These coalesce. He is motivated partly by his personal vendetta and partly by a political cause, indicated by his perception of a similarity to Udham Singh. There are differences between them but the parallels are more significant – the dual perception of their roles (freedom fighter/terrorist) and the militaristic/interventionist side of imperialism in the case of the British and their successors, the Americans, and its impact on the victims and forms of resistance. Almost twenty-one years after the Jallianwala Bagh massacre, Singh kills its architect, Sir Michael O'Dwyer, in London in 1940, but he does not intend to escape. Shalimar reaches his target in America and tries to escape – in vain. Yet he does get out of jail and goes in search of Boonyi's illegitimate child, whom he has also sworn to kill.

India, like Max, is a cinematic figure and an expert in her chosen fields – archery, small arms, boxing, martial arts. Diana-like (I am referring to the Greek goddess), she is glamorous and flinty, not 'slinky'.[6] She later changes her name to Kashmira because she identifies with her mother and Kashmir, going in quest of both. In the final scene, Shalimar enters her house in pursuit of revenge, while she lies in wait to avenge the murder of her father and mother. The mindless, ruthless, traditional supporter of fundamentalism and violence is about to be shot by a weapon (a bow and arrow), lethal but not brutal, graceful, demanding skill not animal strength, handled by India/Kashmira, a synthesis of East and West, a representative of hybridity. The love of Kashmira and Yuvraj, who promotes and makes traditional art profitable, and is of admirable parentage, is a symbol of hope. The nostalgia for, and lament over, pre-fundamentalist Kashmir is not constructive, but it includes a positive message as demonstrating hybridity. Calling attention to the current situation in Kashmir (underscored by Max in his last public appearance) is useful, though Rushdie, like in *Shame*, has nothing to offer to change that which he criticizes, and can suggest no way out of the rival claims of India, Pakistan and 'Kashmir for the Kashmiris'.

Rushdie continues to favour feminist ideals. *Shalimar* features strong women – Firdaus Begum; Hasina 'Harud' Yambarzal; the impressive Gujar prophetess Nazrebadoor; even the comic but tenacious and warm-hearted survivor of repeated catastrophes, Olga Volga Simeonovna. The Grey Rat, Margaret Rhodes, is more important. Her essential decency despite Max's infidelities crumples under the blow delivered by his infatuation with the beautiful and sensually powerful Boonyi (a contrast to her strong love and strong frigidity), yet she has all the physical courage, endurance, toughness and resourcefulness which are considered masculine virtues. India is interested in masculine pursuits and in sex for sex's sake.

Rushdie's desire to cater for a wider audience influences the whole novel. It seems a vintage Hollywood romance, the Hollywood of the 1930s (purveying stuff like *The Prisoner of Zenda*), not the Hollywood of today – (seemingly) a simple and basic sex and melodrama story. This is blatantly clear in the opening (the gruesome murder of Max) and the conclusion. The socio-political concerns regarding the fate of Kashmir, fundamentalism, local/international terrorism, form the Rushdie hallmark of awareness of the tensions and violent politics of today. Yet the personal story bulks so large that the socio-political issues slip from the foreground. It does not 'trivialize the larger issues',[7] but blurs them.

Against the bizarre brilliance of *Midnight's Children* and *Shame*, *Shalimar* appears rather conventionally and elaborately exotic. Its circular structure – recalling the films of Max Ophul's namesake, the German director – is neat and striking; the disordered time sequence whets the appetite – in ways that suit a different and larger readership. Perhaps for the same reason, there are only touches of magic realism, some quite effective ('the iron mullah', for instance); there are long stretches of old-fashioned narrative realism. Terms such as 'comic book'-like[8] and 'cartoonish',[9] repeatedly used by reviewers, identify the thinness and simplified quality of the writing in *Shalimar*. Rushdie confines himself to simple Standard English – not the packed hurtling idiom he created to reflect the fractured realities of history as it happens in *Midnight's Children*. Less frenetically, but as effectively, he employed this technique in *Shame*, *The Satanic Verses*, *The Moor's Last Sigh* and, in a slapdash manner, in *The Ground Beneath Her Feet*. Here he demonstrates an ability to regress from multiplex complexity to two levels of meaning at a time.

Uneven in execution, *Shalimar* does not go deep, but it succeeds both as a competent page-turner and in alerting the reader to illusions of benevolent hegemony.

11

The Enchantress of Florence (2008)

In June 2007, Queen Elizabeth II announced that she was conferring a knighthood on Rushdie. This aroused afresh issues that have dogged him over the past twenty years not only among traditional Muslims around the world (it seemed to them an accolade bestowed on a global symbol of hostility to traditional Islam) but also among British conservatives who believed that he was again endangering Britain's security. Iran reaffirmed the death sentence. A Pakistani government minister suggested that the award justified suicide bombings. Al-Qaeda's second-in-command Ayman al-Zawahari warned that it was preparing a 'precise response' to Britain's decision. Rushdie's political kin were contemptuous that an avowed leftist should accept such an imperial honour. Even to critics, it seemed 'to confirm his rejection of a more radical, anti-establishment position'.[1] Such political interpretations are wrong and unnecessary, though understandable in the context of a politically charged atmosphere. It was not that Rushdie, just as much as Darius Cama, had his British dream or that the British Empire was going down on its knees. The knighthood showed that Rushdie had reached an eminence as a writer and there was no reason for him to refuse it. He was accepting it as an honour due to him. After it was conferred in 2008, he said: 'This is an honour not for any specific book but for a very long career in writing and I'm happy to see that recognized.'[2] In fact, it is not unique but a part of a pattern. V. S. Naipaul accepted a knighthood before Rushdie. It may also be a part of Britain's desire to show even-handedness, to honour eminent writers whether British or not, and to signal that immigrant writers can acquire close connections to British literary culture.

In July 2007, Padma Lakshmi informed him by email that she was leaving him. The announcement was so timed that she would have to be correctly referred to as 'Padma, Lady Rushdie', even after her divorce. Rushdie confessed that writing *The Enchantress of Florence*

(2008) saved him from the 'wreckage' of his 'private life; it was a bit of a refuge. I found that in the end a life-time's habit of just going to my desk and doing a day's work and not allowing myself not to do it is what got me back on track'.[3]

Rushdie has written a different kind of novel. He has gone back to the late fifteenth and early sixteenth centuries. He regards *The Enchantress of Florence* as more 'historical' or 'factual' than his other novels and as his 'most researched book', complete with a bibliography at the end.[4] Having studied history at Cambridge, he has a clear notion of what he can, and should not, invent. He has emphasized: 'It would surprise people to know how much was rooted in truth, how little I had to invent.'[5] He had included the bibliography partly 'to give people an opportunity to explore it further'[6] and partly 'to avoid the sort of accusations made against Ian' [referring to the allegations that Ian McEwan, in his novel *Atonement*, used the research of another writer without adequate acknowledgement].[7]

As in *The Ground Beneath Her Feet*, Rushdie is aware that the origins of globalization go far back. The narrative in *The Enchantress of Florence* covers half the world known at that time: the Indian subcontinent, the sea coast of Africa, the Safavid Empire of Persia, the Ottomans, Europe, England and the newly 'discovered' America. There are characters, major (Qara Koz, Mogor dell' Amore, Argalia, Ago Vespucci) and minor, who traverse and link different worlds, but, at this early stage, there is an intermingling but little impact between worlds. Rushdie said that he 'had originally intended to set the story completely in Europe, but ended up dividing the narrative between two great civilizations that barely knew of each other'.[8] It is true that Florence and Fatehpur Sikri are the major foci of the narrative but he interweaves stories set in other locales as well to create a complex architecture.

The Florentine narrative includes the repeated line: 'In the beginning there were three friends, Antonino Argalia, Niccolò "il Machia" and Ago Vespucci;'[9] these three are the major figures with Lorenzo de' Medici as a strong factor. In boyhood, the three friends dreamed of having occult power over women and in the woods masturbate for mandrakes. Niccolò Machiavelli was known, in his time, for his lewd comedy *La Mandragola* (1513). ('Mandragoras' is the Greek and Latin form of the word 'mandrake'.) The friends display different attitudes towards 'migration'. Argalia is an adventurous traveller, becoming a great warrior in the Ottoman army, returning victorious to Florence and, finally, chosen as the *condottiere* of the city and commander of the Florentine militia. Ago travels when he must, even to America when driven by love for Qara Koz (she flees there to escape the wrath of the Florentines). Machiavelli is profoundly stay-at-home.

The reader sees much of Florence through the eyes of Machiavelli. Furthermore, his life and career reflect its social state. The creative aspect of Renaissance Florence is evident in that he is a writer and a thinker. Its hedonistic aspect is illustrated by his sensuality. Its political ferment, the active intrigue and jostling for power, is shown during his practical involvement in its politics. His rise and fall (when the Medicis ascend to power) reveal the volatility of the political situation. He is tortured and his spirit is virtually destroyed: 'In the city that gave the world the idea of the value and freedom of the individual human soul they had not valued him...' (pp. 239–40). An old man at forty, contact with Qara Koz lifts his gloom (an attraction of which his wife is aware but exercises restraint because of her own surrender to Qara Koz's charm) but only briefly and temporarily. In the faint hope of making a political comeback, he immerses himself in writing *The Prince*, suggested but not named, a Rushdie source book.

The Enchantress of Florence opens with an arresting shot of the entry of Mogor dell' Amore (a.k.a Uccello, real name Niccolò Vespucci) into Akbar's capital city – the bizarre figure of a European stranger with startling yellow hair, wearing a coat of particoloured leather lozenges in the heat, standing tall and upright acrobatically on a bullock-cart travelling on an uneven highway – against the onion-shaped domes and turrets of Fatehpur Sikri. *Shalimar the Clown* and *The Enchantress of Florence* have a strong visual appeal and can conceivably be transmuted into blockbusters. Rushdie has been influenced by cinema, has appeared in films (*Bridget Jones's Diary*, 2001, and *Then She Found Me*, 2007) and is not above being a Bollywood enthusiast. He remembers: 'Some of the most popular Indian movies when I was growing up were about Akbar and his queen Jodhabai – it was the Indian equivalent of *Gone with the Wind*.' He is aware of the 2008 version, *Jodhaa Akbar*, and 'the debate whether Jodhabai actually existed'.[10] Some consider her one of Akbar's Rajput (Hindu) wives (she is so in the 2008 film), while others think she is his daughter-in-law. Interest in her dates back to the nineteenth and eighteenth centuries. Rushdie is sharing in a longstanding Indian fascination with Akbar-Jodha.

Mogor is an enigmatic conjurer, murderer, adventurer and dazzling storyteller. He claims that he wishes to meet Akbar the Great to deliver a message from Queen Elizabeth I (which, in fact, he had stolen from the Captain of the ship to India on which he was a stowaway) but he also wants to claim kinship with the King as his uncle – Mogor being, as he claims, the son of his great aunt, Qara Koz [Black Eyes] and her last man, Ago Vespucci. Mogor is a Scheherazade figure who must tell his story (to Akbar) to avert death, a motif Rushdie understands and has used earlier. *The Thousand and One Nights* has been a major influence on Rushdie as is made obvious in *The Enchantress of Florence* by such references as the thousand and one gardener-cum-executioners in the Turkish Sultan's garden.

The Enchantress of Florence is immortal Qara Koz. Her enchantment has its impact, though it also fades in Florence. The word 'enchantress' in the title affects the reader subliminally: the general effect of the novel is beguiling. The atmosphere derives partly from the influence of the Arabian Nights and from the Italian Renaissance epic, especially the fantasy/magic filled *Orlando Furioso* (1516; 2nd edn 1521; final version 1532). Ludovico Ariosto's poem is a sequel to Matteo Maria Boiardo's *Orlando Innamorata* (1495), but Ariosto has an ironic tone, seldom present in Boiardo, as has Rushdie, particularly with regard to the Akbar-Jodha 'love'. Qara Koz was known later as Angelica, the name of Ariosto's elusive Moorish heroine. *The Enchantress of Florence* celebrates a world of the imagination 'before the real and the unreal was segregated forever and doomed to live apart under different monarchies and separate legal systems' (p. 221).

The portrayal of Akbar is essentially the same in history, in *The Enchantress of Florence* and in L. H. Myers' *The Root and the Flower* (1935). Myers takes into account Akbar's philosophical/devotional attitudes but presents him in a faintly comic light. Rushdie is seriously funny and takes a generally comic approach; at the same time, he is aware of Akbar's worthy qualities. Both Myers and Rushdie describe Akbar as fat. Rushdie is often deliciously comic in delineating the complexities of Akbar's self-doubt as in depicting his credulous infatuation with Morgor and with Morgor's (false) representation of Elizabeth I, the 'faraway redhead queen' (p. 69) (sending her love letters that are never answered, declaring 'his megalomaniac fantasies of creating a joint global empire that united the eastern and western hemispheres', p. 74).

Despite Rushdie's comic slant, Akbar does emerge as a real but not common man, as a king of stature – the most potent, indeed dominant, character in the narrative. He has a vigorous mind and is guided not so much by self-aggrandizement as by idealism. He was not only a military hero but also a practical man, a warrior as well as administrator, capable of running a far-flung empire. He was a lover of beauty and of form, of art and architecture, as manifested in his palace, Fatehpur Sikri; he possessed a taste for literature and an interest in learning. From one perspective, it is his pursuit of beauty that makes him find comfort in the Enchantress at the end. Historians record: 'On some rare occasions his temper got the upper hand and the culprits were summarily dealt with'[11] – as in the case of the Rana of Cooch Naheen, a fictional character who is the ancestor of the Rani of Cooch Naheen in *Midnight's Children*. The traumatic murder of the Rana was Rushdie's 'way of dramatizing [Akbar's] moment of choice', 'his shift toward a synthesized religion' and 'his creation of The Tent of New Worship'[12] – which is based on the historical structure Akbar built at Fatehpur Sikri, *Ibadat-Khana*. Even a tiny detail such as the inclusion of Christian missionaries from Goa in the discussions there is true to history.[13] In history and in the novel, Akbar was 'a firm believer in the policy of universal toleration'.[14] It was in keeping with his promise to the Rana that Akbar created his centre for free thought in religion. There is a bitter little jest in that the admirable liberal thinkers, the Rana ('a feudal ruler absurdly fond of talking about freedom', p. 32) and the Rani are rulers of Naheen [Nothing], an implication of the ineffectuality and impotence of the liberal stance.

The omniscient frame narrator summarizes the contradictions in Akbar's character: 'a Muslim vegetarian, a warrior who wanted only peace, a philosopher-king' [Plato's concept in his *Republic*] (p. 33). The narrator could have added: 'a cultured illiterate'. Akbar is an early proponent of hybridity (though the concept as such was not available in his time). Towards the close, debating whether he could bring Mogor into his inner circle, Akbar envisions 'a culture of inclusion...' (p. 317). Earlier, Akbar had freed his people from the silence imposed on them by his overzealous officials, the opposite of Cultmaster Khattam-Shud in *Haroun*. Akbar was a hyper masculine type in his penchant for flattery and gory violence, yet he was also animated by an idealistic and imaginative temperament.

Rushdie presents a rich, colourful and crowded canvas. Even minor characters such as Tansen, Dashwanth and Abul Fazl, stand out vivid and individualistic, like figures in a Mogul miniature. The reader gets the feel of two Renaissance worlds, Florence and Fatehpur Sikri, in the West and the East, having a vigour physical and intellectual. In both places, the same kind of surge surfaces in the same period. (This was also the age when sea adventurers were meeting the challenges of opening up new worlds, Westerners journeying East and further Westwards. America was a new found land, the America in the novel being a symbol of what they find.) The similarity between Florence and Fatehpur Sikri has both positive and negative aspects: the flowering of the arts, architecture and thinking as well as hedonism, violence, torture. Fatehpur Sikri seems more normal and stable than frenetic and volatile Florence, but Rushdie's basic 'message' is clear: 'there are such things as universals... the worlds were more like each other than unlike'.[15] There are also implied similarities between these two worlds and the present world, underlined by the mirror motif which binds the narrative as well as the three worlds: Qara Koz has her Mirror; the hero in Dashwanth's pictures became the emperor's mirror (p. 117); Dashwanth who paints Qara Koz, and Filipepi who paints Simonetta, are mirrors of one another; Fatehpur Sikri and Florence mirror each other; Mogor explains that Elizabeth I was 'the western mirror' of Akbar (p. 69); the lake at Sikri mirrors the changing fortunes of the city; finally, as Rushdie explains: '... we see ourselves as each other's other, whereas we are much more like each other's mirror image'.[16] Ultimately, Rushdie is making the point that 'the good and the bad of human nature are constant',[17] underlined by Akbar's ahistorical/transhistorical prophecy at the end, which expresses Rushdie's own pessimism: 'The future would not be what he hoped for, but a dry hostile antagonistic place... harshness, not civilization, would rule' (p. 347).

In *The Enchantress of Florence*, gender issues are prominent. Qara Koz makes use of men. She abandons her Indian family to be with the Persian conqueror. She leaves him to join Argalia when he defeats the Persian, who tells his body-servant: 'That a woman so beautiful should not be tender, this I did not expect. I did not expect her to turn away from me so casually, as if she were changing a shoe' (p. 215). She is making use of Argalia at the beginning, but later falls in love with him, which she reveals to him (and the reader) at the end of their relationship. Argalia is in love with her and gives himself to her totally and enduringly. Yet she is faithful only in so far as she will be able to work out her own destiny. Near death, he is aware that she discards him and leaves him to hold the fort while she escapes. Rushdie has confessed that his template for Qara Koz was Padma Lakshmi;[18] he is willing to accept without bitterness the idea of a woman with a future being prepared to pursue her destiny, transcending fidelity. Qara Koz is not an all-conquering beauty. She was all-powerful in Florence but, the 'journey from enchantress to witch being short' (p. 297), the tide turned and she was defeated. Her return to Akbar's consciousness, supplanting Jodha, a great-aunt and phantom, is a kind of triumph, brought about by her strength of will and power of survival.

Akbar's actual wives and his harem could satisfy his loins but they cannot appease his aspiring mind and loneliness. Hence he creates Jodha, an imaginary queen, and later Qara Koz. Jodha is his ideal, and he conceives her as a complement to the male, not as an entity in herself. In fact, he conceives two images of her. When Akbar realizes the possibility of sharing the experience of being an individual, who identifies himself with the first person singular and not the royal 'we' – called for by his apprehension of himself as more than a mere man, and as the force which both rules and protects his people, and so either contains or subsumes them – as he becomes aware of himself as 'I' and goes in quest of Jodha for love, his change presumably changes her. She is no longer all-fulfilling (and undemanding). She is individual too, keen on asserting an image of her own. So their reunion is less than satisfactory since her responses do not correspond to his need. The dialogue in Akbar's mind produced by these two images of Jodha indicates that he feels some kind of lack in his ideal. At the end of the account of Qara Koz, he who feels the need for a new ideal finds it in her. The millennium issue of *Femina* hails Akbar as 'one of the earliest Indians to practise gender equality'.[19]

Rushdie being concerned with 'erotic power',[20] enchantresses are prominent in the novel and include the courtesan Alessandra Fiorentina, Simonetta Vespucci (the model for Botticelli's 'Birth of Venus'), Khanzada Begum. Marietta Machiavelli, however, is a perfectly normal wife. Skeleton and Mattress belong to the type of the pragmatic, good-hearted prostitute.

Rushdie has liberated his imagination more fully in regard to the portrayal of sex. *The Enchantress of Florence* is his 'most sexually explicit book'[21] and the first of his novels to emphasize lesbianism. Here it is given acknowledgement – the relationship of Qara Koz and her Mirror is pointed up – not only in the light satirical vein of the presentation of the harem entertaining each other while Akbar is absent.

Mogor puts across skilfully the impressions of a conjurer and bedazzles the admittedly imaginative Akbar. But his audacity and 'silver tongue' (p. 75) fail him at the close. A hard ray of common sense pierces the haze of Akbar's credulousness when he begins to disbelieve Mogor's version of the story of his parentage and, finally, realizes that Mogor was the child of the Mirror's child, born in incest. Mogor escapes and Akbar does not wish to pursue him. Mogor is a born survivor and the probability is that he will survive. Akbar loses his capital city, but he is the richer for his experience and, undefeated, he is still forward-looking. His vision of the perfect city with Jodha as the ideal woman is lost, but his resilience is such that he attempts a new vision with a new ideal woman.

Rushdie's style changes in *Shalimar the Clown* and *The Enchantress of Florence*. The style of *Midnight's Children* was not reader-friendly, nevertheless it hooked readers. Now his style is less dense and reader-friendly, evincing a desire to communicate with readers not only at brow level but sensuously and emotionally. The style of *The Enchantress of Florence*, despite lapses into overlong sentences, is generally attractive. It is swashbuckling when rendering Mogor's rapidity of thought and action as he copes with his situation on board the ship when he, a stowaway, is discovered. The book possesses 'the virtues of swiftness and lightness' which Rushdie aimed at.[22]

Rushdie's obsessions – free speech, migration, hybridity and globalization – remain in *The Enchantress of Florence*. But he is departing from serious interpretations of the present and liberating himself to entertain, like the old oral artists, creating fantastic arabesques of fancy and humour, dealing with love, beauty and aspiration. The novel is serene and playful. Rushdie now seems to be enjoying being 'totally eligible, single and available'.[23] The summing up of the novel should be Rushdie's own: 'pleasurable funny sexy international story'.[24]

12
Conclusion

Self-exile such as Rushdie's is not a new phenomenon. Whether it is modernists like James Joyce, Joseph Conrad or T. S. Eliot or a postmodernist like Rushdie, the focus of exile is not on pain. But the exile of Western writers, whether Joyce, Conrad or Eliot, took place within the context of European or Western society; if there was a difference in milieu, it was between provincial and metropolitan. In the case of Third World exiles like Rushdie, the difference between the West and the Third World implies a more significant difference – between lifestyles and cultures. Yet, both types find exile an enabling experience.

Physically, Rushdie has left the subcontinent, but his imagination is always, more or less, connected to it. In *Grimus*, India appears in terms of occasional references to Hindu myth and ancient history. *Midnight's Children* takes in North India, Kashmir, Pakistan and Bangladesh; *Shame*, Pakistan; *The Satanic Verses*, India and India-in-London; *Haroun*, Pakistan and Kashmir; *East, West*, India, Pakistan and India-in-England; *The Moor's Last Sigh*, South India and Bombay. All his earlier (and best works, leaving out *Grimus*) are parts of a massive oeuvre which is rooted in, presents and interprets the subcontinent. With regard to India, he is partly an insider. He lived his most impressionable years and formed the deepest layers of his emotional life there. The fact that he left India at the age of fourteen does not mean that he is an outsider. Yet Rushdie is aware of his 'ability to see at once from inside and out...a piece of good fortune which the indigenous writer cannot enjoy'[1] – which is made possible by his position as migrant.

The same position shapes his view of the language of fiction at this stage:

> The language, like much else in the newly independent colonies, needs to be decolonized, to be made in other images, if those of us who use it from positions outside Anglo-Saxon culture, are to be more than artistic Uncle Toms.[2]

He brings in Indian varieties of English – Bombay English in *Midnight's Children* and Cochin English too in *The Moor's Last Sigh* – not just for comic purposes but as a vehicle for serious art. He thus revivifies the language of fiction and shows a method of revivifying it, for writers of his sort.

Britain has been hard on Rushdie, problematic ever since the kipper-eating scene on his first outing there, breakfast at Rugby. He became intellectually an insider in Britain: he absorbed its literature, especially at Cambridge, acquired the ability to analyse its social and political life. But he was never accepted as in insider in society by the white British. The insider's position in society is, after all, determined by a two-way process. Nevertheless, Rushdie does find a political location among the black communities in Britain and his fiction (*The Satanic Verses*, in particular) does derive strength from it. After the *fatwa*, he was disconnected from these communities. After the easing of the *fatwa* and his change of location again, he became a part of the celebrity culture in New York and, during his part-time stays in Britain, a part of London's celebrity culture. He is not lost or isolated, but he is not a member of a closely knit community. Celebrity culture is a group of individuals rather than a unit. Rushdie's social location has become increasingly fluid – and less enabling creatively.

In his earlier novels, Rushdie thought of migration in relation to home, belonging and identity – in keeping with postcolonial theories of diaspora and transnationalism. In his later novels, he is concerned with homelessness, an existential condition without moorings, like V. S. Naipaul in *A Bend in the River*. Rushdie's characters are no longer engaged in a quest for home or a different lifestyle. Rushdie's own earlier authorial insider/outsider position as immigrant is transformed in his later novels: as an expatriate writer, he is able to be 'inside the frame, enough to give you the texture of life' and 'outside the frame'; 'it has nothing to do with India or England, or race or class, it's to do with how you see'.[3] The latter position has been debilitating.

In his later four novels, Rushdie has been experimenting with the global novel. It has resulted in diffuseness and the absence of the kind of intensity found in his earlier novels centrally focused on India, Pakistan and Britain. Moreover, there is a distance between Rushdie and regions such as Fiji, Strasbourg and Florence. India, Pakistan and Britain of the migrants are known to him at close quarters. With reference to the debate, the global versus the local, the global has proved enfeebling in Rushdie's case. In the later four novels, he becomes a commentator rather than someone deeply involved in the issues he is contemplating. I have suggested other, biographical, causes which have, probably, contributed to the changes seen in the later novels. After being incredibly original in his earlier works (inclusive of *The Moor's Last Sigh*), in his later novels Rushdie is experimenting and moving towards older, more relaxed literary forms and catering to a wider, less discriminating readership. Nevertheless these later novels illustrate the trajectory of Rushdie's complicated writing career and, as such, these are an indispensable part of the whole story – and are not without interests/rewards of their own.

Rushdie's political outlook has shifted from the left to the centre (or centre-right). He is increasingly interested in US experience and, in his recent novels, he writes (to uneven effect) about the relationship between globalization and US culture, economics and military presences throughout the world. His later fiction notably features strong and emancipated women. His representation of women becomes increasingly positive. This change in him seems natural – whether he is responding to the changing standpoint of society or whether he is being influenced by his own personal experiences or both.

Rushdie has been influenced by postmodernist ideas and techniques, but he is not a complete postmodernist ideologically: '...they don't accept that literature is referential.... I do think books are about the world.'[4] His work is suffused with a definite political intent: 'Where Orwell wished quietism, let there be rowdyism, in place of the whale, the protesting wail.'[5] Rushdie's 'wail' activates the reader. Rushdie presents critiques and leaves the reader to work out positive alternatives, implying rather than stating these – like other great writers (Conrad in *Nostromo*, for instance). Rushdie's spirit emerges when *The Moor's Last Sigh* implies that the fate of the residents of Benengeli – without will or future – should be resisted. His humanism and innate sense of justice impel him to accept a 'broadly speaking Marxist' political position,[6] but he does not adopt the Marxist standpoint of the writer as a social engineer and does not suggest the ideal state or advocate revolution. Foucault's discourse 'presupposes the impossibility of stepping outside of a given discursive formation by an act of will or consciousness'.[7] But, surely, consciousness of the discourse trap is a key to freedom, as Rushdie finds, and, like Edward Said in *Imperialism and Culture*

(1993) and Homi Bhabha in *The Location of Culture* (1994), Rushdie interrogates and identifies ambivalent or contradictory spaces in the modes of thought and conduct that buttress colonial and neo-colonial hegemony.

Rushdie departs from what Jacques Derrida called 'the law of genre'.[8] As from *Grimus*, Rushdie employs heterogeneous semiotic codes. Indeed, magic realism is in itself an instance of code-switching. By incorporating popular genres such as science fiction and film in his hybrid texts, Rushdie subscribes to the postmodern thrust to bridge the gap between 'high' and 'low' culture/art. His novels seep one into another. The recurrences add depth and richness to his oeuvre. More importantly, it looks as though Rushdie is constructing a unified oeuvre – an exploration of total life as Balzac did in a more stable world in *La Comédie Humaine*. Rushdie is still not far beyond the mid-point of his career and, given his constant responsiveness to the changing world around him, his future work too may throw up multiplex illuminations.

Notes

1. EARLY LIFE AND EARLY WORKS

1. William Wordsworth, 'My heart leaps up ...', in *A Book of English Poetry*, ed. G. B. Harrison (London: Penguin, 1950 edn), p. 247.
2. Salman Rushdie, *The Wizard of Oz* (London: British Film Institute, 1992), p. 9.
3. Ibid., p. 18.
4. Ibid., pp. 9–10.
5. W. J. Weatherby, *Salman Rushdie: Sentenced to Death* (New York: Carroll & Graf, 1990), p. 14.
6. Salman Rushdie, 'Bonfire of the Certainties', interview recorded on 27 January 1989 by Bandung File and broadcast on 14 February on Channel 4, in *The Rushdie File*, eds. Lisa Appignanesi and Sara Maitland (London: Fourth Estate, 1989), p. 30.
7. Rushdie, 'Satyajit Ray' (1990), in *Imaginary Homelands: Essays in Criticism 1981–1991* (London and New Delhi: Granta and Penguin India, 1991), p. 107.
8. Rushdie interview in *Scripsi*, Vol. 3, Pt. 2–3, 1985, p. 116.
9. Rushdie, 'Gunter Grass' (1984), in *Imaginary Homelands*, p. 276.
10. Rushdie, *The Wizard of Oz*, p. 9.
11. Quoted from Weatherby, *Salman Rushdie*, p. 18.
12. Ian Hamilton, 'The First Life of Salman Rushdie', in *The New Yorker*, 25 December 1995 and 1 January 1996, p. 95.
13. Quoted from Weatherby, *Salman Rushdie*, pp. 25–6.
14. Quoted from Hamilton, 'The First Life', p. 97.
15. Rushdie, 'Censorship' (1983), in *Imaginary Homelands*, p. 38.
16. Quoted from Hamilton, 'The First Life', p. 100.
17. *Scripsi* interview, p. 121.
18. Quoted from Hamilton, 'The First Life', p. 100.
19. Ibid.
20. Weatherby, *Salman Rushdie*, p. 35.
21. Rushdie, *Grimus* (London: Paladin, 1989 edn), p. 209; all subsequent references to the novel are from this edition and their page numbers are noted in the text.
22. 'Salman Rushdie', in *Novelists in Interview*, ed. John Hoffenden (London: Methuen, 1985), p. 245.
23. Ibid.
24. Rushdie, quoted from 'Salman Rushdie: Interview by Suzie MacKenzie', in *The Guardian Weekend*, 4 November 1995, p. 12.
25. James Harrison, *Salman Rushdie* (New York: Twayne, 1992), p. 36.
26. Ibid.
27. 'Salman Rushdie', in *Novelists in Interview*, p. 246.

28. Catherine Cundy, ' "Rehearsing Voices": Salman Rushdie's *Grimus'*, in *Journal of Commonwealth Literature*, Vol. 27, No. 1, 1992, p. 135.
29. Mujeebuddin Syed, 'Warped Mythologies: Salman Rushdie's "Grimus" ', in *ARIEL: A Review of International English Literature*, Vol. 25, No. 4, 1994, pp. 136, 139.
30. Ibid., pp. 143–4.
31. M. M. Bakhtin, *Problems of Doestoevsky's Poetics* (1963), in *The Bakhtin Reader*, ed. Pam Morris (London: Edward Arnold, 1994).
32. Ibid., p. 192.
33. Rabkin, *The Fantastic in Literature*, quoted from Catherine Cundy, ' "Rehearsing Voices" ', p. 136.
34. Bakhtin, p. 187.
35. *Scripsi* interview, p. 125.
36. Bakhtin, p. 190.
37. Ibid., p. 192.
38. Ibid.
39. 'Saeva indignatio' is a phrase used by W. B. Yeats to describe Swift, one of Rushdie's literary ancestors – Yeats, 'Swift's Epitaph', in *The Collected Poems of W. B. Yeats* (London: Macmillan, 1961 edn), p. 277; originally, used of the Roman satirist Juvenal.
40. *Scripsi* interview, p. 125.
41. Ibid.
42. Notice, for instance, Rushdie's statement: *'Grimus* enabled me to use fantasy without worrying about it' ('Salman Rushdie: Interview', in *Kunapipi*, Vol. 4, No. 2, 1982, p. 25).

2. *MIDNIGHT'S CHILDREN* (1981)

1. Liz Calder's words, quoted from Ian Hamilton, 'The First Life of Salman Rushdie', p. 101.
2. Liz Calder's words, quoted from 'Salman Rushdie: Interview by Suzie MacKenzie', p. 15.
3. Quoted from Hamilton, 'The First Life', p. 101.
4. Rushdie's words, ibid., p. 102.
5. Ibid.
6. Ibid.
7. 'Salman Rushdie: Interview', in *Kunapipi*, p. 20.
8. T. S. Eliot, 'Yeats' (1940), in *On Poetry and Poets* (London: Faber, 1971 edn), p. 252.
9. *Scripsi* interview, p. 114.
10. 'Salman Rushdie: An Interview Conducted by David Brooks, 6/3/84', in *Helix*, No. 19/20, 1984, quoted from *Span*, No. 21, 1985, p. 184.
11. *Scripsi* interview, pp. 107–8.
12. Kapil Kapoor and Ranga Kapoor, 'Third World Poetics – The Indian Case', in *ACLALS Bulletin*, 7th Series, No. 5, 1986, p. 54.
13. Rushdie, 'The Courter', in *East, West* (London: Cape, 1994), p. 211.
14. Rushdie, 'Imaginary Homelands' (1982), in *Imaginary Homelands*, p. 15.

15. Ibid., p. 17.
16. 'Salman Rushdie', in *Novelists in Interview*, p. 246.
17. Rushdie, 'Outside the Whale' (1984), in *Imaginary Homelands*, p. 87.
18. Bryan Appleyard, 'Portrait of the Novelist as a Hot Property', in *The Sunday Times Magazine*, 11 September 1988, p. 31.
19. Quoted from Hamilton, 'The First Life', p. 102.
20. Ibid., pp. 102–3.
21. Salman Rushdie, *Midnight's Children* (London: Picador, 1982 edn), p. 9; all subsequent references to the novel are from this edition and their page numbers are noted in the text.
22. Shashi Tharoor, *The Great Indian Novel* (New Delhi: Penguin, 1990 edn), p. 17.
23. *Scripsi* interview, p. 115.
24. Rushdie, 'Imaginary Homelands', in *Imaginary Homelands*, p. 17.
25. Ibid., p. 14.
26. David W. Price, 'Salman Rushdie's "Use and Abuse of History" in *Midnight's Children*', in *ARIEL: A Review of International English Literature*, Vol. 25, No. 2, 1994, p. 103.
27. Ernest Renan, 'What is a Nation?' (1882), in *Nation and Narration*, ed. Homi K. Bhabha (London and New York: Routledge, 1991 edn), p. 19.
28. Price, 'Salman Rushdie's "Use and Abuse of History" in *Midnight's Children*', p. 96.
29. Salman Rushdie, '*Midnight's Children* and *Shame*', in *Kunapipi*, Vol. 7, No. 1, 1985, p. 4.
30. Rushdie, '*Midnight's Children* and *Shame*', in *Kunapipi*, p. 8.
31. Ibid., pp. 8–9.
32. Linda Hutcheon, *The Politics of Postmodernism* (London and New York: Routledge, 1993 edn), p. 1.
33. *Scripsi* interview, p. 123.
34. Ibid.
35. Robert Graves, *Greek Myths* (London: Penguin, 1969 edn), Vol. 1, p. 175.
36. 'Salman Rushdie: Interview', in *Kunapipi*, p. 21.
37. Ibid.
38. Ibid.
39. Ibid., p. 18.
40. Salman Rushdie, 'Midnight's real children', in the *Guardian*, 25 March 1988, p. 25.
41. Rushdie, '*Midnight's Children* and *Shame*', in *Kunapipi*, p. 5.
42. Ibid., p. 6.
43. Rushdie, *The Wizard of Oz*, p. 33.
44. Winston S. Churchill, *India: Speeches* (London: 1931 edn), p. 94.
45. *The Mahabharata*, condensed in the poet's own words by Pandit A. M. Srinivasachariar, trans. V. Raghavan (New Delhi: Uppal, 1990 edn), p. 459.
46. 'Salman Rushdie', in *Novelists in Interview*, p. 239.
47. Robert Graves, *The White Goddess* (London: Faber, 1961 edn), p. 303.
48. Gunter Grass, *The Tin Drum*, trans. Ralph Manheim (London: Penguin, 1967 edn), pp. 385, 388.
49. 'Salman Rushdie', in *Novelists in Interview*, p. 240.

50. Hutcheon, *Politics of Postmodernism*, pp. 1–2.
51. 'Salman Rushdie', in *Novelists in Interview*, p. 244.
52. Rushdie, 'Midnight's real children', p. 25.
53. Uma Parameswaran, 'Salman Rushdie', in *Encyclopedia of Post-Colonial Literatures in English*, eds. Eugene Benson and L. W. Conolly (London and New York: Routledge, 1994), p. 1390.
54. Rushdie, 'Imaginary Homelands', in *Imaginary Homelands*, p. 16.
55. Timothy Brennan, *Salman Rushdie and the Third World* (London: Macmillan, New York: St Martin's Press, 1989), pp. 103–4.
56. Gayatri C. Spivak, 'Reading *The Satanic Verses*', in *Third Text*, Vol. 11, 1990, p. 46.
57. 'Salman Rushdie: Interview', in *Kunapipi*, pp. 19–20.
58. Rushdie, ' "Errata": Or, Unreliable Narration in *Midnight's Children*' (1983), in *Imaginary Homelands*.
59. Rushdie, 'Imaginary Homelands', in *Imaginary Homelands*, p. 10.
60. 'Salman Rushdie', in *Novelists in Interview*, p. 239.
61. Rushdie, '*Midnight's Children* and *Shame*', in *Kunapipi*, p. 4.
62. Ibid., pp. 10–11; see also Rushdie, 'Minority Literatures in a Multi-Cultural Society', in *Displaced Persons*, eds. Kirsten Holst Petersen and Anna Rutherford (Denmark: Dangaroo Press, 1988), p. 35.
63. S. Nomanul Haq, 'A Moslem tells Salman Rushdie he did wrong', in *The Rushdie File*, p. 232.
64. Rushdie, 'Midnight's real children', p. 25.

3. *SHAME* (1983)

1. Rushdie, 'Gunter Grass' (1984), in *Imaginary Homelands*, p. 277.
2. 'Salman Rushdie', in *Novelists in Interview*, p. 253.
3. Ibid.
4. Ibid., p. 242.
5. Ibid., p. 243.
6. Rushdie, *Shame* (London: Cape, 1983), p. 61; all subsequent references to the novel are from this edition and their page numbers are noted in the text.
7. Alamgir Hashmi, 'Pakistan', in *Encyclopaedia of Post-Colonial Literatures in English*, Vol. II, p. 1191.
8. 'Salman Rushdie', in *Novelists in Interview*, p. 287.
9. Ibid., p. 256.
10. Hamilton, 'The First Life', pp. 90, 104–5.
11. Omar Khayyam, 'Quatrains', in *The Elek Book of Oriental Verse*, ed. Keith Bosley (London: Paul Elek, 1979), p. 214.
12. Edward Fitzgerald, 'Rubaiyat of Omar Khayyam of Naishapur', in *A Book of English Poetry*, ed. G. B. Harrison (London: Penguin, 1950 edn), p. 346.
13. Omar Khayyam, 'Quatrains' in *The Elek Book of Oriental Verse*, p. 213.
14. 'Salman Rushdie', in *Novelists in Interview*, p. 251.
15. Rushdie, '*Midnight's Children* and *Shame*', in *Kunapipi*, p. 14.

16. D. M. D. Dharmasena and L. D. R. B. Karunaratne, *Report of the Study on Knowledge and Attitudes on HIV (AIDS)* (Colombo: Health Education Bureau, Ministry of Health and Women's Affairs, Sri Lanka, 1992), p. 1.
17. *Scripsi* interview, p. 108.
18. Ibid.
19. Ibid., p. 109.
20. Ibid., p. 111.
21. Rushdie, *'Midnight's Children* and *Shame'*, in *Kunapipi*, p. 18.
22. Ibid., p. 14.
23. Steven R. Weisman, 'Come On, Fire Bullets at Me', in *New York Times Book Review*, 4 July 1993, p. 10.
24. Ibid.
25. 'Salman Rushdie', in *Novelists in Interview*, p. 254.
26. *Scripsi* interview, p. 109.
27. Ibid.
28. Salman Rushdie, *The Moor's Last Sigh* (London: Cape, 1995), p. 352.
29. Aijaz Ahmad, *In Theory: Classes, Nations, Literatures* (London and New York: Verso, 1992), p. 140.
30. *Scripsi* interview, p. 108.
31. 'Salman Rushdie', in *Novelists in Interview*, p. 255.
32. D. J. Enright, 'Forked Tongue', in *The New York Review of Books*, Vol. 30, No. 19, 8 December 1983, p. 26.
33. Romila Thapar, *A History of India* (London: Penguin, 1976 edn), Vol. 1, pp. 280–1.
34. Brennan, *Salman Rushdie*, p. 142.
35. John Dowson, *Classical Dictionary of Hindu Mythology and Religion, Geography, History and Literature* (New Delhi: Manu Publications, 1987 edn), p. 87.
36. Ibid., p. 86.
37. 'Salman Rushdie', in *Novelists in Interview*, p. 255.
38. Harrison, *Salman Rushdie*, p. 69.
39. Ahmad, *In Theory*, p. 146.
40. *Shame* has shown itself to be of continuing relevance. Benazir Bhutto became prime minister twice. She resembled her father in her populist style, charisma and death, being assassinated in 2007. The Bhutto name ended, but family politics goes on: her husband, Asif Ali Zardari, was elected President of Pakistan in 2008.

4. *THE JAGUAR SMILE* (1987) AND *THE SATANIC VERSES* (1988)

1. Quoted from Hamilton, 'The First Life', p. 105.
2. Ibid., p. 106.
3. Rushdie, 'The New Empire within Britain' (1982), in *Imaginary Homelands*, pp. 130–1.
4. Harrison, *Salman Rushdie*, p. 5.
5. Rushdie, 'Outside the Whale' (1984), in *Imaginary Homelands*, p. 100.

6. Mel Gussow, *Conversations with Pinter* (London: Nick Hem Books, 1994), p. 73.
7. Salman Rushdie, *The Jaguar Smile: A Nicaraguan Journey* (London: Picador, 1987), p. 12; all subsequent references to this work are from this edition and their page numbers are noted in the text.
8. Rushdie, '*Midnight's Children* and *Shame*', in *Kunapipi*, p. 16.
9. Frances Wood, 'A Nicaraguan Odyssey', in *Asiaweek*, 8 March 1987, p. 64.
10. Quoted from 'Salman Rushdie: Interview by Suzie MacKenzie', p. 12.
11. Quoted from Hamilton, 'The First Life', pp. 110, 112.
12. Appleyard, 'Portrait of the Novelist as a Hot Property', p. 32.
13. Rushdie, 'In Good Faith' (1990), in *Imaginary Homelands*, p. 394.
14. 'Sean French talks to Salman Rushdie', in *The Observer*, 25 September 1988, p. 43.
15. Salman Rushdie, *The Satanic Verses* (London: Viking, 1988), pp. 4, 10; all subsequent references to this novel are from this edition and their page numbers are noted in the text.
16. 'Sean French talks to Salman Rushdie', p. 43.
17. Quoted from 'Salman Rushdie', in *Novelists in Interview*, p. 232.
18. Brennan, *Salman Rushdie*, p. 121.
19. Thomas W. Lippman, *Understanding Islam: An Introduction to the Moslem World* (New York: Mentor, 1982), p. 152.
20. Farid-ud-din 'Attar, *The Conference of Birds*, trans. Afkhan Darbandi and Dick Davis (London: Penguin, 1984), p. 56.
21. Ibid., p. 79.
22. D. J. Enright, 'So, And Not So', in *The New York Review of Books*, 2 March 1989, p. 25.
23. Brennan, *Salman Rushdie*, p. 164.
24. Quoted from Vijay Mishra, 'Postcolonial Differend: Diasporic Narratives of Salman Rushdie', in *ARIEL: A Review of International English Literature*, Vol. 26, No. 3, 1995, p. 10.
25. Rushdie, 'The New Empire within Britain' (1982), in *Imaginary Homelands*, p. 129.
26. Spivak, 'Reading *The Satanic Verses*', p. 50.
27. 'Interview: Salman Rushdie talks to the London Consortium about *The Satanic Verses*', in *Critical Quarterly*, Vol. 38, No. 2, 1996, p. 52.
28. Ibid.
29. Ibid.
30. Ibid., p. 53.
31. Ibid., p. 57.
32. Rushdie, 'Minority Literatures in a Multi-Cultural Society', in *Displaced Persons*, p. 35.
33. Philip Larkin, *Collected Poems* ed. Anthony Thwaite (London: Marvell Press and Faber, 1988), p. 111.
34. 'Interview: Salman Rushdie talks to the London Consortium', p. 51.
35. T. S. Eliot, 'Hamlet', in *Selected Essays* (London: Faber, 1953 edn), p. 144.
36. John R. Nabholtz (ed.), *Prose of the British Romantic Movement* (New York: Macmillan, 1974), p. 192.
37. 'Sean French talks to Salman Rushdie', p. 43.

38. Ibid.
39. Robert Irwin, 'Original Parables', in *The Times Literary Supplement*, 30 September–6 October, 1988, p. 1067.
40. Milan Kundera, 'The Day Panurge No Longer Makes People Laugh', in *Critical Quarterly*, 38, 2, 1996, p. 43.
41. Ibid., p. 44.
42. 'Interview: Salman Rushdie talks to the London Consortium', p. 58.
43. Ibid., pp. 51–2.
44. Sara Suleri, *The Rhetoric of English India* (Chicago and London: University of Chicago Press, 1992), p. 202.
45. Rushdie, 'Introduction' (1991), in *Imaginary Homelands*, p. 4.
46. Rushdie, 'In Good Faith' (1990), in *Imaginary Homelands*, pp. 409–10.
47. Harrison, *Salman Rushdie*, p. 90.
48. Kundera, 'The Day Panurge No Longer Makes People Laugh', p. 44.
49. 'Interview: Salman Rushdie talks to the London Consortium', pp. 79–80.
50. 'Bonfire of the Certainties', Interview with Rushdie, recorded on 27 January 1989 by Bandung File and broadcast on 14 February 1989 by Channel 4, in *The Rushdie File*, p. 28.
51. 'Interview: Salman Rushdie talks to the London Consortium', p. 55.
52. Rushdie, 'In Good Faith', in *Imaginary Homelands*, pp. 398–9.
53. 'Interview: Salman Rushdie talks to the London Consortium', pp. 56–7.
54. Rushdie, 'In Good Faith', in *Imaginary Homelands*, p. 409.
55. 'Interview: Salman Rushdie talks to the London Consortium', p. 55.
56. Quoted from Weatherby, *Salman Rushdie*, p. 44.
57. 'Of Satan, archangels and prophets', Shrabani Basu interviews Rushdie, *Sunday*, India, 18–24 September 1988, in *The Rushdie File*, pp. 40–1.
58. Amir Taheri, 'Khomeini's scapegoat', *The Times*, 13 February 1989, in *The Rushdie File*, p. 93.
59. Weatherby, *Salman Rushdie*, p. 26.
60. O. E. D. (Oxford: Clarendon Press, 1970 edn), Vol. 6, p. 38.
61. Ibid., Vol. 3, p. 10.
62. Ibid., Vol. 1, p. 659.
63. Mihir Bose, the *Daily Telegraph*, 16 February 1989, in *The Rushdie File*, pp. 115–16.
64. Shabbir Akhtar, 'The case for religious fundamentalism', the *Guardian*, 27 February 1989, in *The Rushdie File*, p. 241.
65. Rushdie, 'In Good Faith', in *Imaginary Homelands*, p. 402.
66. Ibid., p. 401.
67. Quoted from Malise Ruthven, *A Satanic Affair: Salman Rushdie and the Wrath of Islam* (London: Hogarth, 1991 edn), p. 27.
68. Rushdie, 'Choice between light and dark', in the *Observer*, 22 January 1989, p. 11.
69. Daniel Pipes, *The Rushdie Affair: The Novel, the Ayatollah and the West* (New York: Birch Lane Press, 1990), pp. 115–16.
70. 'Interview: Salman Rushdie talks to the London Consortium', p. 60.
71. Rushdie, 'In Good Faith' in *Imaginary Homelands*, p. 399.
72. Rushdie, 'Choice between light and dark', p. 11.
73. 'Interview: Salman Rushdie talks to the London Consortium', p. 62.

74. Rushdie, 'In Good Faith', in *Imaginary Homelands*, p. 408.
75. 'Interview: Salman Rushdie talks to the London Consortium', pp. 62–3.
76. Ibid., p. 63.
77. Rushdie, 'In Good Faith', in *Imaginary Homelands*, p. 401.
78. *Scripsi* interview, p. 125.
79. Rushdie, 'Is Nothing Sacred?' (Herbert Read Memorial Lecture 1990), in *Imaginary Homeland*, p. 420.
80. Ibid., p. 422.
81. Jean-Francois Lyotard, *The Post-Modern Condition* (Manchester: Manchester University Press, 1986), quoted from *Cultural Theory and Popular Culture*, ed. John Storey (London: Harvester Wheatsheaf, 1994), p. 359.
82. Akbar S. Ahmed, *Postmodernism and Islam* (London: Routledge, 1992), p. 32.
83. Ibid.
84. Bruce King, review of *The Rushdie File*, in *World Literature Today*, Vol. 64, No. 3, 1990, p. 529.
85. Ibid.
86. Rushdie, 'In Good Faith', in *Imaginary Homelands*, p. 394.

5. *HAROUN AND THE SEA OF STORIES* (1990)

1. Weatherby, *Salman Rushdie*, p. 108.
2. Quoted from Mehdi Mozaffari, 'The *fatwa* that wasn't', in the *Guardian*, 13 November 1996, p. 16.
3. Anon in *The Rushdie File*, p. 203.
4. Weatherby, *Salman Rushdie*, p. 194.
5. Ibid.
6. Rushdie, *The Wizard of Oz*, p. 9.
7. Michel Foucault, 'What Is an Author?', in *Language, Counter-Memory, Practice*, Michel Foucault ed. Donald F. Bouchard (Oxford: Basil Blackwell, 1977) p. 117.
8. Salman Rushdie, *Haroun and the Sea of Stories* (New Delhi: Penguin and London: Granta, 1990), p. 20; all subsequent references to this book are from this edition and their page numbers are noted in the text.
9. Rushdie, *Wizard of Oz*, p. 10.
10. Ibid., p. 17.
11. J. R. R. Tolkien, *The Lord of the Rings* (London: Allen & Unwin, 1971 edn), p. 854.
12. Rushdie, *Wizard of Oz*, p. 10.
13. T. S. Eliot, 'Tradition and the Individual Talent', in *Selected Essays* (London: Faber, 1953 edn), p. 16.
14. 'This question of divisions in the self, for me, just arises out of the accidents in my life. If you come from over there and end up over here you just have that sense of doubleness, all the time. Even in India, if you come from a minority community inside a majority culture, you have that sense of belonging and not belonging all at the same time' ('Interview: Salman Rushdie talks to the London Consortium', p. 59).

15. James Fenton, 'Keeping Up with Salman Rushdie', in *The New York Review of Books*, 28 March 1991, p. 34.
16. Rushdie, 'Satyajit Ray' (1990), in *Imaginary Homelands*, p. 111.
17. Fenton, 'Keeping Up with Salman Rushdie', p. 34.
18. Rushdie, 'Introduction' (1991), in *Imaginary Homelands*, p. 6.
19. 'I wrote *The Thirteen Clocks* in Bermuda, where I had gone to finish another book. The shift to this one was an example of escapism and self-indulgence. Unless modern man wanders down these byways occasionally, I do not see how he can hope to preserve his sanity.' James Thurber, 'Foreword', in *The 13 Clocks* (London: Hamish Hamilton, 1951), p. 11.
20. Tolkien, 'Foreword', in *Lord of the Rings*, p. 9.
21. Paul Griffiths, 'What he did next', in *The Times Literary Supplement*, 28 October–4 November, 1990, p. 1036.
22. For instance, Alison Lurie, 'Another Dangerous Story From Salman Rushdie', in *New York Times Book Review*, 11 November 1990; Frank Kermode, 'Saving the Streams of Story', in *The London Review of Books*, 27 September 1990; Carlo Coppola, 'Salman Rushdie's *Haroun and the Sea of Stories*: Fighting the Good Fight or Knuckling Under', in *Journal of South Asian Literature*, 26, 1 and 2, 1991.

6. *EAST, WEST* (1994)

1. Rushdie, 'Why I Have Embraced Islam' (1990), in *Imaginary Homelands*, p. 432.
2. Jean-Francois Lyotard, *The Differend: Phrases in Dispute*, trans. Georges Van Den (Manchester: Manchester University Press, 1988), p. 28.
3. Rushdie, 'One Thousand Days in a Balloon', in *Imaginary Homelands*, p. 438. See also Alan Taylor, '1001 Nights', in *Assistant Librarian*, Vol. 85, No. 3, 1992.
4. Rushdie, *East, West* (London: Cape, 1994) p. 15; all subsequent references to this book are from this edition and their page numbers are noted in the text.
5. Rushdie, 'Interview: Homelessness is where the art is', in *The Bookseller*, 15 July 1994, p. 49.
6. Ibid.
7. Ibid.
8. Ibid., p. 50.
9. Hermione Lee, 'Falling Towards England', in the *Observer*, 25 September 1988, p. 43.
10. Rushdie, 'Interview: Homelessness is where the art is', in *The Bookseller*, p. 49.

7. *THE MOOR'S LAST SIGH* (1995)

1. 'The Last Laugh: Salman Rushdie Interview with Maya Jaggi', in *New Statesman & Society*, 8 September 1995, p. 20.

2. Tom Shone, 'Mother knows best', in *The Spectator*, 9 September 1995, p. 38.
3. Rushdie, *The Moor's Last Sigh*; all subsequent references to this novel are from this edition and their page numbers are noted in the text.
4. Salman Rushdie, 'Interview with Will Self', in the *Evening Standard*, 7 September 1995, p. 8.
5. 'Interview: Salman Rushdie talks to the London Consortium', p. 54.
6. Rabindranath Tagore's English translation, quoted from *India 1991: A Reference Annual* ed. and comp. Research and Reference Division, Ministry of Information and Broadcasting, Government of India (New Delhi: Publications Division, Ministry of Information and Broadcasting, India, 1992), p. 23.
7. See Percival Spear, *A History of India*, Vol. 2 (London: Penguin, 1968 edn), pp. 126–7.
8. 'Salman Rushdie: Interview by Suzie MacKenzie', p. 16.
9. Rushdie, 'Bosnia on my mind', in *Index on Censorship*, 1/2, 1994, pp. 17–18.
10. Ibid., p. 17.
11. There is no dog in the film and the title bears no relation to its surrealistic themes. Buñuel is, probably, having a spiteful dig at the Andalusian poets who were his student contemporaries – principally, Lorca and J. Ramon Jimenez.
12. J. M. Coetzee, 'Palimpsest Regained', in *The New York Review of Books*, 21 March 1996, p. 14.
13. Ibid., p. 13.

8. *THE GROUND BENEATH HER FEET* (1999)

1. Salman Rushdie, *Step Across This Line: Collected Non-Fiction 1992–2002* (London: Jonathan Cape, 2002), p. 229.
2. Ibid., p. 237.
3. Ibid., pp. 242–3.
4. Olivia Cole, 'Artists delve into failing love of Salman Rushdie, the purple lobster', in *The Sunday Times* (UK), 10 February 2008.
5. D. T. Max, 'Manhattan Transfer', in *The New York Times*, reprinted in the *Observer* (London), 24 September 2000: Review, p. 2.
6. Pradyumna S. Chauhan (ed.), *Salman Rushdie Interviews: A Sourcebook of His Ideas* (Connecticut: Greenwood Press, 2001), p. 283.
7. Rushdie, *Step Across This Line*, p. 391.
8. Dave Weich, 'Salman Rushdie, Out and About', in *Powell's Author Interviews*, 25 September 2002.
9. Chauhan, *Salman Rushdie Interviews*, p. 282.
10. Ibid.
11. Ibid.
12. 'Interview with Salman Rushdie', 9 September 1999, <www.groundbeneath.com/rushdieinterview.htm>
13. Salman Rushdie, 'The Firebird's Nest', in *The New Yorker*, June 23 and 30, 1997, p. 127.

14. Anthony Giddens, 'The Globalizing of Modernity', in *The Global Transformations Reader* eds. David Held and Anthony McGrew (Cambridge: Polity, 2003 edn), p. 60.
15. Manfred B. Steger, *Globalization* (Oxford: Oxford University Press, 2003), p. 18.
16. Some may feel that film has at least a rival claim. But film stems from painting and theatre – a narrative art. It does not work on the pulse, blood and nerves like pop music, transporting and transforming the listener, gripping and ruling his/her reactions. It promotes mass frenzies; film does nothing like this.
17. Chauhan, *Salman Rushdie Interviews*, p. 286.
18. Salman Rushdie, *The Ground Beneath Her Feet* (London: Jonathan Cape, 1999), p. 91; all subsequent references to the novel are from this edition and their page numbers are noted in the text.
19. Chauhan, *Salman Rushdie Interviews*, p. 294.
20. Ibid., p. 264.
21. Quoted from Scott MacLeod, 'The Life and Death of Kevin Carter', in *Time* magazine, 12 September 1994.
22. Andrew Teverson, *Salman Rushdie* (Manchester: Manchester University Press, 2007), p. 53.
23. Rushdie, *Step Across This Line*, pp. 177–8.
24. Stephen Morton, *Salman Rushdie* (Basingstoke: Palgrave Macmillan, 2008), p. 112.
25. Chauhan, *Salman Rushdie Interviews*, p. 285.
26. Ibid., p. 281.
27. Ibid., p. 285.
28. Martin Amis, 'Rendezvous with Rushdie', in *Vanity Fair*, December 1990, 161.
29. Anshuman A. Mondal, '*The Ground Beneath Her Feet* and *Fury*: The reinvention of location', in *The Cambridge Companion to Salman Rushdie* ed. Abdulrazak Gurnah (Cambridge: Cambridge University Press, 2007), p. 177.
30. Morton, *Salman Rushdie*, p. 26.
31. Shaul Bassi, 'Orpheus's Other Voyage: Myth, Music and Globalization', in *The Great Work of Making Real: Salman Rushdie's The Ground Beneath Her Feet*, eds. Elsa Liguanti and Victoria Tchernichova (Pisa: Edizioni Ets, 2003) p. 111.
32. Teverson, *Salman Rushdie*, p. 184.
33. Chauhan, *Salman Rushdie Interviews*, p. 294.
34. Mondal, '*The Ground Beneath Her Feet* and *Fury*', p. 176.
35. Ibid., p. 177.
36. Chauhan, *Salman Rushdie Interviews*, p. 256.
37. Ibid., p. 259.
38. Rushdie, *Step Across This Line*, p. 299.
39. Michael Wood, 'The Orpheus of MTV', in *The New York Times Book Review*, 18 April 1999, p. 8.
40. Chauhan, *Salman Rushdie Interviews*, p. 281.
41. Viktoria Tchernichova, ' "The outsideness of what we're inside": Double Vision as *Kunstlerasthetik* in *The Ground Beneath Her Feet*', in *The Great Work of Making Real*, p. 72.

42. Elena Rossi, ' "Against an amnesiac culture": Greek and Latin Mythology in *The Ground Beneath Her Feet'*, in *The Great Work of Making Real*, p. 31.
43. Chauhan, *Salman Rushdie Interviews*, pp. 258–9.
44. For an analysis of Rushdie's 'frolics in word-play', see James Wood, 'Lost in the Punhouse', in *The New Republic*, Vol. 220, Nos. 17–18, 26 April–3 May 1999, pp. 96–100.
45. Weich, 'Salman Rushdie, Out and About'.

9. *FURY* (2001)

1. Salman Rushdie, *Fury* (New York: Modern Library, 2002 edn), p. 27; all subsequent quotations are taken from this edition and their page numbers are incorporated in the text.
2. Cf. The Bratz dolls, meant for girls between six and ten, have been transformed from their original concept, popularized in a diversity of products to build a global financial empire, and made into a film by Hollywood in 2007 (Reuter, London, 2 August 2007).
3. Sarah Brouilette, *Postcolonial Writers in the Global Literary Marketplace* (Basingstoke: Palgrave Macmillan, 2007), p. 92.
4. Alfred Hickling, Review of *Fury*, in the *Guardian*, 7 September 2002. Jack Leonard, 'Puppet Show', in *The New York Review of Books*, 4 October 2001, p. 36.
5. Rushdie, *Shame*, p. 29.
6. Rushdie in Weich, 'Salman Rushdie, Out and About'.
7. Ibid.
8. Unpublished interview.
9. See Conclusion for more suggestions on this matter.

10. *SHALIMAR THE CLOWN* (2005)

1. Steve Inskeep, 'Interview: Salman Rushdie on "Shalimar the Clown" taking him back to Kashmir', in *National Public Radio*, 24 October 2005.
2. Salman Rushdie, *Shalimar the Clown* (London: Jonathan Cape, 2005) p. 110; all subsequent quotations are from this edition and their page numbers are incorporated in the text.
3. Samuel P. Huntington, *The Clash of Civilizations and the Remaking of World Order* (New York: Simon & Schuster, 1996).
4. Rushdie, 'Anti-Americanism Has Taken the World by Storm', in the *Guardian*, 6 February 2002.
5. Rushdie, 'A Liberal Argument for Regime Change', in the *Washington Post*, 1 November 2002.
6. Theo Tait, 'Flame-Broiled Whopper', in *The London Review of Books*, 6 October 2005.
7. Michiko Kakutani, 'In Kashmir Toxic Love Breeds Terrorism', in the *New York Times*, 6 September 2005.

8. Tait, 'Flame-Broiled Whopper'.
9. Kakutani, 'In Kashmir Toxic Love Breeds Terrorism'.

11. *THE ENCHANTRESS OF FLORENCE* (2008)

1. e.g. Morton, *Salman Rushdie*, p. 152.
2. AFP, June 2008.
3. Reuter, London, 16 April 2008.
4. Mukund Padmanabhan, 'Imagining the self and the world: Interview with Salman Rushdie', in *The Hindu Magazine*, 13 April 2008, p. 1.
5. Kate Muir, 'Exclusive Interview with Salman Rushdie', in *The Times*, 4 April 2008.
6. Padmanabhan, 'Imagining the self and the world: Interview with Salman Rushdie'.
7. Muir, 'Exclusive Interview with Salman Rushdie'.
8. Reuter, London, 16 April 2008.
9. Salman Rushdie, *The Enchantress of Florence* (London: Jonathan Cape, 2008) p. 134; all subsequent quotations are taken from this edition and their page numbers are incorporated in the text.
10. Muir, 'Exclusive Interview with Salman Rushdie'.
11. R. C. Majumdar, H. C. Raychaudhuri and Kalinkar Datta, *An Advanced History of India* (London: Macmillan, 1950) p. 460.
12. Padmanabhan, 'Imagining the self and the world: Interview with Salman Rushdie'.
13. Majumdar et al., *History of India*, p. 458.
14. Ibid., p. 459.
15. Rushdie in an interview in *The Spectator*, 9 April 2008.
16. Reuter, London, 16 April 2008.
17. Padmanabhan, 'Imagining the self and the world: Interview with Salman Rushdie'.
18. Patricia Cohen, 'Now He's Only Hunted by Cameras: Interview with Salman Rushdie', in *The New York Times*, 25 May 2008.
19. *Femina*, Mumbai, 1 January 2000, p. 364.
20. Muir, 'Exclusive Interview with Salman Rushdie'.
21. Ibid.
22. Padmanabhan, 'Imagining the self and the world: Interview with Salman Rushdie'.
23. Cohen, 'Now He's Only Hunted by Cameras: Interview with Salman Rushdie'.
24. Muir, 'Exclusive Interview with Salman Rushdie'.

12. CONCLUSION

1. 'A Dangerous Art Form', Interview with Rushdie, *Third World Book Review*, 1, 1, 1984, quoted from Ahmad, *In Theory*, p. 130.
2. Rushdie, in a paper presented at a Conference of Third-World Written Books, published in *The Times*; quoted from Wimal Dissanayaka,

'Towards a Decolonized English: South Asia Creativity in Fiction', in *World Englishes*, 4, 2, 1985, p. 242.
3. Chauhan, *Salman Rushdie Interviews*, p. 283.
4. Ibid., p. 69.
5. Rushdie, *Imaginary Homelands*, p. 99.
6. Rushdie, *'Midnight's Children* and *Shame'*, in *Kunapipi*, pp. 17–18.
7. Teverson, *Salman Rushdie*, pp. 21–2.
8. Jacques Derrida, 'La Loi du Genre/The Law of Genre', in *Glyph* 7, 1980, pp. 176–232.

Select Bibliography

PRIMARY SOURCES – RUSHDIE'S WORKS

Grimus (1975).
Midnight's Children (1981).
Shame (1983).
The Jaguar Smile: A Nicaraguan Journey (1987; 2nd edn 1997).
The Satanic Verses (1988).
Haroun and the Sea of Stories (1990).
Imaginary Homelands: Essays in Criticism 1981–1991 (1991; rev. edn 1992).
The Wizard of Oz (1992).
East, West (1994).
The Moor's Last Sigh (1995).
'The Firebird's Nest' (1997), in *The New Yorker*, 23 and 30 June 1997.
(Ed. with Elizabeth West), *The Vintage Book of Indian Writing 1947–97* (1997).
The Ground Beneath Her Feet (1999).
The Screenplay of Midnight's Children (1999).
Fury (2001).
Step Across This Line: Collected Non-Fiction 1992–2002 (2002).
(With Simon Reade and Tim Supple) *Salman Rushdie's Midnight's Children* adapted for the theatre (2002).
Shalimar the Clown (2005).
'The Shelter of the World' (2008), in *The New Yorker*, 25 February 2008.
The Enchantress of Florence (2008).

INTERVIEWS

John Hoffenden (ed.), *Novelists in Interview* (London: Methuen, 1985).
Scripsi, Vol. 3, Pt. 2–3, 1985.
James Fenton, 'Keeping Up with Salman Rushdie', in *The New York Review of Books*, Vol. 38, No. 6, 1991.
Critical Quarterly, Vol. 38, No. 2, 1996.
Michael R. Reeder (ed.), *Conversations with Salman Rushdie* (Jackson: University Press of Mississippi, 2000).
Pradyumna S. Chauhan, *Salman Rushdie Interviews: A Sourcebook of His Ideas* (Connecticut: Greenwood Press, 2001).

OTHER WORKS

Ahmad, Aijaz, *In Theory: Classes, Nations, Literatures* (London and New York: Verso, 1992).

Appignanesi, Lisa, and Maitland, Sara (eds), *The Rushdie File* (London: Fourth Estate, 1989).

Brennan, Timothy, *Salman Rushdie and the Third World* (London: Macmillan, New York: St Martin's Press, 1989).

Gonzalez, Madelena, *Fiction After the Fatwa: Salman Rushdie and the Charm of Catastrophe* (Amsterdam: Rodopi, 2005).

Gurnah, Abdulrazak (ed.), *The Cambridge Companion to Salman Rushdie* (Cambridge: Cambridge University Press, 2007).

Hamilton, Ian, 'The First Life of Salman Rushdie', in *The New Yorker*, 25 December 1995 and 1 January 1996.

Harrison, James, *Salman Rushdie* (New York: Twayne, 1992).

Kundera, Milan, 'The Day Panurge No Longer Makes People Laugh', in *Critical Quarterly*, Vol. 38, No. 2, 1996.

Liguanti, Elsa, and Tchernichova, Victoria (ed.), *The Great Work of Making Real: Salman Rushdie's The Ground Beneath Her Feet* (Pisa: Edizioni Ets, 2003).

Mishra, Vijay, 'Postcolonial Differend: Diasporic Narratives of Salman Rushdie', in *ARIEL: A Review of International English Literature*, Vol. 26, No. 3, 1995.

Morton, Stephen, *Salman Rushdie* (Basingstoke: Palgrave Macmillan, 2008).

Ruthven, Malise, *A Satanic Affair: Salman Rushdie and the Wrath of Islam* (London: Hogarth, 1991 edn).

Steger, Manfred B., *Globalization* (Oxford: Oxford University Press, 2003).

Suleri, Sara, *The Rhetoric of English India* (Chicago: University of Chicago Press, 1992).

Teverson, Andrew, *Salman Rushdie* (Manchester: Manchester University Press, 2007).

Third Text, No. 11, 1990 (Beyond the Rushdie Affair: Special Issue).

Twentieth Century Literature, Vol. 47, No. 4, 2001 (Special Issue on Rushdie).

Weatherby, W. J., *Salman Rushdie: Sentenced to Death* (New York: Carroll & Graf, 1990).

Wilson, Keith, '*Midnight's Children* and Reader Responsibility', in *Critical Quarterly*, Vol. 26, No. 3, 1984.

Wood, James, 'Lost in the Punhouse', in *The New Republic*, 220, 17–18, 26 April–3 May 1999.

Wood, Michael, 'The Orpheus of MTV', in *The New York Times Book Review*, 18 April 1999.

Index